Prais

"Bravo! There were so man~~y~~ honesty; she spared herself ~~very little, and in the end,~~ emerged a winner."

-Barbara Delinsky, Author of 23 New York Times Best Sellers

"I have always admired Nikki's talent as a singer. Now, having found her voice as a writer, she is indeed Ms. Unstoppable!"

-Donna McKechnie, Tony Award winning Broadway actress (A Chorus Line), Author of *Time Steps: My Musical Comedy Life*

"Inspiring and empowering…Nikki's poignant story of her father's battle with alcoholism and her own battle for self love illustrates how running has the power to heal, transform, and save lives. In *Dry Run*, Nikki captures the essence of the relationship between life and running, showing us that ultimately, growth does not come from the flat roads, but from the hills, peaks and rough terrains."

-Daphnie Yang, Personal Trainer/Team Challenge Race Coach/ Creator of the HIIT IT! High Intensity Interval Training workout

"*Dry Run* is a wise and entertaining book that weaves together a story of running the Providence marathon with a parallel story of growing up with an alcoholic parent, its own kind of marathon. The story is told with humor, grace, wit, and self-knowledge, and is essential reading for anyone growing up under less than desirable circumstances and anyone who loves to run."

-Mary Allen, Author of *The Rooms of Heaven*

"If *Dry Run* helps just one person, then I'm all for it."

-Bernard J. MacCallum, Runner of 32 marathons, Fastest Time: 2:46, Clarence Demar Marathon, 1982

DRY RUN
A Memoir

Nikki MacCallum

Auctus Publishers

Copyright © 2019 Nikki MacCallum
Copy editing by Melanie Rud
Book design by Sarah Eldridge
Author photography by David Gazzo

Published by Auctus Publishers
606 Merion Avenue, First Floor
Havertown, PA 19083
Printed in the United States of America

Dry Run is a work of creative non-fiction. The events are told to the best of the author's memory. Some names have been altered to protect the privacy of those involved and in a few cases, two minor characters have been written into one for the sake of clarity.

ISBN 978-1-7327882-3-7 (Electronic)
ISBN 978-1-7327882-2-0 (Softcover)

To Mom and Dad

Thank you for being the tremendous humans that you both are, and thank you not only for your support, but also for your undying encouragement to tell my story.

I love you.

Foreword

My name is Jonny Podell and I'm a recovering alcoholic and drug addict. I've struggled with addiction more than half of my life and after recovering from a dramatic and cinematic bottom due to heroin and cocaine in 1985, I was able to preserve the tapestry of my life.

As a young man out of college, I'd never used a drug. I was drawn to the music business and had what most people would call a meteoric rise. My first four clients wound up being the four biggest artists in the world. At the same time, I started using drugs, and my usage quickly kept pace with my rise in business. It was only a matter of time before the drugs overtook my success. In 1984 I lost everything. I had no place to live, and it was only by the grace of God that my ex-wife continued to allow me to see my two children. I quickly rebuilt my life through the program of recovery, reestablished myself as a father, reestablished myself in business, and re-established myself as a member of the community. Life was good. Twenty-five years later, after a simple surgery on my hand, I wound up on the slippery slope of an addiction to pain meds. I was taking two-hundred-fifty extra-strength pain pills a week. I had multiple doctors, pharmacies, and prescriptions— a definite legal no-no. I was filled with paranoia about getting caught, lying to everybody that I was still clean, and afraid to leave my house for in my mind the police were waiting outside to nab me.

Feeling alone and hopeless was an understatement. I didn't know where to turn and I was unwilling to admit my plight. I was truly trapped in a hell on earth. This bottom, emotionally, was even greater than the very dramatic bottom I'd experienced twenty-five years prior. My children intervened, and when I finally admitted the truth, as the saying goes, it set me free. Once again I went to rehab and there, in addition to participating and paying very close attention to everything, I experienced a spiritual awakening—the type of which we all read about. But this time I wasn't reading. It happened to me. My sobriety coupled with this profound spiritual experience that I've had has allowed me to live again, love again, and thrive again. At seventy years old I've brought a new son into the world to join my two grown children and two grandchildren. I am living a life beyond my wildest dreams.

Dry Run touched me on multiple levels. What resonated with me the most is its rawness and authenticity. MacCallum didn't hold anything back and the book excels at depicting the challenging family dynamics that arise when addiction is involved. Reading this as someone in recovery, I found it powerful to hear these things from a daughter's perspective. Above all, *Dry Run* is relatable. The book is edgy, authentic and poignant. The comparison of running a marathon to the fighting of addiction is profound. Through this device, MacCallum succeeds in giving both of her parents a voice. And, it's funny! I laughed out loud several times. I can see *Dry Run* being particularly powerful for addicts, or for anyone dealing with someone with an addiction (particularly ACOAs) but this book will carry weight with anyone who has had to overcome adversity. It is an important and inspiring reminder to persevere. *Dry Run* is a perfect tribute to the beautiful imperfections of humanity.

Jonny Podell is currently the head of the Podell Talent Agency. Over the course of his career he's represented: George Harrison, John Lennon, the Allman Brothers Band, Alice Cooper, Van Halen, Cyndi Lauper, Peter Gabriel, Britney Spears, NSYNC, and the Backstreet Boys, to name but a few.

Preface

My father is a recovering alcoholic. He has also run thirty-two marathons. After battling alcoholism for twenty years, my father suffered a near death relapse. This led me to the starting line of the Providence Marathon. Though I wasn't a competitive runner at the time, and certainly wasn't thrilled about my decision to run twenty-six point two miles, it was the only thing I could think to do as a Hail Mary pass to save him. He'd been in rehab twice and hospitalized for alcohol poisoning over ten times. I didn't know how else to communicate with him, and I hoped that such a feat —a feat that was important to him and dear to his own heart —would get his attention. So, I ran.

Dry Run has twenty-six point two chapters and is organized around that particular Providence Marathon. Each chapter represents one of the twenty-six point two miles of that race in real time, and also covers a coming-of age story comparing the physical and emotional challenges of running a marathon with the struggles of growing up as an only child with an alcoholic parent.

"Crossing the finish line of a marathon makes me feel unstoppable." That's what my dad told me, even long after he stopped running. Well, even after he stopped walking, for that matter. Before I was born, he ran a total of thirty-two marathons including Boston, which he completed in two hours and forty-eight minutes. He still has the official certificate to prove it. My parents never wanted children but according to my mother, while pushing up the infamous Heartbreak Hill (AKA Heartbreak Hell) during her third Boston Marathon she thought, "Giving birth can't be as bad as this." I guess you could say running is in my blood.

PART I:
TWENTY-SIX
POINT TWO

MILE 1

The gun goes off and I can't believe I'm actually doing this. So many simultaneous thoughts are running through my head, all trying to upstage one another, each with more vibrato and volume than the last. Will I make it through this entire marathon without walking? Will I win? What will I say to my dad when I cross the finish line? Is he well enough to stand outside for four hours while I run this thing? Regardless, he'd still do anything for me. Will my dad be proud of me? Will I puke and die from dehydration before I see him? Was it weird that I didn't go over and say hello to my parents when I spotted them at the starting line? What will I eat after the race? Will I meet a hot dude while I'm running? Will I crap my pants? What if I meet a hot dude running while I'm running while crapping my pants? Is my dad sober? I don't even realize until halfway through the first mile that I've been running on an incline this whole time.

-Providence Marathon, 2011.

I was six years old and full from dinner to the point where my stomach was about to break through my skin and split my belly button in two. Too young to appreciate the joy of a food comma, my biggest goal was shrinking my stomach to make room for the Halloween candy I planned on consuming within the hour. My solution was to sprawl out on my front in hopes that the physical pressure of the living room floor would magically fast-track my digestion. In the kitchen, my dad was clearing the dinner table and my mom's slender figure was hovering over the sink, rapidly rinsing dishes covered in the gloppy parts of the tomato sauce that no one wanted to eat; she started loading the dishwasher.

"Great dinner!" Dad delivered the line to her in a playfully disingenuous tone. Then he paused for just a second, like he was waiting for the laugh track on his own sitcom (or to get a reaction from me). When he didn't get any laughs, he added, "The meatloaf was great. Good stuff." Standing at the dinner table, my father caught my attention through the doorway that separated the kitchen from the living room; we shared a secret smirk and he subtly rolled his eyes. To ensure that I saw exactly what he was doing, he rolled them again, this time moving his head around on his neck in large circles, like an actor on stage at The Old Globe who wanted to make sure the back row could still see him. The eye roll was a very import-

Dry Run

ant skill my dad instilled in me because he knew I'd use it for the rest of my life, and to be fair, he was correct. I returned his eye roll and couldn't help but let out an audible giggle.

"What are you laughing at, Nik?" my mother called through the window above the kitchen sink that looked into the living room.

"Nothing," I replied, trying to stifle another laugh.

"You know I don't like it when you two gang up on me," she said.

It wasn't our fault Dad and I had formed an alliance. Even at the age of six, I knew when a meatloaf was overcooked.

"What's so funny?" my mother asked my father privately and the two of them started to bicker, my mom seriously and my dad playfully. Still sitting on the black-and-white living room carpet, I looked at the board game, positioned right next to a coffee stain, and transcended into my own world.

I played *SORRY!* three or four times a week. As an only child, not wanting to be held back by just Solitaire (which, for the record, I was quite good at), I became very well-versed in solitary versions of board games. When I played *SORRY!* I'd race all four pieces, blue, red, yellow, and green to see which color would win. I'd sometimes sit there for hours at a time, apologizing to myself for sending myself back four spaces over and over again. "I'm sorry. I'm sorry. No, I'm sorry. I'm really sorry. Sorry." The great part about my solo board game endeavors was that I always won.

"Nik, what are you doing?" my mom asked from the kitchen snapping me out of my *SORRY!* haze. A small cluster of soapsuds had floated up from the sink and landed on her frizzy brown bangs.

"Playing *SORRY!*" I yelled back in my stage voice so that she could hear me over the running water.

"That's neat," she replied tentatively. It was as if she was half concerned that I enjoyed playing multiple person board games alone, and partly thrilled that I could entertain myself. My dad finished transferring the last tomato sauce-infested plate from the dinner table to the kitchen counter so my mother could rinse it, and joined me in the living room. After turning on the new television and finding the end of an episode of *Roseanne*, he knelt down next to me and picked up a deck of Uno cards.

"Did you like your dinner, Nik?" he whispered to me conspiratorially, rolling his eyes again for the third time that evening. He really didn't want to give up on the dinner bit. I rolled mine back at him like the good eye roller-in-training that I was and heard the faucet turn off. Mom retreated into my parent's bedroom, which was at the opposite end of our house, and I took the deck of cards from my father and dealt us each seven. Dad let me go first. I picked up a blue three and discarded a blue six. Somehow, over the next several minutes, I watched my pile of cards diminish while my dad's stack grew; I was winning. I couldn't believe that I was only six and so much better than he was at this game. Dad was a lawyer which meant he was really smart, too. Since I beat him, I must've been a genius.

"Uno!" I shrieked as the *Roseanne* credits rolled.

That was the moment my dad let me win. The moment my dad was *able* to let me win. There's a distinct difference between losing and letting someone win.

"It's six-thirty," Dad said looking at the digital clock below the television. "Shouldn't you be getting into your costume?"

"Yeah," I answered loudly with a slight Boston accent, which had developed the year I started going to pre-school in Revere, where both of my parents worked. By the first grade, I was attending the local public school in Hamilton and thank God because I didn't care for Revere. When I got older, my parents admitted that on multiple occasions I came home from pre-school thirsty and crying because other kids would threaten to shake me down for my milk money. To this day I'm confident this is why I don't drink milk. But at the time, Revere made sense because my mother taught music at Revere High School, and my dad was a defense attorney with an office in Revere (since it was such a hot bed for crime). "And your cahwstom," I continued, "is laid out on your bed. I put it there after school."

I always loved a good costume party and October 31, 1990 was no exception. I'd waited all week for that night and it had finally arrived. It was time to get my six-year-old self and my entourage ready for trick-or-treating. To be clear, my entourage consisted of Freckles, my stuffed beagle, and my father, who always took me trick-or-treating. After a quick-change into my brown button-down dress and black Mary Jane shoes to transform into Dorothy from Kansas, pre-tornado, I grabbed Freckles, who I was dressing up as Toto.

That night I had to be careful to carry Freckles on my left side in order to hide his recently injured right ear. The week prior I'd accidentally dropped him in a puddle while getting into my mom's car after school. He almost drowned. My mom tried to fix him with a hair dryer, which left a giant burn mark on his ear. Whether a stuffed animal or a meatloaf, my mom always tried to fix things. It was okay, though. I still loved Freckles even if he was on injured reserve. And, at least she hadn't decided to cover up the burn with tomato sauce or something.

Toto and I marched into my parents' bedroom and planted ourselves on their queen-sized bed, facing the giant mirror with the ugly green frame that took up the majority of the wall above their dresser. The dresser was more hideous than the mirror and the same shade of bright lime green. It looked like it was rescued from a 1970s yard sale. But I looked into that mirror and thought about how my pale complexion and dark hair made me look just like Judy Garland, though I could've used a little blush. Halloween was my favorite night of the year because it was the only time, aside from being in a play, when my mom let me wear makeup. And I liked wearing makeup because I wanted to look like all of the *real* actresses who wore makeup, because I wanted to be one someday.

My mom sat on the bed behind me and started doing my hair while my dad took his shower. I really wanted Judy Garland pigtails with the twists, like Dorothy had in the movie, but I was too young to do them myself. I stared in the mirror while Mom parted my hair and brushed out the snarls. I hoped she was better at doing Judy Garland pigtails than she was at cooking meatloaf. The sound of running water stopped and from the bathroom my dad yelled, "Is Nik in here?" He probably wanted to get dressed in private so once in costume he could have a big reveal.

"Let's finish your hair in the living room so your dad can get ready," Mom suggested. Holding the half-completed right pigtail in place, we maneuvered ourselves to the living room and I kept trying to imagine what my dad would look like in his costume. My pigtails were a little too tight but I didn't feel like asking her to redo them; she'd done enough work for one night. Besides, even though they hurt a little, at least I knew they wouldn't fall out.

The smell of burnt meat lingered in the living room and kitchen and the sound of light rain tapped against the roof. To pass the time while Mom and I waited for my dad, she got out her video camera and filmed me dancing around the house belting out "Somewhere Over the Rainbow" in a variety of different keys while simultaneously flashing my undies at the camera. I wasn't sure why I was flashing the camera, but at the time it felt like the right thing to do. I also thought there was a chance that dancing would help my digestion.

After my third rendition of "Somewhere Over the Rainbow," this one with distinctly more vibrato (a term my mother had taught me) than the previous two versions, I yelled at the top of my lungs, "Dad, are you almost ready?"

"Almost ready, Nik!" he shouted back. Our house only had one floor not counting the basement and wasn't that big, so even from the living room I could hear him rummaging around the bedroom.

Earlier that week, in anticipation of my favorite holiday, I'd carefully selected his costume pieces from the play accessories Mom kept in plastic tubs in the basement. When his door finally opened with a creek, the sound echoed through the entire house. I listened with baited breath as shuffling footsteps came slowly down the hall.

Based on an inconsistent number of seconds in between his shuffles, it sounded like he was having trouble walking. I knew the shoes would be several sizes too small for him, but they did match the rest of the outfit. They were open-toe and made of plastic, but the best part was the large blue jewels perched in the middle of the thick straps that covered the front of the foot.

His footsteps grew louder and sloppier and eventually my dad turned the corner for his big reveal, posing with his hands on his hips and feet parallel, standing in the living room doorway where earlier he had performed eye rolls. I marveled at my masterpiece. His head was cocked slightly to the right and he looked towards the sky. I smiled at him and he batted his eye lashes dramatically. My mother and I both applauded, though my applause seemed far more sincere than hers.

"Daddy!" I said jumping up from the couch, still clapping. He strutted across the room, tripping every few steps, but I figured I'd give him a pass since the shoes were a children's size eleven. He ran races all of the time so his legs were in pretty good shape and looked good under the pink satin strapless dress I'd picked out from the princess kit I'd gotten for Christmas/Chanukah last year. Unfortunately, the dress didn't come up past his waste so it looked more like a skirt, and he didn't have a shirt on. He was also wearing my little Orphan Annie wig from my Halloween costume circa 1989, which was actually a flaming reddish-orange wig from the clown section of Toys 'R' Us. It barely covered his blond hair, which he'd been bleaching for as long as I could remember. While I had nothing but the greatest intentions, looking back, I essentially dressed my father up as a slutty, grown-up Orphan Annie drag queen. My mother's eyes grew wide and her jaw dropped. She looked disturbed, but did her best to remain stoic.

"Let's go, Daddy!" I said. Jumping up and down, I grabbed the wooden basket that would double as a prop for Dorothy and a trick-or-treating bag for candy.

"Okay, Nik. Let me just change my clothes."

"Thank God," my mother said.

"But Dad, I thought we were going out in costume, together. I've been planning your outfit for weeks!"

"You have?" he asked as his cheeks softened, making him appear as if he was trying to buy some time to come up with a more satisfying response. "Oh. Well, it's awfully frigid out. Your dad doesn't want to catch cold in this little dress." He looked at my face for a few long seconds and his skeptical expression melted into a defeated smile. He hung his head, shook it back and forth very slowly, as though he was pained by the thought of letting me down. He tried rolling his eyes, seemingly hoping that making me laugh would get him off the hook.

Finally, realizing that the only cure for my pout was sticking to our original plan, he changed his tune. "Never mind! I like my outfit!" He threw a ski parka over the dress, grabbed a pair of running shoes, and we were off—through the garage door—to see the wizard. I turned around just in time to see my mother standing at the living room window with a big smile on her face. The smile said both, "Why the hell did I marry this man?" and "Thank God I did." I waved goodbye to her just like Dorothy waved goodbye to Munchkin Land and continued down our not-so-yellow-brick driveway.

My father and I walked the dark driveways of Old Cart Road as the light rain misted on our heads. Poor Freckles got damp. We progressed from door to door and after five houses, no one had yet commented on Dad's costume, which was disappointing.

"I'll race you to the front, Dorothy," Dad challenged me. Before I had a chance to explain to him that Dorothy only ran when flying monkeys were chasing her, he was sprinting up the Riley's driveway.

"Dad! That's not fair!" I shrieked, piercing the air of Hamilton, Massachusetts. The finish line seemed to be the bottom step leading to the Riley's front door, or at least that's where Dad stopped.

I chased after him as quickly as my Mary Janes allowed and I was so tickled by the image of my dad racing in that dress that I didn't even realize I was running uphill.

"I won, Nik!" he declared, as if it was an actual accomplishment.

"Good for you Dad. Now let's get some candy!" Running was the only thing dad never let me beat him at, and quite frankly, my endgame wasn't to win a race, it was to amass chocolate.

There were two pumpkins sitting on opposite sides of the top step. Before I even got a chance to ring the doorbell I heard an evil laugh from behind the screen door. Over the course of eight seconds or so the laugh became bellowing and hysterical.

"Hey man, you make a good lady! Your wife must be thrilled. Tell her I say hi."

"Thanks, Al. Will do!" my dad replied in a kind tone, without skipping a beat.

I grabbed some M&Ms, put Freckles in my basket on top of the rest of the candy and reached for my dad's hand. Al's wife was calling him from the other room and he closed the screen door. We retreated down the stairs, back down the Riley's driveway, and prepared to regroup for our next conquest.

Large water droplets started hitting my tightly braided hair and one landed right on the part of my white sock exposed through my shoe. After two more houses, it became too rainy, even for me. I rustled through my basket for the package of candy corn I'd gotten at the first house, opened it, and started eating. I always tried to eat whatever candy I could before I got home because my mom never let me keep it. Every year she made me trade in all of my Halloween candy in exchange for a present. That year I was gunning for a Cabbage Patch Kids doll named Maggie—that, or the *Les Misérables* soundtrack. It had swear words in it which made it infinitely more appealing than other musicals.

Dad, Freckles, and I got home just in time for my dad to catch the new episode of *Walker, Texas Ranger*. He took a seat on the couch and cracked open a beer while my mom helped me loosen my pigtails and pulled off my muddy shoes, socks, and damp dress so I could shower and go to bed. After my shower, Freckles and I were safely tucked away in my warm sheets, both of us with hair that was still a little damp. I kissed his ear and closed my eyes. My head felt good now that I was free of the pigtails that had been pulling at my scalp all night.

Dry Run

My mom came into my room to say goodnight and put on a Broadway tape so that I could fall asleep. Ever since I could remember, she'd played musical soundtracks to help me fall asleep. I loved the ones with inappropriate words like "Tits and Ass," from *A Chorus Line*. That night I fell asleep to Donna McKechnie singing "The Music and the Mirror," a song that I'd performed in our living room, often. I wanted to be just like Donna when I grew up and dance in a beautiful red dress, in a role that was written especially for me, and win a Tony. As I started to doze off I thought about how I was so happy my dad wore his costume and that he liked it. I hoped it made him proud. Who needed a brother or a sister when I had a Dad?

MILE 2

My mom advised me to start out slow even if the natural adrena-line of the marathon gave me the impulse to go fast. People only really pay attention to how fast you're going at the finish line, anyway, and you don't want to tire yourself out early and have to quit. Pacing myself, something I've never been good at. Luckily I'm not experiencing an urge to go fast since it's pretty close to the starting line, and besides, I'm still surrounded on all sides by hundreds of footsteps patting the pavement, which is physically forc-ing me to stay slow. I'm not even going to try to calculate my pace. Also, who are we kidding, I'm not going to win. Really, I just want to finish. What if my dad isn't at the finish line after all? Could this torture be for nothing? Since this is my first and last marathon it will be a Personal Record, as long as I cross that finish line.

–Providence Marathon, 2011.

A blast of cold air gushed out from the vents below the dash-board when Dad started the car. The frost on the window slow-ly started to melt, revealing the grey Thanksgiving morning. He looked over his right shoulder and guided the silver Isuzu Rodeo out of the driveway without hitting the tree that my mom often tapped with her car. Over the past several years she'd taken out a tail light, a rear-view mirror, and some paint.

My scrawny, eleven-year-old legs were covered with goose bumps and I kind of regretted wearing my thin navy blue soccer shorts that wouldn't have warmed a hairless Chihuahua. But Dad always said that real runners wore shorts, even if it was only thirty degrees outside. Perhaps that was his version of 'fake it 'til you make it,' another important skill he taught me at a young age. He himself was sporting a pair of neon green shorts that barely covered his butt cheeks, but he was thin and could kind of get away with it; it passed as embarrassing dad attire.

"Nik, can you look in the backseat to make sure I brought our race registration forms?"

I reached behind me, comatose, and grabbed the entry forms for the 18th Annual Turkey Trot: 1995. They were hiding under the greasy, brown peel from a banana my dad must've eaten on the way home from work yesterday. Gross.

Dry Run

"Got them," I said.

"Are you ready for your first Turkey Trot, Nik?" His excitement was palpable.

"I wish it weren't so early," I told him.

He laughed, a deep, piercing, slightly nasal laugh consisting of a bunch of staccato chuckles that sounded like they were coming from the back of his throat. It was unclear to me what he found so funny. I hit the FM button on the radio panel and changed the station from boring talk radio to top 40. I'd have given anything for him to stop talking that morning so I could've dozed off. I wished I'd never agreed to the Turkey Trot. That morning was an example of why I preferred theater rehearsals. They never started before six o'clock at night and the rehearsal spaces were heated.

"How was this morning's waffle?" my dad asked, obviously trying to make conversation.

My father's job description, in addition to defending the criminals of Revere (whose children had probably had a lot of milk on my dime), included a chore I wouldn't wish on my worst enemy—getting me up in the morning. Dad had done this dutifully for the past several years, and we'd established a routine that seemed to be working. Every day he'd wake me up about twenty minutes before I actually had to be up for school. Then I'd get into a hot shower, after which I'd return to my twin bed, and let my fleece blanket absorb the water on my body while I fell back to sleep. About ten minutes later, like clockwork, Dad would come back for take two, this time luring me out of bed with a waffle, which was almost always burnt. Every morning, after I was successfully up and running, I'd get into the car, burnt waffle in hand, and Dad would drive me to school. I'd start to eat around the crunchy charred perimeter; I always liked saving the middle for last. The most curious piece of the puzzle was that after years of this charade, my dad still continued to burn the waffles. I guess he never mastered how to use a toaster.

The morning of the Turkey Trot there wasn't another car on the road as we drove through Ipswich, passing horse farms and huge, barren, frost-covered fields that stretched on for miles. Though my parents settled in the area because of the strong public school system, the town of Hamilton was known for its horses. Rumor had it the horse that threw Christopher Reeves was ensconced there. Like the residents of any rural Massachusetts town, everyone was sleeping, as they should have been at that ungodly hour. Everyone, it seemed, except for my father and I.

"You know, your mom and I ran a marathon together once and she was so slow that your dad was able to finish, go home and shower, drive back, and re-park the car just in time to see your mom cross the finish line." He loved telling me that story. Every time he did, his face lit up and I could never decipher what his favorite part was. Did he love the fact that he and my mom ran together? Was he proud that he was able to get so much accomplished within the time frame between their finishes? Or did he think it was funny that she was so much slower than he? I looked at him, and wondered why he often referred to himself in the third person when he talked to me. "And your dad's fastest marathon time was two hours and for-ty-two minutes. Your dad is quick." He loved to remind me of his most successful marathon whenever he got the chance, but not in a boastful way, it was more like solemn reminiscing about his prime. I was trying my best to wake up, and rested my feet on the dashboard right above the vent which was now blowing hot air. My mom always told me, "get your dirty feet off my clean dashboard," but since Dad left brown banana peels in his back seat, he couldn't possibly care that much about his dashboard. We drove another twenty miles or so in silence and I mentally prepared myself for the race. It was a 5K, which, according to my new-found sixth grade knowledge of the metric system, was 3.1 miles. I'd never run three miles before. In fact, I don't think I'd ever gone further than a mile. I ran a lot during soccer practices, but the only time my distances had ever been measured were during the end of the year walkathons in elementary school, where kids would solicit parents to sponsor a phantom cause. Sometimes it was ten cents per lap, maybe a dollar if you were lucky. And those laps were walking. I figured if I started dying in the mid-dle of the Turkey Trot, Plan B was to walkathon it.

A few minutes later we pulled into the race parking lot, where an overly enthusiastic volunteer wearing a drumstick hat and a goofy smile directed us to a spot. Dad turned off the engine and I stepped out of the car into the freezing air, as goosebumps immediately at-tacked my legs. My violet jacket barely served as a shield against the wind that ripped through my seventy-five-pound body and I started jumping up and down to stay warm. I threw my black winter hat over the pigtails I'd French braided myself, and grabbed my Walkman, cueing up the *Les Misérables* Act I cassette. Dad and I set out to walk down the hill, avoiding rogue orange cones that matched his artificially-tanned skin. We jumped over a wooden fence and crossed the street to where the registration line was forming. We got our numbers and headed to the starting area, the frost-covered ground crunching beneath our feet.

"Nik, I'm going to go and try to find my friend, Mitch," Dad told me. I'd been hearing about this guy for my entire life, but only the same three things. One: Mitch and my dad met while running races in Revere together about ten years before I was born. Two: When Mitch went to Africa to join the Peace Corps, he stored quite a bit of furniture in our garage. Three: Mitch looked like Jesus.

I wanted to meet my dad's mystery Jesus-friend just to confirm his existence, but I was way too cold and tired to try and carry on a conversation, let alone one with a stranger. I put on my headphones, pressed play on my Walkman, and pretended to stretch as Act 1 of *Les Misérables* (The London Cast) began. I saw my father walk back in the direction of the car, which struck me as odd since we'd just come from there. Maybe Mitch liked to hang out in parking lots, proselytizing. Maybe that was his thing and my dad knew just where to find him. Dad disappeared into the crowd of runners, some of whom were wearing absurd-looking turkey hats, and I started to feel a little anxious. Even though I hated running next to my dad because he always went so fast and I could never keep up, the idea of running my first race all alone was daunting. But my dad always said that running wasn't a group activity; racing was something you did alone. Plus, when I looked around I noticed that there seemed to be a lot of other kids my age, some even younger, running with their parents, so it couldn't be that hard. If they could do it, so could I.

"All runners please report to the starting line. Repeat, all runners please report to the starting line." I looked around. Dad was nowhere to be found and I followed the masses of people through a frozen field, like the ones we'd passed on our drive, to the line of yellow tape where the race would start. Still able to see my breath, I stood behind the tape with all of the other runners; there must have been 2,000 people there. About five minutes passed and I wished my dad would appear.

"Is that Nikki?" A voice said in a deep South Boston accent. "You should have run to the stahting line, not walked there, Miss!" I turned in the direction of the bothersome voice. "It's Mitch!" Well, at last, there he was—Mitch. I'd be lying if I said I wasn't a little annoyed by his preachy commentary, and the way he said 'starting line' was especially irritating since I'd worked so hard in my singing lessons to learn how to pronounce my Rs. Mitch slowly reached out to give me a hug, like Christ in the parable of the little children. His beard was long and brown, draped over the front of his black hoodie, which matched his black tights and sneakers. The effect was alarming. I wouldn't have been shocked if you'd told me he also had a criminal record.

"Good morning, Mitch," I said politely, removing my head-phones and over-pronouncing the "r." Suddenly my dad emerged from the crowd and tapped Mitch on the shoulder.

"You ready?" Mitch gave my dad a confident nod and turned back to me.

"Staht your wahm-ups, Miss" he said. Being a Jew, like my mom, I didn't feel that I needed to do what Jesus told me so I laughed it off and continued to just stand there. I'd have done what Andrew Lloyd Webber told me, maybe, but not Jesus. As time passed I became infinitely more nervous about being able to finish the race. I hadn't realized until we got there that it was a cross-country race, which basically meant over the river and through the woods, rather than on flat pavement.

"Nik," Dad said, "I can't wait until you start running mara-thons. When your dad crosses the finish line of a marathon it makes your dad feel unstoppable."

"No thanks. That will never happen. I'm never going to run a marathon."

"Is Nik nervous?"

"You already asked me. No." I didn't know why I was being so short with him, but he never got mad at me for it. When I was curt with my mother, she always told me that I was being fresh.

"Good. The best thing about races is that you're only ever really competing against yourself. It's all about PRs, Nik. PRs!" I had no idea what PR meant aside from peanut butter roll, but may-be I'd ask my mom later. I looked down to make sure my sneakers were double-knotted, like Dad taught me the time we went running around our neighborhood as practice. Just as the starting gun went off, my dad reminded me, "Remember, even if you're slow during the actual race, the part people see is the big finish. You always want to run the fastest at the very end. And don't go too fast down those hills just ahead. Even if you want to fly down them, you must pace yourself at the beginning." I noted his first-person communication, as he and Mitch sprinted ahead since they were more seasoned runners. I decided to take my dad's advice and hang back and take things a little bit slower. I might've only been eleven, but I wasn't an idiot. Last night, while she made us a spaghetti dinner, my mom had given me the same warning: If I started off too fast, I might not be able to finish the race, and not to be afraid to take it one step at a time, even if my dad left me behind. She wasn't as fast as my dad, but she had run five marathons, so she clearly knew what she was talking about. She was also the one who taught me about carb loading, or, as Mitch would say, cahhhb loading. Another very important skill that my parents taught me at a young age. Parenting at its finest, truly.

You could hear the pack of runners and thousands of feet stomping across the field. You could taste the Thanksgiving excitement, but I kept a slow and steady pace and tried not to get swept up in all of the adrenaline. At the end of the day, I just wanted to finish. Given my competitive nature, it was hard to be okay with others running ahead of me, especially when it was a golden retriever, being pulled on a leash by a kid half my age. But, like my dad said, this wasn't a group activity and the only performance I needed to worry about was my own. Once across the field, the crowd thinned out into more established pace groups and I seemed to be surrounded by people running closer to my speed, since the faster ones had already run ahead.

I was running under tree branches, over rocks, and through puddles and I was pretty miserable. About five minutes into the trot, I felt a sharp pain in my lower left side that hurt the most when I inhaled. It was so cold I could still see my breath in front of me. My calves started to hurt and I wasn't sure how I was going to keep this up for however many more minutes I had left. I also felt like I had to be on extra high alert to avoid tripping over the branches that were sometimes in my path. One step at a time. In the distance, about a hundred yards ahead of me, I saw a large white X painted on the trunk of a tree. It must've been a distance marker of sort. Maybe if I could just get to that X I could deal with the rest of the race later. But in that moment, all I had to do was make it to that X. Simple. About a minute later I passed that white X. About a hundred yards further ahead I saw what looked to be a little bridge built over a stream. Okay. I just had to make it to that bridge. Landmark by landmark, I would get myself through that race.

I wondered how far ahead of me Dad and Mitch were and whether or not they were running together. The woods after the bridge were decorated with spectators, some holding cameras. "Master of the House" was playing, so I knew I'd been running for about twenty minutes or so; I must've been about halfway through the course. Ten feet ahead of me on the left, I saw an older man trip over a branch. He sat down on a stump and clutched his left knee. I wanted to stop and help him, but my instinct was to keep running. Too many cooks in the kitchen was never a good thing, and I was sure adults would be more effective in coming to his aid. Also, helping him would've slowed me down and I didn't want Dad to be embarrassed by my time. And I had to think about the PR, whatever that meant. While it didn't feel entirely right in my gut, I passed him. I looked ahead and saw people sitting on a giant log that had fallen along the course. The log: my next landmark.

My head started pounding and I thought it might've been because I was so tired. Why did my dad love this so much? The whole thing was painful and all I could think about was how much I'd rather be on stage. I tried to pretend I was playing the role of a runner and that I wasn't actually there myself. What if I were Jean Val Jean running through the sewers of Paris? For a second I thought about slowing down, as if I were about to sing my big ballad, and walk the rest of the way, but again, I didn't want to disappoint my dad. He'd been so excited for me to run this race, and I liked that he was proud of me. Not finishing my first race, or even walking during part of it, wasn't really an option for me. I was a straight A student and something about walking part of it felt to me like getting a B, or maybe even a C. Several landmarks later, my eyes settled on the opening to a field I could see through two larger trees.

By the time I neared the finish line, my sneakers were covered in mud and I was still dodging tree stumps, sticks, and holes. My breath was growing short and the pain in my left side, which I'd managed to block out for the past several minutes by pretending to be Jean Val Jean, became too agonizing to ignore. I couldn't believe that within the next few minutes I would have completed just over three miles. I'd never run this far, ever, and it seemed like an eternity. Lines of parents, spouses, and siblings formed on both sides of the

Dry Run

path that led to the finish line. About one hundred yards from the end I saw Mitch in the crowd; he'd obviously finished and come back for me. Let's be honest, Jesus was pretty hard to miss, especially since he was also unusually tall. He was standing along the path to the finish line, flanked by spectators on both sides. His head was moving back and forth as his eyes tried to focus on each individual runner.

"Great jawb, Nikki! Keep going!" he yelled, slow clapping as I passed him.

I didn't know why I was so annoyed by him. He'd done nothing wrong, but it bothered me that he was acting like he'd known me my whole life, when we'd only just met. I guess he was just trying to be supportive of his best friend's daughter but I felt angry that he was intruding on what was supposed to be a father-daughter date, though I still didn't see my dad anywhere. I could hear his words echoing in my brain: "Even if you were slow during the actual race, the part people see is the big finish. You always want to run the fastest at the very end." I tried to forget about the burning sensation in my thighs and took a deep breath, trying to muster the willpower to take me up that last hill. In the future, I'd rather stick to our father-daughter dates at the mall.

I sped up and sprinted to the end and crossed that finish line. My final time was thirty-six minutes, and while I had no concept as to whether that was a good or bad time for a 5K, there were still people behind me, so it couldn't have been that bad. I also couldn't believe that I'd run for thirty-six minutes straight. My voice lessons weren't even that long. Someone was handing out waters to all of the runners at the finish line. I grabbed one and saw my father coming from the direction of our car in the parking lot.

"Nik! You finished!" he yelled across the crowd, in a pleasantly surprised tone of voice.

"Yeah, Dad. I finished!" I yelled back, irritated by his tone which suggested that he didn't seem to think I would.

"I didn't think you'd finish for another few minutes. I can't believe I missed you."

"Did you go home, change and shower, and come back?" I said, trying to break the tension, which was probably just in my head. I couldn't help but wonder why the man who had historically hung onto my every word left the finish line during my first race. What was he doing in the car?

"Very funny," he said nodding his head. "I'm such a proud dad! You finished your first race! How do you feel?"

I felt tired. Hungry. Treacherous. Those were a few of the adjectives that came to mind. Not wanting to ruin his euphoria, I just said, "Great, Dad!" We said goodbye to Mitch and piled our muddy, exhausted, freezing selves back into the car. Hoping I didn't miss Carol Channing on television, we got home in time to catch the end of the Macy's Day Parade and to start the preparations for Thanksgiving dinner, which was at our house that year. I was so hungry.

MILE 3

I'm cold. I'm wearing a white tank top, which is definitely one size too small, and shorts that are absolutely two inches too short, but running a marathon gives me license to wear whatever the hell I want, and I'm hopeful I'll warm up soon. I wonder if there's any form of mac and cheese near the finish line. A girl can dream. About one hundred yards ahead of me on the left is a water station. I just need to get to the water station, and then I'll pick my next landmark to run to. I'm starting to feel a tiny bit light-headed, which is likely a product of anxiety and nerves more than anything else. I decide to pop my first gel shot, tucked away in my runner's pack. These shots are supposed to give me energy in lieu of eating food—allegedly. After tearing open the wrapper, I pull out my first shot; it's small, green, and reminiscent of a Juicy Fruit gummy candy. It tastes pretty good and I revel in the anticipation of an energy burst as a light wind hits my face. For an instant I feel like a little girl again, free from it all. What are my parents going to do for the next four hours? I can't imagine my dad is that mobile with his walker.

- Providence Marathon, 2011.

The wind kissed my twelve-year-old face and freed a few strands of frizzy hair (which I'd styled with just enough gel to make crunchy). I was sporting my infamous half-ponytail look, which I loved so much at the time because it allowed my long curls (inherited from my mother) to fly free down my back, while the top stayed slicked back and out of my eyes. 1996 was the year of my most committed—and most unfortunate—hairstyles. I had this strict routine where I'd take a shower, immediately slick my hair in that half-pony as tight as it would go, no bumps, coat the top with gel, and then not put any product in the rest of my frizzy hair. It bore a striking resemblance to the hairstyles of a handful of men (from New Jersey, eye roll) that I'd go on to date in my twenties.

That afternoon, Suzie, my best friend in middle school, and I were jumping up and down on her family's new trampoline. It was a Wednesday in late October, which was the best kind of Wednesday. It was early release day at school and the weather was still warm enough to play outside. Suzie's mom said that as long as we did our homework first, we could go in the backyard and jump.

"I'm going to try a back flip!" Suzie yelled, signaling for me to get out of the way. I bounced over to the perimeter and sat down cross-legged, wanting to stay out of her way in case she jumped a little too high and things got out of control. She jumped a few times before torpedoing herself into a giant backflip. Her long red hair flew wildly as she flipped and landed on her feet, then bounced on her butt, giggling, as her braces twinkled in the sun.

I had to try that backflip. Without missing a beat, I stood up and made my way to the middle of the trampoline, bouncing two feet at a time. I thought about how some kids at school would be too scared to do a backflip, but I, on the other hand, could just do it. I couldn't jump *that* far; there was really no way I could fall off the trampoline. What was the worst that could happen? Had I known how fleeting that sentiment would be, I'd have clung to it longer.

"Go, Nikki, go!" Suzie cheered.

I started with smaller bounces, with about a foot of air between my feet and the net. Then I bent my knees and hit the trampoline harder, sending my body sailing into the air. I experienced a moment of panic just before the third bounce, but in that split second, I also knew I couldn't hesitate. My legs flew over my head and for a second I was weightless. Before I knew it, I was back on my feet bouncing, just like Suzie was. We jumped together for the rest of the afternoon, taking turns doing back flips. Once the first one was out of my system, the rest were a piece of cake.

It was getting dark and my dad was supposed to pick me up on his way home from work. He'd taken over the role of family chauffer, among other things, since my mom had breast cancer a second time, earlier that year. She seemed fine, though she'd definitely scaled back her activities. None of us talked much about it, but I knew the surgery was successful. With a lot of help from my dad, and a little help from me, Mom was on the mend. Mostly, she just seemed tired.

At the time I didn't have enough life experience to grasp that life itself was and is fleeting. I remember feeling sad that my mom wasn't feeling well, and I remember her having a massive bandage under her left arm. But it never occurred to me that the cancer was life-threatening, probably because my parents never positioned it that way. It was just an annoying surgery and healing process my mom had to go through and that was that. Looking back, I don't know

Dry Run

whether she thought I was too young to comprehend cancer, or that maybe she just wanted to shield me from her trauma and did so by not talking about it.

Sometimes when my dad picked me up from a friend's house I liked to pretend that I was a Broadway star, like Donna McKechnie, and that he was my driver picking me up at the stage door of a theatre. That night he was going to take me to my musical rehearsal at the local community theatre. I usually drove with Mom, since she was the musical director of that season's production of *A Swashbuckling Pirate Revue*. (It was what it sounded like, an hour-long musical revue about pirates. To this day, it's unclear to me how *A Swashbuckling Pirate Revue* had a sold out run, but apparently the town of Hamilton went nuts for pirates.) That particular Wednesday she was going early to teach a smaller group of soloists the harmony part to "With One Hook" a musical parody of Andrew Lloyd Webber's "With One Look," which I wasn't in. Lately she'd been scheduling more and more rehearsals to start around the time my dad got home. They ran later into the night, and even though she always complained about being tired and driving after dark, I loved any excuse to stay up past my bedtime.

The air started to get a chilly, making the hairs on my arm stand up straight. October days were always hard to predict; as soon as you settled into a warm afternoon, the wind picked up. I put on my Red Sox Hoodie, the one my dad had given me for Christmas the year before. He was happy to encourage my infatuation with his favorite team. We were hoping to catch a game together in the spring.

"So I have something to tell you," Suzie said, with a guilty look in her eyes. She sat down in the center of the trampoline, waiting to speak until I zipped up my sweatshirt and was settled. She wanted my undivided attention.

"What?" I asked. I scooched a little closer so that I was sitting exactly opposite her.

"I did something," she said.

"Okay. What kind of something?"

"I might've slipped a note in Dave's locker asking him if he'd like to go out with me, in the form of a multiple-choice question."

"What? What does that even mean?" I laughed and pulled my hands into my sleeves for extra warmth.

"I wrote a note asking him if he'd like to go out with me," she clarified. "I then added some empty boxes with optional answers next to them. I instructed him to check off the box next to his answer and return it to my locker."

"What were the options?" I couldn't even begin to guess what choices Suzie had given Dave. Before she could answer, her mom interrupted our juicy conversation.

"Girls, can you come here for a second?" Mrs. Mason yelled out the back door.

"Be right there, Mom!" Suzie bent over the side of the trampoline face first, grabbed the metal perimeter, and did a slow summersault off, landing on her butt on the ground. Taking what I felt was the safer approach, I shimmied off feet first and sat down on the grass next to my sneakers. I jammed my feet into my shoes, but didn't bother tying them because I knew I'd just have to take them off again inside Suzie's house.

"Hurry up girls!" Suzie's mom called again. My hands were dirty from the grass and the trampoline but I didn't care. Suzie and I would probably have to finish the Dave conversation on the phone because I was sure my dad was waiting for me in the driveway. It was dark enough to be close to six; he was supposed to come at 5:30. Suzie and I ran to her mom so she didn't have to shout at us anymore. She was standing on the back porch holding the portable phone with a somewhat concerned look on her face. Her forehead looked wrinkled.

"Suzie, come inside for a second, please," she said in a loving but stern voice. Mrs. Mason was a painter who also played the harp. She was one of those artsy people who always sounded passionate and emphatic no matter what she was talking about. She could've been talking about oatmeal, and the concern and love she had for that oatmeal would be unparalleled. "Nikki, honey," she said to me. "Your mom is on the phone and would like to speak with you." I wondered why she'd be calling me from rehearsal.

It was apparent to me by the tone of Mrs. Mason's voice that something was wrong. I wondered if maybe my mom, waiting on the other end of that cordless phone, might've been upset or angry with me for some reason. Had I forgotten to make my bed that morning? Was she calling to tell me that I wouldn't be able to play at Suzie's anymore because I left my room a mess? Had I forgotten to feed our pet bunnies? Knots formed in my stomach and I slowly reached for the phone. Mrs. Mason's pale freckled face remained unchanged as she turned back to the kitchen as if to give me some privacy. I put the receiver to my ear and could hear my mother breathing through the static.

Dry Run

"Hi, Mom," I answered casually. What's up?"

"Hi, I already spoke to Mrs. Mason and you're going to stay there for dinner, okay?" I'm going to pick you up later but I may not get there until eleven or so. If you want to sleep over there, you can."

This was unexpected and insane. My mom never let me have sleepovers on a school night. I wasn't even allowed to go on AOL instant messenger after ten o'clock. Also, what about rehearsal?

"Okay," I answered, unsure of what to say next. The pace of the conversation was off. My mother usually talked so fast that I could barely get a word in. We rarely shared silences, except for when she'd had cancer. Was that all she was calling about? Why was she letting me sleep over Suzie's? I waited for her to hang up, and after a few more seconds of silence, she didn't. "Is something wrong?" I managed to ask, even though I didn't really want to hear the answer, nor could I imagine what could possibly be wrong. At that point I had the feeling it was something far worse than an unmade bed. Was cancer back?

My mom's trembling voice said, "Dad is sick."

"Oh." I paused. "With what?" The knots in my stomach grew larger and started to twist around my intestines. My face felt hot.

"Nikki," she said. Her voice started to break and I could tell she was using all of her strength, the same strength she used to beat cancer twice, to resist crying. "I don't expect you to understand this at your age, but it's very important that you don't tell anyone what I'm going to tell you. If I find out you even told Suzie, you're going to be in big trouble. If I find out you told anyone what I'm about to tell you, you'll be in big trouble."

Then I felt scared. "Okay, Mom. I promise I won't tell."

"Your father has a drinking problem. He's an alcoholic. He's very sick and in the hospital right now. I'm with him and won't be able to come get you until eleven or so. Please, you cannot tell anyone.

"I got it, Mom. Jesus. Who do you think I am?" I wasn't sure why my response was so defensive. "Okay," I continued, trying to make my end of the conversation sound a little bit kinder in case Suzie's mom could hear. "I'll stay here until you come get me. I love you. Bye." I hung up the phone and stood there, staring into Suzie's backyard at the trampoline where I was just doing backflips. I was so confused. I wanted to run and look up *alcoholic* in the dictionary so that I had a clear understanding of what exactly my dad was sick with. That was how I'd learned about masturbation. I heard the *Rent* soundtrack, and looked up *masturbation, sodomy,* and *AZT.* I didn't recall there being any alcoholics in *Rent.* I could've asked to see a dictionary, but I'd promised not to tell Suzie and I didn't want her to ask me what I was researching. Instead, I handed the phone back to Mrs. Mason and forced a smile.

"So, Nikki," Mrs. Mason said. "What would you like for dinner? I was going to make macaroni and cheese because that's Suzie's favorite but if there's something else you'd like you just tell me."

"I love mac and cheese," I said.

"Suzie is that okay with you?" Mac and cheese makes everything better, and for a second I wondered if my mom told Suzie's mom that my dad was an alcoholic and that was why she was being so nice. But then I thought my mom probably didn't tell her because she was so adamant about me not telling anyone.

"Yay! You're staying!" Suzie said. "Let's go up to my room until dinner is ready." We went upstairs to her room and locked the door. I'd always been jealous that Suzie's bedroom door locked because mine didn't. But then, I had my own phone line in my room and Suzie didn't.

"So, the options I gave Dave were as follows: A.) Yes. B.) No. C.) I need to think about it. D.) No, but I will slow dance with you at the next dance. E.) Yes, but in a group. F.) None of the above." I forced out a laugh a beat later than I should've. What was an alcoholic exactly? How sick was my dad? Would he ever pick me up from Suzie's again? Was this temporary?

I willed my attention back to Suzie. "You gave him all of those options?"

"Yeah! With boxes next to each one so he can check off which ones apply."

"Yeah, you said that outside. You're brave." I wished I could slip a note to my dad at the hospital with empty boxes where he could check off the answers that applied. Are you going to be okay? A.) Yes. B.) No. C.) I will be after I get out of the hospital. D.) Yes, once I get the right medicine. E.) None of the above.

"Anyway, what did your mom want, Nik?" Suzie asked me.

"Oh nothing." My mother's warning weighed very heavily on me because the last thing I ever wanted was to be in big trouble. "My dad just got tied up at work and isn't able to get me so she's going to come later."

"Yay! More time for us!"

"Yes!" I responded hollowly. More play time. That was all I needed. More play time and some of Mrs. Mason's mac and cheese and maybe a dictionary.

MILE 4

My next landmark is a giant church-like building that's maybe a quarter of a mile ahead. I lock eyes on it and run toward it. There's a boy to my left who looks to be about twelve; he came up behind me and is now keeping pace with me. I hate when people try to run next to me because then I feel pressure to keep up with them. I'd rather the kid hurry up and pass me so I can do this my way. I slow down even more and he slows down with me. I speed up and he speeds up with me. What the hell is his problem? Run your own marathon, kid asshole. Why is this random twelve-year-old making me so angry? Have I given him too much power? And it is only Mile 4. Incidentally, marathons don't bring out the best in me. I never ran long distances when I was his age, just at soccer practices when my dad made us do laps around the field, four laps each practice, which equaled a mile. By the time I complete the mile I'm on now, I'll have run the distance of four soccer practices and only have twenty-two soccer practices left to go.

—Providence Marathon, 2011.

Mud and damp grass kept getting stuck to the bottom of my cleats as I dragged the mesh bag full of soccer balls across the parking lot to the game field. There were two balls that didn't fit into the equipment bag so I kicked them in front of me. Being the coach's daughter, I was in charge of making sure the first aid kit, goalie gloves, and starting lineup also made it to the game—even when the coach didn't.

My dad was away for about three days before I saw him, the length of a holiday weekend. After my mom picked me up at Suzie's that night, he spent two days at the local hospital in what my mom called "detox." He was then transferred to a rehab facility about a two hour drive from our house, which didn't feel much like a home without Dad in it. Mom and I were going to make the trek to visit him after my soccer game.

I dribbled the two balls while my mom walked next to me, dragging her massive lawn chair to the field so she could watch the game comfortably with the other parents who'd all be cheering on the Renegades. Mom and I walked side by side, both staring straight ahead. I was sure we were thinking the same thing—there hadn't been one Renegades game in the history of my short-lived soccer career that my dad had missed, but I guess there was a first time for everything. The awkwardness between my mom and me was palpable, at least to me. Looking back, I'm sure she didn't know what to say in that moment either, but she made sure I played in that game. My brain was spinning like a luggage carousel. And every time I thought I saw my bag, it was the wrong one, so I kept waiting for the right one to arrive, while it kept spinning. What should I tell my team-mates? What had my mom told their parents? What if people asked me where my dad was? I finally blurted out, "Mom, what should I tell the team when they ask where Dad is?"

She paused for a second, standing in place with her heavy lawn chair on the ground behind her, and I could see her trying to craft the perfect response. I knew she was stressed when she start-ed to twirl one of the curls under her left ear. Her short hair was tucked under a purple winter hat that didn't quite match her red, knee-length, puffy parka.

"Just tell the team that Mrs. Trenton is here to pitch in if anyone needs anything." Mrs. Trenton was the team's assistant coach, one of those cliché soccer moms with a short square haircut who always wore wind pants and polos. She'd occasionally attend our practices, since her daughter was also on the team. Mom started moving again, and I took my cue from her as we continued to head in the direction of the field. "Are you excited, Nikki? What position are you playing today? Are you going to score some goals?" Her tone was cheerful, and it was clear she was saying anything to fill the silence.

"But what if the kids ask me where he is? He's our coach. We're in the playoffs. People are going to ask," I persisted, over-whelmed by the fear of getting into *huge* trouble. I was more worried about being in trouble than I was about the actual state of my father's well-being.

"Just tell them he's in the hospital with a very bad case of the flu," she retorted almost maniacally. "I can't wait to watch you out there. Do your best, and maybe later we can go shopping, after we visit Dad. I love you and I'm proud of you." Why was she proud of me, I wondered. She put on her sunglasses and we parted ways. I watched her head to the far sideline, almost tripping in the wet grass, hauling that stupid clunky chair, but she was able to regain her bal-ance and after a small and slightly dramatic gasp, kept walking.

"Hey, Nikki!" I heard a voice yell from across the field in front of me. "Do you need help?" It was Suzie running toward me with that red ponytail once again flapping in the wind. I was sure she was excited about today's game because Dave's soccer team also had a game on the same field at some point. We knew this because our other friend Amy had overheard Dave and his friend Chris talking. It had been three days since Suzie slipped that note in Dave's locker and so far, no response.

"Yeah! Thanks!" I yelled back and she kept running toward me. I wished it hadn't rained the night before because everything was wet and cold. At least the sun was trying to peek out. There was already a patch of mud on my left thigh that must've rubbed off from one of the soccer balls I was kicking. I was glad that I had shin guards to keep part of my legs warm because my shorts barely covered my butt. Suzie picked up the two balls on the ground and kept pace with me.

"So I have confirmation that Dave's team is playing on our same field right after us," she informed me. "How crazy is that?" Considering we were a small town with only four intramural soccer teams that all played on Saturdays, the scenario did not seem that far-fetched to me, but I let her have it.

"Are you going to talk to him?" I asked her.

"Not sure. How's your dad?"

"He's fine. Still sick."

"Is he going to be okay? Hasn't it been a few days?" Suzie asked.

"He went to the hospital on Wednesday so technically I guess three. Yeah."

"What's wrong with him?"

I so badly wanted to tell my best friend that my dad had a drinking problem and that I didn't entirely understand what that meant, and I didn't want to ask my mom because I didn't want to make her more upset. The dictionary defined alcoholism as: *an uncontrollable and compulsive consumption of alcoholic beverages*, but that was confusing because I never saw my dad drink aside from an occasional beer in the evening and I didn't think I'd ever really seen him drunk. An alcoholic just didn't seem like my dad.

Instead of telling her he had apparently had made some poor decisions, I told her, "He has the flu. He's just really sick with the flu. Hopefully he'll be coming home soon." That was the first lie I ever remember telling.

"Well that's good news, my mom seemed really worried," she said.

I didn't say anything and just kept dragging that bag of balls behind me until Suzie and I got to the game field.

"Hi, Nikki!" A few girls from the team yelled.

"Nik, do you have the bag with the goalie gloves?" Suzie asked me.

"It's back in the car," I told her. "But I can go back and get it. My mom always left our car unlocked."

"I'll go get it!" Suzie offered. She ran energetically toward the parking lot, her shorts hiked up to showcase her muscly legs in case she ran into Dave. I saw Mrs. Trenton filling out the pregame paperwork on her clipboard while some of the other girls started to dribble balls up and down the field. The sun managed to push its way through the clouds and one of our players, Katy, ran up to Mrs. Trenton and dumped a giant plastic bag of orange slices at her feet. That was disappointing. I much preferred pizza to orange slices, but at least there was a snack at all. Katy was a nice girl, a grade below me and Suzie. She was blond and petite, one of those popular girls who was nice to everyone and, naturally, brought orange slices to sporting events.

"Hey, Nikki," Katy said to me softly, leaning forward as if to have a serious and private conversation. "What's wrong with your dad?" Before I could answer, other girls chimed in with the same question. The Renegades had had essentially the same roster for the past three seasons. We had played games on Saturdays and practiced on Tuesday and Thursday nights for the past year and a half, for all of which my dad had had perfect attendance. My dad missed our final practice yesterday and now he wasn't here for our first play-off game, making it apparent to everyone that something was really wrong. Megan, who played the right forward, reached in her sports bag and pulled out a card that read "Get Well Soon!" on the front.

"Here," Megan said handing me the card. "My mom got this so our whole team could sign it and give it to him after we win!"

"Thanks! That's so nice!" I said, sincerely.

"He must be really sick. What's wrong with him?" Megan asked. "I heard he was in the hospital." Word traveled fast. Megan was a nice girl, too. She was a good enough soccer player and strikingly beautiful for a seventh grader. She wasn't the sharpest tool in the shed, but she was smart enough. One of those people who was good enough, in general.

"Yeah, he just had a bad case of the flu so they brought him in."

"Must be pretty bad," Megan continued, "I didn't know people went to the hospital for the flu. Is he super dehydrated or something? Tim was out sick last week. Sounds like maybe there's something going around. I guess it's that time of year."

Feeling thankful that Megan had justified my own lie for me, I responded, "Yeah, he's super dehydrated. It's a tough time of year too, with the weather changing," I told her, feeding off of her suggestions. I was starting to get the hang of lying. It wasn't as hard as I thought it would be and it seemed less wrong when I pretended I was playing a character that lied a lot. Kind of like the priest in *Les Misérables* who told the French police that he gave his candlesticks to Jean Val Jean so that he could start a new life, even though they were really stolen. Maybe that was a lie that would help my father, just like the priest helped Jean Val Jean. The vision of myself in nineteenth-century France was interrupted by a piercing whistle signaling that the referee was ready for the coin toss. Our team convened on the sidelines for a brief good luck cheer and then dispersed to our usual positions. I took my normal place as left forward.

For that next hour of my life I just had to focus on the game. All I had to do was run, kick the ball, and get it in the net. I didn't have to talk, or lie, or explain myself to anyone. The edge of the field was lined with excited parents getting ready to watch their children; I saw my mom waving at me and pretended not to see her. I wasn't sure why I did that.

We won the coin toss against the team from North Andover and chose to start with the ball. My dad always liked it when we got to start with the ball. He would've been excited if he were there.

"Let's go Renegades!" Mrs. Trenton cheered as we all settled into our starting positions. I could hear my mom cheering and clapping from her lawn chair and I avoided looking at her for a second time. I didn't want to connect with her in that moment, but I was also glad she was there. I knew soccer games were never really her cup of tea. She much preferred watching me sing on stage or perform at a piano recital. But she made sure she was in the audience at that game. It was important. A cold, light wind brushed my ears but soon we'd all be running fast enough that it wouldn't matter. I thought about my dad, and how if he were there he'd be running up and down the sidelines, reminding kids to be aggressive or yelling at the referee whenever an unfair call was made. Nobody loved to win more than my father.

Wondering what the doctors could possibly be doing for him at the hospital or rehab to make him feel better, I looked down to

Dry Run

make sure both of my shoes were double-knotted as the whistle blew. I passed the ball to Megan and the game began. I ran up the field. The hour that I was looking forward to as a relief from my life was over in a flash and I was back where I left off, forced to face my team and deal with my father's absence.

Immediately following our win, we formed a circle on the sideline and stuck our right hands in the middle, our fingertips all touching as we yelled our victory chant. My mom came rushing over as fast as she could from across the field to give me a big congratulatory hug. She was still pulling that lawn chair.

Mrs. Trenton caught my attention, congratulated me, and gave me a pat on the back. "You won us the game! Your dad will be so proud when he hears you scored that last goal." Megan handed me the card that the entire team had signed and I thanked both her and Mrs. Trenton. Against my better judgement, I grabbed an orange slice, since that's what everyone else was doing; though I didn't love the texture or oranges in general, I did like the juice. Suzie, Mrs. Trenton, and Mom helped me drag the soccer team's equipment across the long field back to my mother's car.

"Thank you for coaching the team today, Kathy. My husband would've loved to be here but unfortunately he's just bedridden for a while." My mom exchanged pleasantries with Mrs. Trenton while I arranged the equipment so that the trunk would close. Suzie and I had a quick pow-wow about her Dave strategy. Unfortunately, I couldn't stick around to watch her execute it since I was going to visit my dad. I climbed into the front seat of the car and my mom wedged herself and her jacket—not so gracefully—into the driver's seat with a thud and started fishing for her keys in the depths of her gigantic mom purse.

"Jesus Christ, I can never find anything in this bag."

"Maybe you should get a smaller bag?"

"But I like big bags so I can fit all of my stuff."

"What do you actually carry in there, other than your keys and too many tissues?"

Mom didn't answer, but did find her keys, as unused tissues fell out of her purse, littering the front seat. When she turned on the car, heat from the vents immediately blasted my face. She started to back out of the parking lot and abruptly hit the brakes when she realized there were two young boys in her blind spot.

"Jesus, Mom," I said. I'd learned that "swear" from her. I think it was a Jewish thing. I knew a lot of Jews (mostly middle-aged moms) who used the savior's name in vain and something about it just felt satisfying. Jesus Christ.

"I'm sorry, Nik. I just didn't see them. Please be nice to me. I've had a tough few days.

I looked at my mother and saw something I'd never seen before. She wasn't looking directly at me. In fact, she didn't seem to be looking at anything specific. She stared in my general direction, outside the passenger window, and looked lost, desperately searching for something to look at without fixating on one thing. I felt helpless and lost too, and guilty because I couldn't do anything about anything, but I just didn't feel like talking. "I'm sorry," I said.

"Should we go to Brigham's after we visit Dad and celebrate with some milkshakes?". Mom seldom let me have milkshakes but we both loved Brigham's. She'd take me maybe twice a year when we felt like being bad. I started dreaming of a grilled cheese on wheat doused in butter, cut into triangles, served with fries and ketchup.

"Yeah. That sounds fun," I told her. I removed my damp shoes and shin guards and rested my right foot on the dashboard to blast it with the heat from the vent.

"Nikki, please take your feet off the dashboard. I just had the car cleaned."

"Sorry." I lowered my foot.

Dry Run

MILE 5

My feet start to ache and I wonder if I'd tied my shoes too tight. They're double-knotted so to untie and retie them more loosely would be a hassle. I thought this race would get my father's attention, but now I think it falls into the category of what I classify as a PLD, which stands for "Poor Life Decision." PLD is a term coined by yours truly in 2007 when I drunkenly entered myself in a topless contest at a transvestite bar in Buffalo at a cast party for a production of "Grease." My nipples hurt a little bit and I'm confident it's because of the cutting air, not because of chaffing or anything, at least not yet. It's too early for that. Plus, I'd decided to wear three sports bras today because sometimes my jugs really do get in the way and can be uncomfortable. The extra support also helps minimize chaffing. "La Vie Bohème" starts playing, which I'd thrown on my play list for good measure. It has a consistent beat and is one of those songs that always puts me in a good mood. It's nuts to me that I'm actually in the process of running twenty-six point two miles. I've literally only ever gone that distance in a car. Thank God I have my music.

—Providence Marathon, 2011.

Back on the road after the soccer play-off game and a quick change, we cruised down Route 128, my mother lifting her foot off the gas pedal every few seconds, making me nauseous. The sun was gone, it was completely overcast outside, and I was trying to focus on Act Two of *Rent*. I had Cassette Two ready to go in case Cassette One finished before Mom and I reached our destination; I didn't want there to be any silence. I'd heard somewhere that a car is the worst place to be trapped with someone you don't feel like talking to, a confined space where it's hard to create distractions. There were only so many activities you could do in a car and I was just trying to focus on the music. In that prison cell on wheels, my only option was to escape to a fantasy world of singing cross-dressers and homeless New Yorkers. It got me excited about someday living in the Big Apple and maybe even being in a production of *Rent*. Despite my best efforts to transport myself to an alternate universe, "Goodbye Love" came on and it was the part about the character of Mimi going to rehab.

"I talked to Dad this morning before the game," my mom told me, staring at the highway in front of her.

"Okay," I replied.

"He's excited we're coming to visit him."

"Okay," I said apathetically, reaching for the volume to turn up "Goodbye Love."

"Nikki, I'm trying to talk to you. Can you please shut that off for a minute?" She jabbed at the eject button on the tape deck twice before successfully stopping the music. Silence. There was a pit in my stomach. I was desperate to turn the song back on. But I knew that would upset my mom more, so instead I did my best to swallow the quiet and stared out the passenger window, counting all the cars we passed. I felt uncomfortable and I wasn't sure why. I wanted to know the details about my dad but I didn't want to hear them from her. Something about hearing them from her made me feel pressure to react in a certain way, in the right way. And I didn't know what that was. She also got so upset whenever she brought it up and I didn't want to be her shoulder to cry on. Rain droplets started hitting the window and I could hear my mom turn on the windshield wipers while letting out a "Jesus Christ." I didn't look at her for the next few minutes, but I could still sense the tears silently rolling down her cheeks. At first I ignored her, but she slowly started to cry harder. "What?" I snapped, immediately regretting it. I sounded so angry and annoyed, but really I was just uncomfortable and unsure of what I should do.

"Nothing," she said, her cracking. "It's just." She paused for a moment, then whimpered, "This has been a really hard week. That's all."

I felt like I should have been taking care of my mom, but for some reason my instinct was to push her as far away from me as possible. I inched my left hand towards the tape deck and slid Act II of *Rent* back into the cassette player, making sure the volume was low. Very faintly, the chorus of cross-dressers and gays came back on and I felt better. My mom and I didn't say a word to each other for the next half hour or so, as our car continued to jerk forward whenever my mom took her foot on and off that gas pedal. Finally, she broke the silence.

"Nik, you put Dad's bag in the back seat, right?"

"Yes." I'd packed the bag earlier that morning when Mom told me he'd asked for some clean clothes to wear in rehab. He'd specifically wanted his favorite black running bag that allegedly already had clean clothes in it, probably from his last trip to the gym. I was proud that I was able to find it next to some banana peels in the back-seat of his car (which was essentially a landfill). Instead of rummag-ing through the bag to see what was already in it, I just threw in his running shoes and an extra pair of socks, in case he wanted to go for a run around the rehab campus.

When we turned off the highway and onto the back roads somewhere in Western Massachusetts, the rain let up. It was about three o'clock in the afternoon and all I could think about was how I'd hoped we'd make it back home by eight, in time for *Dr. Quinn Medicine Woman*. Watching *Dr. Quinn…* on Saturday nights had been a favorite pastime of mine for a while now. I'd have a cheese pizza, a Diet Coke, and a bag of popcorn. My parents always bought the kind without butter, but Suzie had taught me how to melt my own butter and add salt, creating the perfect popcorn concoction. The rehab facility was a few minutes away—at the end of a long, poorly paved road. My mom drove too fast, ignoring the speed bumps, and there at the end of the road, waiting for us in all its glory, was rehab. I was surprised by how nice the landscaping looked. The building was lined with small evergreen trees and there was a barren lawn out front that I imagined looked nice and green during the summer. It took her two tries to fit into a parking space straight enough so that other cars would still be able to park on either side of her.

"Can you grab Dad's bag out of the backseat?" she asked me. I liked knowing that I was going to be the one carrying the bag because I wanted Dad to know it was from me. When he opened it I wanted him to see the running shoes and be excited. He'd know I was the one who put them there. I opened the passenger side door directly in front of a giant puddle, and had a hard time balancing, trying my best to not get my feet wet, when I got out of the car. I'd decided to wear a new pair of heels that were on sale and my mom let me buy the other day, but they were hard to walk in. The store didn't have my size, but I loved them so much I got them a half size larger and told my mom they fit. They were black leather with a rounded toe and a skinny heel and I thought they looked grown up—much more fashionable than my soccer cleats. Mom was already halfway across the parking lot by the time I opened the backseat door to grab the bag. I threw it over my shoulder and teetered across the parking lot toward the main entrance, jumping over puddles as quickly as possible to catch up to Mom. We arrived at the entrance at the same time, and, much like the gates of Emerald City, the automatic doors opened for the big reveal—rehab.

Rehab looked like a resort. The reception desk was pink marble and there was nice artwork everywhere. The entire front side of the lobby was covered in windows, making the room bright. It was the type of entrance that made you expect to see slot machines or an indoor pool around the corner. The halls in both directions were carpeted in a light shade of grey and the walls were a pristine white. My mom darted for the front desk where a woman wearing a nametag that read "Laurie" asked in a southern accent, "Can I help you, Miss?"

"We're here to see my husband," Mom said somewhat frantically, while tucking her short brown curls, which were extra frizzy from the rain, behind her ears. Her brown-rimmed glasses still had some droplets of water on them and her purple hat had shifted off-center from where it sat earlier. Laurie asked to see Mom's driver's license and then opened a thick book and scribbled something on the page.

"Yes," Laurie said, chewing a piece of gum that appeared to match the pink countertop. "He's in room 16B. The elevators are over there to your left." She pointed towards them, but before we took more than three strides, she stopped us.

"Wait a moment, Ma'am. I didn't see that bag there." She pointed to the black running bag I was carrying. "If you don't mind, Gerald just needs to take a look." Next to Laurie was a tall clean-cut man who looked to be around my mom's age, late forties. He was dressed in a navy blue uniform and was somewhat intimidating. He definitely looked like he'd broken up, or maybe even started, a few fights in his day, and I was willing to bet that he had at least two tattoos under that uniform. I remember him being the type of guy that you'd probably swipe right for on a dating app, if you felt like you weren't getting enough matches, but then once you connected, you wouldn't actually message him. I walked over to Gerald and handed him Dad's running bag. Slightly out of sorts, Mom continued towards the elevators and I figured I'd just meet her upstairs. Gerald propped the bag on top of the pink counter and unzipped it.

The painting hanging on the wall behind Gerald caught my eye; I knew it was called *Starry Night* because we'd just done a unit on it in art class. While I patted myself on the back for recognizing the

Dry Run

painting, Gerald started rummaging through the bag and removed the pair of shoes I'd packed. Laurie chewed her gum rhythmically and stared at her computer screen. I could see she was involved in a riveting game of FreeCell Solitaire. My Grandma Thelma and I played that computer game all the time. I wondered why Laurie didn't just move the queen of spades on top of the king of spades.

"Excuse me, Miss," Gerald said to me interrupting my Free-Cell fixation. "Where did your mom go?"

"I think she's by the elevators," I told him. "Why?"

"I need to speak with her, please." Gerald was the most politely intimidating security guard I'd ever dealt with, though I hadn't dealt with many.

I turned and walked briskly to the elevators and retrieved my mom. I told her that Gerald wanted to talk to her.

"Who the hell is Gerald?" she asked me, the way a quasi-frantic Jewish mother on a mission would. I told her he was the security guard. Mom speed-walked back to the front desk; it was evident that she was very anxious to get to room 16B and very annoyed by this delay.

"Is there a problem?" she shrilled. "I just want to see my husband."

"Ma'am, do you know what's in this bag?" Gerald asked. Laurie's eyes didn't move from her computer screen and it was clear she didn't want to be part of that conversation.

"Just some clothes. My daughter packed it," she told him.

"Did you know that there's beer in this bag?" Gerald pulled out two cans of beer, the kind my dad drank, and placed them on the pink countertop. I felt the floor drop out from under my feet; I couldn't quite comprehend what I was seeing. I would've given anything not to be there in that moment, and to be back on that soccer field running back and forth. I wanted to disappear.

"Oh my God," my mother said. She started shifting her body weight back and forth, as if she wanted to pace around the room but couldn't. She put her right hand on her forehead and took a few deep breaths. More and more wrinkles appeared on her face, as her eyes flickered back and forth from the floor to the *Starry Night* painting, out the wall of windows, and back at the floor. Her skin looked so tan against the white walls. Hers was darker than mine; I definitely inherited her hair, but must've gotten my fair complexion from my Irish dad. I was frozen, not so much in fear of what that meant for my dad, but out of panic and responsibility for my mom. I'd never seen her so unhinged and I needed to do something to make her pain stop. I had to calm her down but I didn't know how, and my body was still numb, unable to move, with no floor below me. I stood there like an idiot, unable to go to my mother or to say the right words. I was useless.

"I'm so sorry. I had no idea that was in there, you have to believe me! My daughter packed the bag. My husband must've had it in there and somehow we missed it." Gerald looked at me and then back at my mother. Laurie was still mostly hiding behind that computer screen, her beady eyes hovering just above the monitor. All of a sudden it occurred to me that maybe I did have a chance to be useful. I could tell Gerald that I'd packed the bag, which I kind of did. No one would get mad at a kid, or not let a little girl in to see her father, and my mother was acting hysterical and crazy. At least if he thought that I packed the bag, both of my parents would be off the hook. I had no idea where those beers came from. And I didn't think my mom put them in there, but I didn't know for sure. If they were already in there and I just didn't see them, Gerald didn't have to know that my dad had specifically asked for *that* bag.

"Ma'am," Gerald addressed my mother, "you do realize the seriousness of this issue, correct? This is a substance abuse rehab facility and there is a substance in this bag."

I didn't want us to not be able to see my dad so I followed my instincts and took matters into my own hands. I'd apologize, avoid conflict, and move on. How much trouble could I *really* get in if I took the blame? "Sorry," I chimed in. "It's my fault. I packed the bag and I'm the one who didn't see the beer." Ironically enough, it was the most truthful and adult statement I'd made all day.

Gerald looked at me, begrudgingly handed back Dad's running bag sans beer, and spoke to my mom and me in a stern voice: "This is an unforgivable offense and must never happen again. Our patients work extremely hard here to get clean. The way to help them isn't to set them back by giving them the thing that put them in here in the first place." He then gestured to the elevator and finished with, "Please don't let this happen again. There will be consequences." I felt awful. All I wanted to do was make things better for my mom, but what if Gerald told Dad that I was trying to hurt him by bringing him beer? I hated that Gerald would think that I'd want to sabotage my own father. And if I didn't put the beer in the bag, who did? Was it Mom? Was I just covering up for her? Or was the beer in the bag from before, when Dad was drinking it? I should've looked through the bag so I guess at the end of the day it truly was my fault anyway. If I'd been more diligent that altercation wouldn't have happened.

Mom and I walked quickly to the elevator, got inside, and I hit 16. Neither of us said anything and on the sixteenth floor, a few doors down on the left, we found room 16B. I knocked, as my mom pushed the door open and brushed ahead of me without waiting for an answer. The room was dark and not quite as nice as the lobby. My dad was perched on a bed reading the sports section of *The Boston Globe.* His eyes were wide and face looked serious, more like he was reading a deposition than a recap of last week's Patriots game. His rectangular reading glasses looked like they were about to fall off the tip of his nose when his eyes looked up.

"Hi, guys!" he said, as if we were just getting home from a routine trip to the grocery store.

"Hi," my mother replied curtly. I said nothing and sheepishly placed his running bag on a chair in the corner. It was one of those chairs that had a seat cushion and wooden armrests.

"What did you bring me?" He asked.

"Your stuff," I told him.

"There were two beer cans in that bag. Did you know that?" my mother said sternly, cutting right to the chase. I'd never heard her speak that forcefully to my father.

"No," he told her, and looked at me and playfully rolled his eyes. The eye roll he used to do all of the time when I was a child. I remember thinking I *was* a child until about five minutes ago. He got up, opened the bag, and pulled out his running shoes, "Oh great! My sneakers!" he stared at them and his eyes grew wide with relief, like he was happier to have his running shoes than he was to see us. "Good stuff. I'm going to need these."

"Nik," he said to me, completely ignoring my mother, "I have so many friends in rehab!"

"That's great," I said in a monotone. Even though I wasn't looking directly at her I could feel my mother's eyes cutting into my father, and when his shoulders got stiff and crept up to his neck, I knew he could feel them too.

"Your dad is the most stylish boy in rehab," he said ignoring my mother. He waved his left hand, showing off the man bracelets he always wore. Occasionally he'd get new ones because the old ones had rusted, since he never bothered to take them off in the shower. It continued to irk me when my dad spoke in the third person. It almost seemed like it was his way of separating himself from the situation, like I'd sometimes pretend I was a character in a musical, doing or saying things that were written by someone else for that role. It also bothered me for the first time that my dad was referring to himself as a boy. He wasn't a boy, he was a grown man who had done something bad that involved drinking too much beer, and wound up here. Boys didn't do things like that, men did. So why was he calling himself a boy? Why couldn't he just say man, like every other father I knew?

I wanted to shake him. I wanted to scream in his face. Instead, I just said, "We won our game."

"That's excellent. I'm a proud dad." I guessed dad was better than boy. My mom turned her back on him and darted out of the room. I wasn't sure whether to follow her or to stay put. Desperate to break the tension with some sort of movement, since anything felt better than just standing still, I took a seat on the edge of the chair with the wooden arm rests.

The next ten minutes of small talk were a blur. Something about the Patriot's starting lineup and Drew Bledsoe, and then about who'd be coming to our house for Thanksgiving. He even asked me for the first time how my Bat Mitzvah preparations were going, and my Bat Mitzvah wasn't until the spring. We covered every topic, except the two cans of beer and him being in rehab. He told me about his new friend Christina, a female in her early twenties struggling with an eating disorder, and how the two of them liked to talk politics. At one point he pulled a folded piece of paper out of the back pocket of his jeans and showed me a stick-figure drawing he'd done in which he had given himself orange hair. Apparently drawing was part of his therapy: drawing, making new friends, reading the sports section. I remember thinking that if this was alcoholism, I should start drinking. After what seemed like an entire first act of a play, my mother slowly walked back into the room, looking a bit more composed. Her presence was angry, but calm and firm, almost like she had given herself a pep talk outside.

"Nikki, do you mind giving your father and me a few minutes?" I stood up and exited, in my high heels that were not rain appropriate and probably too mature to be worn in the seventh grade, making a clanking sound against the tiled floor as I tried not to fall out of them.

Dry Run

I stood in the hallway for about five minutes and tried to eavesdrop on my parents' conversation. The name Marianne came up, who I knew was my dad's secretary and it sounded like my mom might have been relaying work related messages. I wondered what my dad's clients did without him and decided that it seemed most of them were in jail anyway. For all I knew, some of them were in rehab, too. All of a sudden my parents' voices dropped so low that I couldn't hear what they were talking about anymore. Sudden harsh footsteps that I knew belonged to my mother came my way and she asked if I was ready to leave. I went into the room and said goodbye to my dad, relieved to be heading home. On our way out of the building I thought about saying goodbye to Laurie and Gerald, but figured that would be weird. So I departed silently, lagging a few steps behind my mother, my heels making it hard to keep up with her. We got in the car and I put in Act I of *Rent* to start from the beginning. The repeating strum of the guitar was comforting to me.

"Nikki, can you turn that off?" Mom asked. "I have a headache."

I turned the music down as low as possible, testing the waters to see if Mom would make me turn it all the way off. She didn't.

MILE 6

The rogue twelve-year-old is still in sight, but now about twenty yards ahead of me. I'm relieved. I certainly didn't need a stranger putting pressure on me to run a certain pace. Turning left on what appears to be a bike path through the woods, unfortunately one with minimal shade, a techno version of "Carol of the Bells" starts playing in my ears and I wonder why on earth I included this on my marathon playlist. PLD. I don't want to skip the song because my playlist is perfectly timed to my expected finish, which should be at around four and a half hours, and I plan on crossing the finish line to Donna Summer's "Last Dance." Since I don't want to risk running out of music for that last .2 miles, I dig deep for some Christmas spirit and get on board. I'm still a little chilly but, again, I only have myself to blame. Still, I do think my dad would approve of my outfit since he always endorsed fashion over comfort. A child on the sideline holds out her hand offering a high five and I veer right and accept the gift. It definitely gives me more energy than that gel shot, though I know it's important that I keep eating those. Six miles, we're almost at a 10k.

—Providence Marathon, 2011.

It was a snowy afternoon in 1997 and Dad and I were on our way to the mall to pick out gifts for Mom. I'd always loved Christmas time at the North Shore Mall. This was ironic for many reasons, the first being that I'm Jewish, the second being that Christmas carols give me anxiety because they're rarely sung in tune. Last but not least, I couldn't stand Santa Claus. I thought it was stupid that he always wore the same outfit, and he just seemed like a highly unintelligent being. I also never understood how he allegedly fit down chimneys and why he never tried to lose weight. Despite all of those things, I still loved Christmas; more specifically, I loved the happy facades people put on, even if it was just for one day. Those were the same facades that I'd come to detest later in life. But at the time, I loved the food (still do), the presents, and that cozy family feeling. Most of all, I loved Christmas shopping with my dad.

Even though I was Bat Mitzvahed earlier that year, Dad loved reminding me that I was half Catholic. It infuriated me because I didn't suffer through five years of Temple Ahavat Achim for "half" of anything. Twice a week, I'd travel thirty minutes to sit in the basement of a temple so that Rabbi Gellar's wife could teach me the

Hebrew alphabet and then feed the class carefully rationed portions of dried apricots and grape juice. Sometimes, on Wednesdays, we'd get two animal crackers instead of two apricots, if we were lucky. At the end of the day, it was all worth it for my Bat Mitzvah celebration, which featured more show tunes than Hebrew prayers. I orchestrated my Haftarah portion, mix-belted it, and wrote in a key change. It was basically a one-woman show.

We almost didn't go shopping that afternoon because the roads were so slippery and snow covered; it made Mom nervous, but Dad convinced her it would be fine. And it was fine. I was hoping that this Christmas would be better than last year. Not that last year's Christmas was bad, but it was different. Mom watched Dad like a hawk to make sure he didn't drink anything with alcohol in it. I watched her move half-empty wine bottles to the garage as she told family members there was a problem with the fridge in our kitchen. Then she told me my father he wasn't allowed to go in the garage. I watched her make a small portion of pasta salad just for him, with a store-bought dressing that didn't have balsamic vinegar in it. As far as I knew, Dad had stayed sober for the past year, which was good. He never talked about it and I never asked. I saw how irritated he got when Mom interrogated him about why he was twenty minutes late coming home from an AA meeting, or why he didn't answer his cell phone when she called from the grocery store. He also seemed to hate it when she grilled him in detail about his AA meetings.

She asked the type of questions you asked someone who's read a good book or seen a good movie. Who was there? What did you talk about? What was your favorite part? At the time, I found it unbelievably bothersome to listen to. Why did she need to know every detail about the meeting? Was she on the lookout for a good AA meeting recommendation? Now, looking back, it occurs to me that maybe she wasn't so interested in what happened at the meetings as she was in wanting assurance that he actually went. As a thirteen-year-old, I never wanted him to get annoyed with me the way he got annoyed with her, so he and I both chose to avoid the topic of his drinking. And I'd successfully kept my word to my mother that I wouldn't tell a soul about dad's alcohol problem, even though holding onto that felt lonely at times. Well, all of the time.

Dad parked the Rodeo perfectly and neatly into a small space near the outskirts of the parking lot. The snow was still falling as we sloshed through puddles and I hoped my jeans wouldn't get too wet;

there was nothing more annoying than trying on new clothes while dealing with wet jeans. Dad's jeans looked like they were staying dry, although they were so tight that they probably wouldn't have looked any different even if they were wet.

Entering the mall, we were met by a manic crowd of obligated shoppers lugging more bags than most of them could carry. I could already see Santa, prominently positioned right by the entrance this year, just sitting there. That lazy fuck. I looked up at Dad and smiled. He didn't look at me.

"Where should we start, Nik?" he asked.

"Why don't we start with Mom's present," I said. "What should we get her?" I really wanted my mom to have a good Christmas that year.

"That's a good question, Nik. Mom thinks she knows what she wants but I always tell her that she needs to start wearing different colors. You know, start dressing more unique. She asked for some sweaters but I think we find her something more fashionable. I don't want to get her just another ordinary sweater. Boring," he said with a classic eye roll. I often wondered where my dad's obsession with clothing came from. He wasn't particularly flamboyant in his mannerisms, but for as long as I could remember, he'd always dressed like a walking mid-life crisis. He seemed more intent on finding loud articles of clothing rather than ones that looked good or even ones that fit properly.

"I hope we find something that stands out as much as that orange velour track suit you got her last year," I said.

"It looked chic!"

"It looked hideous."

"Oh. Huh."

We chuckled and my stomach growled. "Dad, can we stop for a quick snack?"

"You want a snack? Sure, Nik. Whatever you want. Your dad will plop his little self down at that table." He motioned to an empty table on the outer perimeter of the food court and handed me two twenty-dollar bills. "Here's some money. Go get what you want."

"Dad, I definitely won't need two twenties."

"Are you sure?" he said, looking at the ground, as his cheeks sagged.

I returned one of the bills and ran around the food court, scoping out prospective snacks. Eventually I decided on a plate of chicken lo mein from Umi of Japan and a croissant from Au Bon Pain. Quite the combo. I returned to where Dad was sitting in his designer jeans and black hooded V-neck sweater. His gut spilled over the pants, and as soon as he saw me heading back in his direction I noticed him sit up straight and attempt to suck it in. I tried to give him back the remaining $5.25 in change but he told me to keep it. After I scarfed down my food we were ready to embark on our shopping journey.

Not too far from the food court we passed a kiosk that was selling earrings. Dad stopped—perhaps it was the glitz that caught his eye. I took a few steps past the jewelry cart before noticing that I was alone, and turned around to see exactly what had captured his attention. The girl working the kiosk was happy to come over and assist, thrilled to have a potentially interested customer.

"You know, Nik, Mom did say she'd love a pair of earrings. Do you think she'd like any of these?"

I scanned the selection and pointed to a pair of giant earrings made of silver dollars. "I think she'd like those. They don't need backings and they're big and will stand out against her giant curly hair."

"Smart, Nik," he said. "Let's get them. Maybe we can give them to Santa on the way out and he'll put them in her stocking."

We continued, but before we could get much further Dad managed to lead us into Structure, the male version of Express. He admired the shirt on a mannequin, quickly found it in a size small, and threw it over his arm.

"Are you going to get that?" I asked. "Should Mom and I get that for you for Christmas?"

"I might get this as a present for myself. I don't trust Mom to pick this out for me." It was an unusual looking shirt to say the least. It was bright yellow with giant silver buttons down the front.

"Dad, don't you have another shirt just like that?" It dawned on me that I was starting to sound like my mother.

"No. That one doesn't have silver buttons."

"Oh. Right."

"I think I'm going to throw in this scarf, too," he said, grabbing a black scarf off the table next to the mannequin. When we got to the register, the college-aged salesman pointed out that the shirt my dad was buying was actually buy-one-get-one fifty percent off.

"What other color should I get, Nik?"

Slightly hesitant, I went and selected an orange version of the shirt; I knew that orange was Dad's favorite color. With his new clothes in hand, we left Structure and continued on our quest for more Christmas gifts.

"Want to pop into Express to look at stuff you might like?" he asked me.

"Right now? Shouldn't we be shopping for Mom?" I reminded him.

"Express is right here. Why don't you take a look and see if there's anything you'd wear?"

"Like, for Christmas?"

"It could be for Christmas. But see if there's anything you'd want right now," he suggested. We went into Express where Dad insisted that I try on a black V-neck top with silver-lined holes up and down the outer edge of both sleeves. I went to the dressing room to try it on, not because I really wanted to, but because my dad just seemed so excited, though not in an inappropriate way at all. Sometimes it seemed like he encouraged me to buy clothes that my mother would oppose. Other times it seemed like he just liked spending money to spend it, wanting to be the cool dad, winning my affection with his "young" sense of style and generous wallet. He wanted to be the hip, best friend parent. There was always one.

"That looks great, Nik" he said when I emerged from the dressing room. "Let's get it!" I strongly disagreed, it reminded me of something one might wear if they were in a motorcycle gang or dating a member of a drug cartel. But I didn't want to hurt his feelings so I figured I'd get it and maybe wear it on Halloween. Who knows, maybe one year I'd want to go as Pablo Escobar's mistress. Besides, it was on sale (even though my mom always said that you should never buy something just because it was on sale, that it was still money spent).

On our way to the register to buy the shirt, I noticed that there was a sale on winter coats, something I actually needed. I spotted a brown suede jacket with wool lining. It was short and had a zipper in the front. I stopped to try it on and both Dad and I agreed that it was an excellent coat. Not necessarily practical for warmth, but it looked good on and I knew I'd wear it. Without blinking an eye, Dad added it to the pile, though I did suggest putting back the black V-neck biker gang top. Dad insisted we take it all, and we checked out and moved on, carrying non-Christmas gifts for ourselves and one pair of earrings for Mom. It didn't feel right. I felt guilty and wasn't really sure why.

We continued our errands and the day turned out to be successful. We were able to find several things for Mom, our favorite being a black blazer with rhinestones on the lapels. I had my doubts about whether or not she'd like it but I agreed with Dad that it was definitely stylish. We also found her a nice purple cashmere sweater I knew she'd love because purple was her favorite color. While I looked in Macy's for perfumes we could throw in her stocking, Dad bought her a beautiful bracelet he spotted at one of the jewelry counters. We also bought her a one-hundred-dollar gift certificate to the Gap, plus another gift certificate to J. Crew. After our day's work, we grabbed our bags and exited the same way we entered.

The snow had let up a bit and we were able to get to the car mostly unscathed. We piled the bags into the trunk and headed home, where I knew mom would be preparing spaghetti and meatballs, one of the dishes she made well. Dad let me listen to my *Scarlet Pimpernel* cassette the entire way home and I rested my feet on the dashboard. By the time we pulled into the driveway it was dark outside, and Dad's silver man bracelets glistened over the steering wheel when the outdoor lights hit them as he pulled the car into the garage.

Before going inside, Dad immediately ran around the back of the house to check on our pet bunny rabbits and monitor their water supply. I started bringing the bulky shopping bags into the house. I smelled fresh tomato sauce and heard meatballs sizzling on the stove. It smelled like home and it warmed me up. My mom was standing over the meatballs, stirring the sauce in the pot beside them.

"How'd you do?" she asked me.

"We did well," I told her. "You're going to love your presents. And dad got me this great coat and a top that I'm going to wear someday."

"He got you a coat *and* a top? Are they Christmas presents?"

"No, he said they were just for fun." I ran to my room to change out of my wet jeans. "You're going to love your presents!" I yelled on the way to the other end of the house. A few minutes later, I was on my way back to the kitchen in a dry pair of sweatpants when I heard my parents bickering. I stopped in the hall and listened.

"How much did you get?" I didn't know why she was asking.

"I got you a lot of presents," he told her. "You deserve them."

"That's nice but I told you I don't need a lot of presents. And what are you doing buying Nikki clothes a week before Christmas? We don't have that kind of money. I thought you'd agreed to be better about this. I'm so disappointed."

"Relax. Live a little." He sounded irritable.

I shifted my weight and the floor creaked and blew my cover. My mother went back to monitoring the meatballs while my dad gathered the shopping bags and left the kitchen. I could feel the tension, even from the hallway. Sometimes I felt like none of the three of us could ever do anything right for one another. I begrudgingly dragged myself to the baby grand that lived in our dining room because I knew it always made my mom happy to hear me practice the piano, though it wasn't an activity I particularly enjoyed. But she seemed upset and I thought it might help. A few years ago, after she retired from teaching at Revere High School, she opened a private piano studio in our home. I'd tried to quit the piano numerous times because all I wanted to do was sing, but she always told me that I would ultimately regret that decision one day, so I kept at it. I knew that I'd only have enough time to run through a few scales since dinner would be ready soon. I quickly placed both hands on the ivory keys, starting with As one octave apart, hoping that my perfect double scale would put a smile on my mom's face. I accidentally hit a C natural instead of a C sharp with my right hand and stopped for a moment.

"Sorry, Mom!" I yelled.

"You missed the C sharp." She could tell just by listening.

"I know."

"It's okay. Start again. Take it slower." I obliged and repositioned my hands to start the A major scale once again. I was interrupted by her announcing it was time for dinner and I practically leapt to the table.

"Should we wait for Dad?" I asked.

"Let's start without him."

MILE 7

Physically, I'm feeling pretty strong, aside from a tiny bit of chaffing-induced pain on my inner arms, just under my armpits. It hadn't occurred to me this morning to put cream under my arms, I'd just put it in between my legs. I shake my shoulders, and throw in a few high knees as the delirium of long distance running starts to set in. I'm not so much fazed by the seven miles I've completed; it's the nineteen I have ahead of me that are so daunting. I could quit now. I could slow down just to a slight walk. Whenever I feel the urge to quit I think about my mom and how she never let me quit the piano. She also told me that her favorite parts of marathons were the hills, because even though inclines are difficult, they're far more interesting and gratifying than a flat road. Well, I'm on a hill now and I still play piano, so might as well embrace Mom and keep on going. Despite being in a little pain, something about running today is oddly liberating, even running up this hill. As taxing as it can be on the body, it really is a break for the mind. It's just so straightforward. Funny how I have to run so hard in order to feel so easy. I wonder if my dad misses this feeling.
—Providence Marathon, 2011.

Much like trumpets might announce royalty, the squeaking of the (ungreased) door leading to the garage opening announced my arrival home from school. I immediately slung my backpack off one shoulder and onto a chair, and removed my Doc Martens so as to not track more mud on the black-and-white carpet that had yet to be replaced. Sue Chang's mom was sitting on our couch listening to her daughter pound out Debussy's, "Arabesque" in the next room. I'd met Mrs. Chang a few times and she seemed nice, but I wasn't in the mood to chat.

"Play lighter." I could hear my mom say from the next room. "There's no need to bang, Sue. Lighten up the left hand." Sue started over, at a slightly slower tempo. I knew that she was one of my mother's favorite students primarily because she practiced a ton. Or, at least she said she did. For the past two years, she'd been the grand finale at my mom's piano recitals. I, on the other hand, was not my mother's shining pupil; when I played "Arabesque" in last year's recital it was mildly traumatizing. The truth was that I hadn't practiced enough and messed up the fingering. Paralyzed, about sixteen measures in, I remember taking a deep breath, backing up to the beginning of the phrase, repositioning my hands and pressing down on the correct keys with the right fingers. I never used sheet music and always played from my memory during recitals. There was a second, during that deep breath, that I prayed that my muscle memory would kick in and that my fingers would find the right keys. Eventually, I made it through the piece, but I was mortified. It was completely unacceptable, especially considering I was the piano teacher's daughter. I was so disappointed in myself, upset for letting down my mom, and ashamed in general. I should've worked harder. That scenario was a great example of why I much preferred singing—because I never messed up, and I didn't have to work as hard.

Mom told me that something similar had happened to her during her Master's recital and that sometimes things happen, no matter how well we prepare. According to her, she froze in the middle of the second movement of "Moonlight Sonata." Instead of giving up, she turned and addressed the jury, and gave a speech about how she was pursuing a Master's degree in education and that part of education is making mistakes and learning how to get back on the horse when you fell off. She then finished the piece and got her Master's degree. That story made me feel a little bit better, or at least less alone. The reality is, I had practiced for that recital, just not enough. But it was more than that; for the first time in my life I felt anxious.

I left my shoes on the mat by the door, slung my backpack back over my right shoulder, and smiled politely at Mrs. Chang before heading to my bedroom to start my homework. Dad had stayed home sick that day and I couldn't remember the last time that had happened. He had an immune system made of steel, which I liked to believe I inherited. I'd started my freshman year of high school a few weeks earlier, and had since been buried under notebooks and important-looking textbooks covered in paper bag wrapping. I'd met Suzie in the art room after school so we could work on our paper-mâché model of the Earth's internal layers for our science class. The crust, the mantle, and the cores never looked so good. I waved to my mom as I passed through the kitchen, which opened up into the dining room where she was standing behind Sue.

"Sue," she said in a matter-of-fact tone, in the voice I knew well, the one she used when she was trying to mask her frustration. "That should be the third finger there. You're using the fourth."

Trying not to disrupt anything, I tiptoed past the piano lesson to my bedroom. When I dropped my backpack on the floor it landed with a thump and I decided to go to my parents' bedroom to see how my dad was feeling. He'd stayed home yesterday too, and didn't even make it to his AA meeting. According to my mom, he never missed an AA meeting. He also hadn't gone on any of his typical early morning runs last weekend. Even after he hung up his marathon career, he historically ran at least ten miles every Sunday.

Careful not to wake him in case he was sleeping, I tapped lightly on his bedroom door. He didn't answer. The television was murmuring, so I turned the doorknob and peered inside. The lights were on. And what I saw was not my father.

A man was sitting in my dad's bedroom, a man who seemed to have stolen my father's body. He was naked, crawling around on all fours on top of my parents' queen-sized bed. He was ruffling the comforter. The top of his head was facing the window and, thankfully, the blinds were drawn. His ass was sticking up in the air, and he was rubbing his scalp on the quilt as if he was trying to relieve and itch. His skin was pale, his entire body was quaking, but I couldn't see his eyes because they were pointed toward the quilt. I stood there, frozen, as this image burned itself into my brain, like an egg dropped on a scalding hot sidewalk frying instantly. I was cemented to the ground, I was unable into go into the room, unable to look away.

Down the hall, "Arabesque" got faster and faster while my mom's corrections got slower and more deliberate. Her voice sounded like she was under water and I couldn't take my eyes off the naked version of my father on my parents' bed. Should I get my mom? I still couldn't move. I didn't want to worry her over nothing, but also didn't want to do nothing if this was serious. It was also embarrassing that he was naked. Maybe he was just having a bad dream. I could've called Suzie and asked her what to do, but then she'd probably have to ask her mom and then it would get back to my mom that I was telling people about my dad- even if this had nothing to do with his drinking—and I'd still risk getting in trouble.

I'd gone about two years without telling a soul about my dad's drinking problem. I didn't intend to break that promise, primarily because I wanted to be a good kid and do the right thing. I could call 911, but I'd have looked so stupid if I called for nothing, and my mother wouldn't like that either. Maybe he *was* just having a bad dream and I happened to walk in on him. I'd never seen my father naked before, let alone any man, but I reminded myself that this wasn't my father. It couldn't have been. It was someone else. It was someone else's father.

Finally able to move, I slowly took two steps back into the hallway, closed the door to my parents' bedroom, and retreated into mine. I sat on the floor and my mind went blank. My eyes wandered, landing on a newspaper clipping taped to the wall. A few months ago, my dad had found some pictures of my favorite New England Revolution soccer players in *The Boston Globe* sports section and cut them out. Together, we'd turned them into a collage by taping them to my bedroom wall, starting at the floor and working up to about three feet below the ceiling. The picture directly in front of me was a photo of the goalie, Jeff Causey, guarding the net, ready to stop the ball. His mouth was open slightly and he looked both prepared and scared at the same time. I wondered what he was thinking when that picture was taken, as I'd never stared at it quite that closely before. My dad wasn't coaching soccer anymore since I'd outgrown intramural sports. I did make the junior varsity soccer team at my high school, but it wasn't as fun as when I played for the Renegades. The girls on the team were cliquey and I wasn't really friends with any of them. The ones on the team in my grade were popular girls and I was intimidated to talk to them. They always gossiped about kissing boys; meanwhile, I'd been so focused on singing and theatre, and the boys in theatre who I wanted to kiss, didn't have any interest in kissing me. I was nice to everyone, and everyone was nice to me, but at practices and games I mostly kept to myself. They just weren't my people. And it was fine. The following year I'd have to choose between fall soccer and the fall production of *Fiddler on the Roof*, and the latter obviously won. Who'd want to play soccer when you could sing dramatic ballads in minor keys about Jews being forced out of their shtetls in Russia?

Still sitting on the floor in my bedroom, I reached into my backpack and pulled out my copy of *The Mill on the Floss* to get started on my English homework. I turned to chapter seven and tried to focus my attention on the words on the page. The piano stopped. I heard the bench scrape against the wooden floor and I assumed that meant that Sue's lesson was over. I couldn't concentrate. I knew I needed to get that reading done by the next morning, but I

53   *Dry Run*

just couldn't do it then. I couldn't. My brain was preoccupied with thoughts of the man in my parents' room.

Sometimes my mom would come to check on me and say hello between her piano lessons, but not that day. Down the hall in the dining room, someone else started sloppily playing the E flat major scale. My guess was that it was Tyler, the boy from next door. He usually took lessons on Thursdays.

"Make sure to play your notes evenly," I heard my mom say. For the second time, Tyler started his E flat major scale, with a half step instead of a whole one. Better Tyler than I. Unfortunately, the key difference between Tyler, Sue, and me was that my mom always knew when I wasn't practicing. I had tried to quit piano for a third time last week because I was struggling to find time to practice between soccer and musical rehearsals, but my mom wouldn't let me. She insisted that I'd make time. She said that if I wanted to grow up to be on Broadway, I should have a solid foundation in music theory because I'd have a better chance at getting cast in musicals if I could sing harmonies. Also, according to mom, if I ever wanted to teach voice, I really needed to be able to play the piano in order to do so. She said I might regret it now, but that she was sure I'd thank her for it later. Piano was the one activity in all my fourteen years on the planet Earth that she wouldn't let me quit.

My mom corrected Tyler again. I still couldn't focus on *The Mill on the Floss*. Maggie Tulliver failed to hold my attention and I contemplated going back into my dad's room to see if he was still having a nightmare, but I couldn't move. Instead, I went back to staring at Jeff Causey. Thirty minutes went by and when Tyler's lesson was over, I heard my mom clomp down the hallway, her heels banging on the wooden floor. Then I heard her burst into her bedroom. A few seconds later, she burst into mine.

"Hey, Nik," she said, looking chipper and completely unaffected by the man in her bedroom. "How's the schoolwork going?"

"It's fine," I told her. "How's Dad feeling?"

"He seems to be sleeping soundly. Probably just needs a lot of rest." She rubbed her forehead and massaged her neck, stretched her arms above her head, then started twisting one of the curls behind her ear. "Thank God Tyler's lesson is over," she said. "That kid never practices and his scales are painful to listen to." I nodded and forced a smile, even though my face felt numb and about as pliable as a clay pot.

"Alright, my next student should be here in a few minutes. I'm going to go have a snack. Just wanted to say hi. We'll probably do dinner around seven. I finish teaching at six forty-five today."

"Cool," I replied. Mom returned to her teaching lair and I processed what I'd just learned. Dad was sound asleep. Probably just needed some rest. I needed to confirm that for myself so I decided to peek inside my parents' bedroom one more time. I gave the door a little push and peered inside. A rerun of that morning's episode of *The View* was on the television and sure enough, my father was sound asleep underneath the quilt. It was as if the other version of him from forty-five minutes ago was nothing but a mirage. Thank goodness I hadn't called 911. I returned to my bedroom and resumed reading. The phone in my bedroom rang and another E flat major scale began in the living room. I answered the phone.

"Hey Nikki," Suzie said. "Did you look at *The Mill on the Floss* questions yet?"

"No," I told her.

"They're so annoying. I hate this book."

"Yeah."

"I might just sparknote the reading for Monday."

"Yeah."

"Do you think that's bad?"

"Nah, I think as long as you read it before the quiz you'll be fine."

"Okay, cool. That's all. I just called to see if you'd done the questions."

"Yeah, I haven't yet."

"Are you okay?"

"Yeah, why?"

"You sound funny."

"I'm just tired."

"Okay. Well, have a good night, Nikki!"

"You too."

MILE 8

My phone, currently stored in my runner's pack next to the gel shots, is vibrating against my left lower stomach and I wonder who on earth would be calling me now? I've been aggressively posting Facebook statuses about this marathon for weeks. Even Ashley Damon, whom I haven't spoken to in over ten years, "liked" my status and knew I was running this now. I bet it's my dad checking in to see how the race is going, which would be totally on brand for him. When I'm angry, running is usually a great thing to do because I can exhaust myself, typically resulting in me becoming less angry. Sometimes I try to think angry thoughts when I run so I'll be able to go longer. Irrationally irritated by the mystery phone call, I run harder and then consciously slow down, remembering that if I start off too fast (unbelievably, I'm technically still kind of 'starting' the race at mile seven), I might not finish. The chaffing below my armpits is now really starting to bother me but the only thing I can do is pretend it isn't happening. I wonder how far ahead of me the twelve-year-old kid asshole is. I reach into my pack and pull out a second Cliff gel shot. This one is yellow.

–Providence Marathon, 2011.

By the time Black Friday 1999 rolled around, I was an exhausted, cranky, fifteen-year-old. I'd woken up at the crack of dawn on Thanksgiving morning in order to run the Turkey Trot with my dad. My first thought had been: "Why did I stay up so late watching reruns of *The Nanny* while eating cookie dough I'm so fat and tired what am I doing with my life I better go run off that cookie dough." After I trotted off the cookie dough, I put down some turkey, kugel (which I'd made), Jell-O mold, salad, stuffing, macaroni and cheese, and green bean casserole. Then I then stayed up again watching reruns of *Frasier*, and around midnight, went in for round two of Thanksgiving dinner, also known as Thanksgiving Late Night Snack. That Friday, when my mother cheerfully woke me up at the ungodly hour of eight o'clock so we could get to our annual Black Friday brunch at the Cheesecake Factory on time, I wanted to punch her in the face. Running on six hours of sleep and not having fully digested my food was my teenage version of a hangover. I was in a mood and the last place I wanted to be was in a car, with my mother.

When I was a little girl I loved car rides with my mom because we'd always play our own made up version of "Name That Tune." The rules were that one person had to think of a song and the other person had to ask for two, three, four, five, or six notes. The person thinking of the song would then sing the number of notes requested by their opponent. You were awarded the same number of points for however many notes it took before you guessed the song, and the person with the fewest number of points would win. I usually won by picking obscure show tunes that my mom had never heard of. She tended to pick songs she knew I'd be able to guess like "The Sun Will Come Out Tomorrow" or a popular Beatles song. Occasionally I'd pick a song with a swear word just to make my mom laugh. I loved to see her laugh. My mother and I always joked about how she introduced me to inappropriate musicals at such a young age. When I was five, she took me to see a high school production of *A Chorus Line* that she had music directed, after which I ran around singing "Tits and Ass" at the top of my lungs for a solid week. She couldn't get me to stop. When I was nine, she took me to see *Les Misérables* and as long as I sang my intervals correctly around the house, it didn't matter to Mom that I was singing about prostitution. I wasn't sure why we ever stopped playing "Name That Tune;" it used to make hour-long car rides feel like minutes.

That Friday morning, the sky was overcast, but so far it wasn't raining, which was a good thing since I'd straightened my hair for the brunch occasion. I leaned my head against the headrest and closed my eyes, zoning out to the *Chicago* CD (the Revival Cast) playing in the background. My mom had gotten me the CD as a surprise gift the week prior.

My mother's right arm skimmed my ear as she swung around, grabbing the back of my headrest. She adjusted her body so she was able to look over her right shoulder to check her blind spot, simultaneously putting on her turn signal to indicate that she'd be switching lanes. Her curly hair fell into her face, obscuring her peripheral vision, and she was wearing the silver dollar earrings Santa had given her a few years ago. They used to be shiny, but that day they were tarnished and blended in with her grey jacket.

"Nikki," she said, "can you look to see if anyone is coming? Jesus Christ, I can't see." She took one hand off the wheel to reposition her glasses on her nose, as if that might help her see things more clearly.

I turned around. "You're good, Mom."

"Are you excited to see Charlotte and Amy?" she asked. Charlotte was one of her best friends from her college days at Boston University and a founding member of Black Friday Brunch. The two of them had actually met in the cafeteria at BU because Charlotte used to date my mom's brother, Uncle Dale. Charlotte loved telling the story of how one day this "hot chick" went up to my Uncle Dale to return his car keys. Charlotte was relieved to learn that said "hot chick" was his sister, and she and my mom became fast friends. For the past five years, my mother and I had met Charlotte and their friend Amy, the third in the trio, for this annual brunch. My mom had met Amy during their first fall term teaching in the Revere school system. My mom taught music and Amy taught first grade.

My mom introduced Amy to Charlotte, and they'd been best friends since those humble beginnings man-handling their twenties in Boston. The three had been together for nearly forty years. All three had daughters, and they raised us to think of each other like cousins: Leanna, Laura, Alex, and me. And they were like my cousins, the kind you saw three times a year and always got excited when you did. Since I was the youngest of the four, I always tried extra hard to impress them. I'd even dressed up that day, debuting a new shirt that Dad and I had bought the week before. It was black with a scoop neck, and probably a little too tight, but all of the popular girls at school were wearing shirts like it. I wanted to fit in and at least give myself a shot at having a boyfriend before high school was over. I'd taken my time that morning applying just the right amount of blue eye shadow, which meant too much. I looked like the distant, awkward teenage relative of Cher and Tammy Faye's baby, if they were to have one. Regardless of what I looked like, my faux cousins always paid extra attention to me because I was the youngest, and they always told me how pretty I looked even when I didn't think I did.

"Nik, answer me. Are you excited to see Charlotte and Amy?" My mom asked again. I wasn't really paying attention the first time she'd asked.

"I am, Mom, I'm just super tired. That's all"

"Ohhhh," she said in a playful tone. "Are you going to get cheesecake?" Despite growing more and more nauseated from the jolting of the car as a result of my mom's driving habits, I still managed to fantasize about a slice of Oreo cheesecake. I'd been picturing it for months, a perfect 3D triangle of white with black specks. In my fantasy, there was some strawberry sauce drizzled on the plate.

I wasn't sure why I was so flippant with my mother those days. I supposed most teenage girls go through a bitchy period, but this felt different. I felt some anger and resentment toward her and I didn't understand why. Maybe it was because she never played games like "Name That Tune" with me anymore. Or maybe it was because she always asked me questions when I didn't feel like talking, and I never felt comfortable asking *her* the questions I really wanted answered. Everything felt like it was on *her* terms. The older I got, the more anxious she seemed, and that started to make me anxious.

"Mom, do you think you could just keep your foot on the gas pedal like a normal person? Your driving sucks and it's making me sick. It always has and my friends think so, too." I immediately felt remorse and hated that I was so mean to her, but couldn't seem to control it. She hit her hands against the steering wheel and we didn't speak until she slammed the CD player with the palm of her hand, ejecting *Chicago* right in the middle of "All I Care About Is Love."

"What the hell, Mom?"

"Can we just turn that off for a second?" It was always ironic to me that the person who instilled in me my love of music was also always the person who wanted to talk instead of listen to music. "There's something I want to talk to you about," she said. Picking at my cuticles, I l groaned a cliché teenage groan and rolled my eyes as she started to talk. "I don't want to make you nervous, but I do want you to know that I had our house transferred to your name. I just want you to know that, in case anything happens to me, the house will go to you and not Dad." Well that came out of nowhere. And once again, on her terms; the last thing I wanted to be doing was having a serious conversation with my mother in a car that she was driving. I also wasn't quite sure what to make of that statement, so I didn't say anything. After a few drawn-out seconds of silence that seemed much longer than they actually were, she continued. "I just want to protect you, in case anything happens," she tried to clarify, but actually created more confusion.

"What do you mean if anything happens?" I asked.

"Remember when your dad had a problem with alcohol?"

Did I remember? How could I not remember? It tortured me every single day that there was this part of me my friends didn't know about. I'd kept that secret for four years. I thought about it all of the time, but never wanted to bring it up because I didn't want to upset either of my parents, and also didn't want to find out that something else was wrong. Sometimes I wished I never knew anything at all.

"The good news is Dad doesn't drink anymore," my mother went on to explain. "But he's developed somewhat of a spending problem. I learned at an Al-Anon meeting recently that sometimes when addicts lose access to one addiction, they develop another." Al-Anon was my mother's latest obsession, a twelve-step program for individuals with family members who were alcoholics. I continued to listen, deliberately not reacting to what she was saying, and reached for the knob to lower the heat. It was a sauna in that car and I didn't want my straightened hair to get sweaty and frizzy before I saw the Black Friday Brunch bunch.

"Nikki, are you listening to me?" she asked.

"Yes, Mom, I'm listening. God." I rolled my eyes again.

"Basically, your father started spending a lot of money we don't have. I made sure he can't touch your college funds and God forbid anything happens to me, you know, if the cancer ever were to come back, I want to make sure you're protected. That's why I transferred the house to your name. We also both know that your dad loves to shop. He loves to take you shopping more than anything and that needs to stop. I really need to be able to trust you to not let Dad buy you clothes anymore unless I'm with you." I was immediately plagued with guilt as I thought of the top I was wearing, which Dad and I had bought a year ago. I never would've let him buy that shirt had I'd known it meant our house would be transferred out of his name and into mine. My mom turned the heat back on; ten seconds later, I switched it back off. She then stayed completely still, aside from her right foot moving on and off the gas pedal.

"It's really important you don't tell anyone about this, not even family members." Another secret.

"I won't mom. Jesus Christ. Who do you think I am?"

"Okay," she said. We spent the remainder of the drive in silence.

The entire Black Friday Brunch bunch was waiting for us when we arrived. I spotted Charlotte almost immediately, coming out of the ladies room and walking to our table. Her black hair was perfectly shaped in a bob and she was wearing a slimming turtleneck sweater that looked nice with her pair of straight-leg, loose-fitting jeans. Charlotte always looked immaculate; there was never a hair out of place and there was always a shade of red polish on her nails. Her face was always bright; she perpetually looked like she was about to smile. I saw that Amy had hung up her fur coat, revealing a deep sapphire knee-length sweater dress. She wore giant diamond stud earrings, and I knew that when I got close enough to her I'd be able to smell her perfume. Amy liked to pretend she was royalty and every time I saw her she looked more regal than the last time. When princess Diana died a few years earlier, my mom said Amy wore black for a week.

Mom and I made our way to the table and the series of emphatic female "hellos" began. We all hugged and in high-pitched, excited voices told each other how skinny we looked for longer than we needed to.

"Miss Nikki," Charlotte said to me in a dramatic voice, "You look so beautiful!" Her eyes went to my chest. "And that's quite a top!" Apparently, my tits were so hard to miss that she had to say something. That's how it felt anyway. I'd just started growing boobs my sophomore year.

"Thanks!" I told her. All I could think about was how I shouldn't have that top at all. Apparently, my father never should've bought it for me. Should I go and return it and see if I could get his money back? I felt like this was my fault.

Trying to bury the guilt, I managed to make it through and even enjoy the entire meal of compliments and laughs. The three founding members caught up on life while us daughters caught up on boys. I filled them in on my crush on Adam Weinberg from the Tenor section of the New England Conservatory weekend choir; Leanna asked me if he was gay. I knew all about gay people from *Rent* and I honestly didn't think there was any way that Adam Weinberg was gay. He had a girlfriend, which was part of the whole problem. She was from the Alto section and I thought he thought Altos were cooler than Sopranos, which is what I was. I sweated Adam pretty hard. He went to school a few towns over but worked at Godiva Chocolate at the North Shore Mall on Friday and Saturday nights. Some Fridays I could convince my parents to eat out at Legal Sea Foods at the mall; between the salads and our entrees I would excuse myself and execute a stake out. Williams Sonoma was directly across from Godiva, and I discovered that if I hid behind the flatware, I had a direct line of vision to the register at Godiva where Adam Weinberg worked. Sometimes when I was feeling brave, I'd wait to make sure he wasn't with any customers, then casually stroll in to say hello. Occasionally, he'd even give me a free chocolate-covered strawberry and I'd save the stems. Suzie thought that was strange. Fast-forward to 2010 and Adam Weinberg was in the Broadway cast of *Wicked* and married to a man.

There were a lot of cute boys in my choir, which rehearsed in Boston every Saturday morning from nine until eleven. My mom had driven me into Boston proper every weekend for the past year and a half. She was always so dedicated to my passion for music. When I was in the eighth grade, she made sure I had the best voice teacher in the area and that I was singing and auditioning as much as possible so that I'd have a shot at getting into NYU's musical theatre program, the only place I ever wanted to go to college. Maybe that's why I always got so annoyed with my mom in cars, because we spent so much time together in them, her driving me to every audition and rehearsal I wanted to go to. I didn't appreciate it at the time.

After about an hour of catching up over eggs and toast, our waiter came to take dessert orders. Without hesitation, I asked for my Oreo cheesecake and handed the waiter my menu.

"You know," Leanna chimed in, "I think I'll just have a bite of Nikki's. I certainly don't need an entire piece." The waiter looked to Charlotte next.

"I think I may just have a bite of Nikki's as well," she said. My face got hot and my heart started racing.

"I certainly don't need all of the calories either," Amy added. "I'll have a little taste of Nikki's, too." Now at that point, if I was doing the math correctly, there were three people who were allegedly going to take bites of my one slice of cheesecake. I saw where this was going and I didn't like it. A few moments later, the waiter came back with my slice of heaven. A second of horror overcame me as my worst nightmare came true. Like vultures, Charlotte, Amy, and all three of their daughters took their little forks and reached for a bite of my cheesecake. Charlotte was even so bold as to attack the crust. My life was over. I was wearing a top that was too tight and I didn't deserve, I had a father with a spending problem, and I had no dessert. I supposed I had just inherited a house, though.

No one noticed that I'd been robbed of my dessert, the one thing I'd been savoring in my imagination for months. I sat there, silently figuring that maybe it was karmic punishment for letting my dad buy me the shirt. It was almost one hundred dollars, but he insisted on buying it for me anyway. The bill came and I watched my mother's face, searching for her reaction to the total. Without hesitation, she handed over her credit card for our portion of the meal. I'd ordered eggs because they were one of the cheaper items on the menu in case we were really hurting for money. I was too afraid to ask if we were. I almost didn't want to know.

MILE 9

I'd trained for this race both on the treadmill and in Central Park on Saturday and Sunday mornings. I started with shorter distances on the treadmill, then tried to get myself to do longer distances in the park by listening to the double-disk soundtracks of shows like "Ragtime" and "Into the Woods." I've found that when running short distances, I need a beat to pump myself up, but when running longer distances I need something that holds my attention. I'd tried books on tape for a while, but the lack of rhythm couldn't sustain me and, let's be honest, "The Help" isn't much of a pick-me-up. My right calf starts to feel tight and I try to block it out by reminding myself how hard I trained for this. In a sense, I've been preparing for this day my whole life, Turkey Trot after Turkey Trot. This marathon is actually a little less than nine Turkey Trots. My brain starts spinning and all of a sudden I start to feel overwhelmed. What if I pull a calf muscle and can't go on? What if I start having trouble breathing and have to stop? Can other people look at me and tell that I'm freaking out? Right now, I'm okay. Breathe, and keep going. Don't let the anxiety win.

—Providence Marathon, 2011.

The night before my grandmother's funeral, my dad was forty-five minutes late to our family meeting with the Rabbi.

"Where is he?" Mom whispered, pulling me aside and twirling a curl behind her ear and pacing the kitchen floor, while the rest of our family sat in the living room of Rabbi Feldman's home. I had no idea where he was. Up until the recent turn of events with my grandmother's death, Dad and I were supposed to have been shopping for my senior prom dress that night. It was easier for me to mentally obsess over prom than it was to deal with thoughts about my dead grandmother. I was originally planning to go to prom with Mike Walsh, but he'd called the day my grandmother died asking if it was okay if he went with Megan instead. According to him, he and Megan had romantic chemistry, but he and I were just friends. I didn't know anything about romantic chemistry since I'd still never even kissed a boy, but I did know that I was officially unasked to my senior prom. Another unexpected turn of events. Since there were no other boys at school I felt comfortable asking, I called in the reserves, Solomon Eskinazi from the bass section of the Boston Conservatory

Choral Camp, who lived about an hour away. At least I wouldn't have to go alone. Suzie was going with Dave and the four of us planned to go together.

All things considered, I thought my mom was handling the death of her mother rather well. I couldn't imagine what I'd do if my mom died, although I guess it was a bit easier when your mother was eighty-four. While the loss was still devastating, it was probably safe to say that she'd had a full life. And Grandma Thelma was a pistol up until her last breath, even during the cancer. Uncle Dale was just telling a story about how she got pulled over for speeding three weeks before she died. When the policeman asked her if she'd realized how fast she was going she told him, "I do, and with all due respect, Officer, I don't have much time left."

Grandma Thelma outlived her late husband, my Grandpa Jack, by five years. They had three children together: Dale, my mother, and their little sister, Donna. My Uncle Dale was tall and stoic. He never said much, but when he did, whatever came out of his mouth was profound and/or hilarious. He was a musician just like my mom. My Aunt Donna was always trying to catch up to her older brother and sister, and while she did not inherit the musical gene, she didn't let that stop her. Determined to fit into the Von Trapp family mold, she started taking piano lessons in her late forties. Between the three siblings, they had four children. Ted, Cara, Jackie, and I were always quite the foursome, and the older I got, the more I clung to them, especially since they were the closest blood relatives I had to siblings.

While my aunts and uncles and cousins sat in the living room swapping stories, my mom and I stood in the kitchen. I didn't really want to be in there with her, but also didn't feel right abandoning her. The rain pounded against the one window above the kitchen sink. "Mom, maybe he's not answering his phone because he's driving and it's storming outside. Not everyone talks on their phone while they drive like you do." I immediately regretted my snarky comment, but I didn't know how to fix the situation and just so badly wanted for her to stay calm. She used to be so grounded in life, and then, one day, something changed; she became more frazzled with age. Even Rabbi Feldman's cat didn't want to be anywhere near her. It was like the only thing her body could do to feel proactive was to pace about that kitchen and keep twirling that curl. She should've been mourning the loss of her mother, but was instead fixated on the absence of my father. She turned away from me and paced back into the living room where her brother and sister were sitting with their spouses, my Aunt Moira and Uncle Ray, reminiscing. Uncle Dale brought up the time his son, my oldest cousin Ted, hijacked Grandma's (who was prim, proper, and Jewish) AOL Instant Messenger account and messaged our Aunt Donna: "I'm leaving your Grandfather and running away with a strapping young black man." (A joke that landed in the 90s.) And there was the night of Thelma and Jack's surprise fiftieth wedding anniversary party when, elated from the evening, Thelma drove off, leaving Jack on the sidewalk not realizing he wasn't in the car until she had had a good two minute conversation with herself and realized Jack wasn't responding. Dale's wife, my Aunt Moira, started laughing about how when my mom brought my dad home to introduce him to her parents, Grandma Thelma said she hated that he wasn't Jewish but loved that he had good table manners, and for that reason, had her blessing. Grandma was immaculate and table manners were of the utmost importance to her. She was the one who taught me to put a napkin in my lap, after all.

"Any word from him?" I could hear my mom's sister ask in a brash, loud voice.

"No, Donna," she said quietly, trying to conceal her nerves.

"Well, calm down, I'm sure he'll be here," Aunt Donna continued slowly in her thick Boston accent, which was ten times more prominent than anyone else in my family. It was as if Mark Walberg and Whitey Bulger had had a baby and named it Donna. "He's probably just trying to drive. This weather is bad."

"You're right, Donna," my mom said quietly, her inflections rising at the end of the sentence. I could hear the weight in the way she said "right" and knew it was not right. I also knew why she was about to cry, and I wondered if she'd told anyone in our family about dad's drinking issue. She probably hadn't. She and I barely talked about it. That March my father had officially been sober for just over five years, at least from what I knew. So what was the point of bringing it up after the fact? And amongst the three of us, the topic seldom came up. I knew he went to AA meetings every day but he and I barely discussed it; that was my fault. Whenever my mom raised the subject of my dad's alcoholism, whether it was twelve-step related or about his over-spending, I always masterfully changed the topic. She'd give me information and I'd memorize every word, as if it were text I needed to prepare for an audition: The house was transferred to my name. Dad was over-spending. Dad was going to two AA meetings day. And while I knew those nuggets by heart, where my mother was concerned, I also pretended not to care. It felt safer. I guess I took after my dad in that way, having the ability to appear apathetic. Another life skill.

Eventually I followed my mom and joined my family in the Rabbi's living room, but didn't sit down. Something about sitting felt too committed and I was upset that my dad's absence was detracting from what should've been an evening of honoring and remembering my grandmother. My cousin Cara could tell I was distressed and tried to lighten the mood by asking me what I was going to wear to Grandma's funeral. The truth was I'd already picked out my sensible black ensemble. That made Jackie, our youngest cousin, laugh too. Cara was going to speak at the funeral, as was her brother, Ted. They were both great in front of a crowd and got their comedic timing from their dad, my Uncle Dale. Just yesterday, Cara and I were driving my grandmother's car to the drugstore, making the most of Grandma's handicapped parking permit. After finding a five dollar bill in the glove compartment, Cara insisted we buy some candy and made a comment about how nice it was for Grandma to buy us things, even after she was dead. I wanted to be present in the conversation with Cara, but I was distracted by a side conversation that had started between Moira and my mom. I tried to do that thing where you're talking to someone, but simultaneously listening to someone else; it was like an advanced acting exercise.

"You seem really anxious," I heard Aunt Moira tell my mother, more concerned for her than for my missing-in-action father.

"I'm fine, I'm just a little worried."

"Does he know the address of this place?"

"Yes," my mom answered, looking at the floor. She kept twirling that curl and shuffling her feet, unable to sit still.

"Then he'll get here when he gets here. Dale and I hit tons of traffic on 128 and it's a good thing he's not trying to talk on his phone and drive at the same time. You remember how you always used to get so agitated when he did that?" Aunt Moira's presence was always commanding and she had the power to make anyone believe every word that came out of her mouth. She reminded me of

Suzie's mom. Moira was great during a crisis and I was glad she was there that day, even if she didn't understand the real reason why my mom was so upset. As an only child, I relied heavily on my extended family, at least on my mom's side. My dad's parents both died when I was eight years old so I never got to have the relationship with them that I had with Grandpa Jack and Grandma Thelma. My dad's father died of a heart attack and his mother died of liver cancer, both within the same year. My dad had two brothers, but there was a huge feud over their parents' property after they died, and since my dad was the lawyer on the estate, he took the brunt of it. After the falling out, he only talked to one of his brothers who lived in Vermont with his wife and two adopted children, so while I liked them, I didn't get to see them often. I was closer to my faux cousins from the Black Friday Brunch bunch than I was with my cousins on my dad side.

"Shall we start with the photos?" Rabbi Feldman asked cautiously, trying to be sensitive to whatever drama I'm sure he could sense was going on, but also wanting get the show on the road. I got the sense he was a bit overwhelmed by our family, we all had large personalities, to say the least, and I was sure he wanted us out of his home at some point.

Growing up, I'd spent every summer with my mom's side of the family at my grandparents' cape houses, which we'd come to name "Camp-What-the-Fuck." Though I didn't really appreciate it until I was older, those houses are the reason my family is so close. We acquired "Camp-What-the-Fuck" in the 1950s when Grandma Thelma purchased a dirt cheap house right on the water on Buzzard's Bay. A few years later, the house right next to it went up for sale, at almost as cheap of a price as the first one. Having visions of hypothetical loud and disruptive neighbors, Thelma insisted that she and Jack buy that house, too.

I'll always remember my grandmother's fear of us kids tracking sand into those houses. She had an orange bucket at the top of the steps that led down to the sandy beach. The cousins took turns filling it with water from the ocean so that there'd always be clean water to rinse our feet. Occasionally, one of us would hide a hermit crab in the bucket and somehow we were always shocked when those crabs died. It never occurred to us that the sun would fry them without plants and sea life to come to their aid.

Each house had a piano in it, and I'm pretty sure I was her favorite grandchild because Grandma Thelma loved it when I sang.

Grandpa Jack was a phenomenal jazz pianist and we'd always perform standards together. He'd gig at local restaurants and started calling me up to sit in with him when I was six years old. I was always a hit. I mean a six-year-old singing "Someone to Watch Over Me" in the style of Broadway was always a treat for the other patrons, I'm sure. After he died, Uncle Dale took over as resident family jazz pianist, and now he and I sing and play together. During Grandma Thelma's last few months, in between cancer treatments at the hospital and her final week of hospice care at home, I visited and sang to her acapella; I sang whatever material I was working on at the time, which was mostly show tunes by Frank Wildhorn or Jason Robert Brown. And I didn't just sing them, I full on performed them, with dramatic intent and everything. Can you imagine what her hospital roommates must've thought? But she'd always smile and ask for an encore. The very last time I performed for her was on the first evening of Passover. She was sitting on her bed, pale as a hermit crab's claws, and wearing bright orange lipstick that matched the buckets at the cape. I don't think I ever saw her without lipstick, not once.

"Nikki," my mom whispered to me from the couch, "Can you go into the kitchen and keep trying dad from my phone?" She covertly passed me her cell phone, and I went back into the kitchen and stood at the sink so I could see out the window. I called my dad, but there was still no answer and it went straight to voicemail. It was an hour drive from his AA meeting to Rabbi Feldman's and the rain was coming down hard. Was it even possible that he was drinking? It bothered me that my mom was so nervous and it forced me to be calm for her, even when my heart was also racing a million miles a minute. Treating it like an audition, I tried to appear calm in front of her and hoped she couldn't see my disgruntled and sweating insides. It was as if our roles as mother and daughter were reversed. I was the one trying to keep her anchored, and I felt like the onus was on me to be more of a friend or partner than a daughter.

Suddenly, bright lights flashed across the Feldman's driveway as a car pulled in. My mom bolted to the front door as my dad came in.

"Where were you? What took you so long? Why didn't you answer my calls?" The barrage of questions that flew out of my mother's mouth were quiet enough that I bet she thought the rest of the family couldn't hear.

"There's no need to panic. Have you seen it outside?"

"I talked to you two hours ago. You knew we were all getting here at six."

"My phone died. The weather is terrible. What do you want me to say?" He reached into his back pocket and pulled out his phone to show my mom that it was, in fact, completely dead, and my mom studied him, silently. He seemed both agitated and sincere. He walked into that house defensive because he knew exactly what he'd be walking into, and I actually felt bad for him. But I also didn't fault my mother, because I didn't trust him either. Nobody did. It was like no matter how many times he told the truth, he'd never be able to make up for the times he didn't, whether it was about beer cans in a bag at rehab, or about how much money he spent on clothes. Maybe he was just late and in traffic with a dead phone.

"Hello, everyone!" Sorry I'm late." My dad stepped around my mother like she was a puddle he didn't want to step in, and walked into the living room, joining the rest of our family. "The weather was horrible and I hit bad traffic. Sad about Thelma." It struck me as odd that he grouped all of that into one thought.

"Have a seat!" Aunt Moira welcomed him. My mom excused herself to the restroom and I resumed my place next to cousin Cara. Dad looked at me with a playful smirk and rolled his eyes, like he used to when I was a kid, only that time he did it smaller so no one else could see. I didn't roll them back, even though part of me wanted to.

How do you know someone is lying when there's no proof? Does it mean they're telling the truth? I hated not knowing. And it angered me to see my mom interrogate my dad, and it infuriated me to see the way my father's behavior sent my mother into a tizzy of anxiety. Throughout most of my childhood, until the end of high school, really, she'd been a pillar of strength. I looked to her for confidence, even though I never told her that. She was the one who taught me to put myself out there. She was the one who made me finish playing "Arabesque," even after I messed up. She was the one who made me play in my soccer game while my dad was in rehab. She was the one who relentlessly drove me to every audition and would calm my nerves before I sang.

There was one audition in particular that stuck out in my mind because I think it marked the first time I ever really remember experiencing self-doubt. And I mean *really* remember passing judgement on myself and feeling it. As a performer, I'd put myself out there on stage many times but that day, during the fall of my junior year of high school, was the first time I remember hearing negative feedback, and realizing that the words were coming from inside my own head. My knees were shaking and I couldn't tell if the shivering was just in my head or if the judges could see it. I was standing in a high school hallway, bathed in bright florescent light, my throat was closing up and having trouble swallowing. There were two other students ahead of me in line. Did I look composed and normal to them? I decided to take one more trip to the water fountain because I thought it might help my throat stop closing. I'd tried to straighten my hair for this audition, but it was raining and by the time I'd made it from my mom's car into the auditorium, and it had started to curl. Though still not ideal, by the time I'd turned sixteen, I'd (luckily) graduated from the half-pony hair style to hair completely down with a little bit of product. Thank God. When I looked down to see if I could see my own knees shaking, I noticed that I had a run in my tights above my right knee and all I could do was pray that I didn't run into Adam Weinberg looking like this. Thankfully he'd told me that his appointment wasn't until the afternoon, and it was only ten in the morning. The tenors auditioned in a different part of the building anyway. Up until that point, I'd never felt that nervous to sing in front of anyone. Maybe it was just because I was getting over a cold and that handicap was making me more jittery than usual.

Mom had assured me that getting accepted to the Northeast District Chorus, a select group of the best singers from different high schools in northeast Massachusetts, was not going to make or break my getting into NYU, but I was still determined to collect every possible accolade to help my cause. And even though it would turn out to be a blip on the radar of my life, at the time, it felt like my career was riding on this audition.

What I loved about having my mom around, as it pertained to performing specifically, was that she always told me the truth, even when I didn't want to hear it. I knew this because she corrected my piano playing constantly and was always giving her opinion in terms of which song best suited my voice. Deep down, I don't think my mom wanted me to pursue theatre professionally, probably because she wanted to spare me the rejection, but that didn't prevent her from driving me to every audition I'd ever asked her to take me to. My

Grandma Thelma wanted my mom to be a secretary, but she defied her and followed her passion and got a Bachelor's Degree in music. After she met my dad she took some time off from work to go back to school and earned her Master's in education. My dad financially supported her during that time. Maybe some part of her would be proud if I followed in her footsteps.

The very first audition she ever took me to was for a production of *The King and I* when I was seven years old. I sang "Part of Your World" from *The Little Mermaid* and sang to a piano track that my mom had pre-recorded for me. She drove me to that audition too, and the last thing she said to me in the corridor before I walked in was, "Nikki, remember there will always be people in your life who are better than you, and you'll always be better than other people, too. It doesn't matter, all you can do is your best." I thought about that advice all of the time. And I used to be more confident. When I was eight, my mom took me to audition for a community theatre production of Oliver and I made it to final call backs for the role of *Oliver*. Being so young, and, at the time, flat chested, I guess they figured they could pass me off as a boy. I lost the role to Dominic Priolo and was flabbergasted. My mother had to explain to me that they probably went with an actual boy to play Oliver, since Oliver was actually a boy and Dominic could sing the role. At the time, it didn't make any sense to me. My rendition of "Where is Love" was profound. But somewhere along the way I lost my confidence, too. Like mother, like daughter.

Outside that audition room, I leaned over and stuck my face in the bubbler and pushed the button. A stream of water shot out higher than I'd anticipated, dousing my nose and cheeks and landing on the neckline of my shirt. Jolting backwards, I used my fingers to wipe away the excess water from the sides of my mouth and pushed the button again, leaning in slower this time, taking a few more sips of water. I stood there for a minute in front of the silver water fountain. I took a deep breath and slowly exhaled. The hardest part of auditioning was that when I was nervous, my breath was the first thing to go and I needed to be able to sustain the long phrases I was about to be judged on.

Each audition seemed to be taking about three minutes. The audition itself involved singing the vocal line of a brief song, which was "Linden Lea" that year, and there was a short sight-singing test. I tended to do well on the sight-singing each year, not only because my mother was hot-to-trot for the Circle of Fifths, but because I was usually stronger at things that were impossible to prepare for. Sometimes I over-rehearsed and psyched myself out. The way I'd always viewed sight-singing was that you can either read music or you can't. It was that simple. Put the sheet music in front of me and I'd show you what I could do, there was just no way to plan for it.

I hated that I got so nervous doing something I loved so much. When did that start? What happened to just assuming I'd be cast as Oliver? Whenever I got nervous, my mother reminded me of the time when I was eight years old and she wrote a part for me in the variety show she'd musically directed at Revere High. I played Melody (I named myself after the character from the hit Nickelodeon sitcom *Hey Dude*), the little sister of one of her students, whose character had terrible stage fright. I sang my go-to eleven o'clock number, "Part of Your World." Apparently, before I walked on stage my mom asked if I was nervous. I looked at her and said, "What, do you have to be nervous to be in this show?" In that moment outside that classroom, I would have given anything to be able to go back to that night in my black and white checkered dress with the cherry pin that Grandma Thelma had sewed on when there wasn't a nervous bone in my body. I didn't know what judgement was. Walking out on stage, the lights hit me and I knew I was home. I took the microphone like I was real singer and started the song, reveling in the fact that everyone's eyes were on me. I got to be the one to tell them that I wanted to be part of their world! It was the most liberating feeling, even for an eight-year-old. I remember feeling my mother's powerful presence in the wings stage right, and seeing my dad smiling in the first row. He was grinning a gigantic grin and started applauding before the song even finished. And there I was, eight years later, outside that audition room, sixteen years old, Ariel's real age, and my right knee wouldn't stop shaking. One more soprano and then it was my turn.

Knots plagued stomach and my mind started to race, the thoughts almost crippling me. What if I ran out of breath and went flat? What if I panicked and sang a wrong note or missed a cut-off? What if I psyched myself out and screwed up the sight-singing part? Don't let them know you're nervous. Stop the thoughts. Just keep moving forward. My knee was out of my control and that was okay. I was okay. All of a sudden, the singing from inside the room stopped and I heard footsteps coming toward the door. A girl came out of the room, made brief eye contact with me and smiled. "Good luck, guys," she said to the three of us waiting. It was my turn.

I smiled as I passed the audition monitor and greeted the judges with a friendly hello. They were seated behind a long table, their backs against the chalkboard. Auditions had only been going on for an hour and these judges already seemed exhausted and, most likely, sick of "Linden Lea." There were two women and two men and none of them seemed interested in small talk, especially the woman on the end sitting with her arms crossed with a cup of coffee in front of her and a scowl on her face. The bald man on the far left side at least tried sitting up straight and wearing a pleasant look as he asked if I was ready to begin. I nodded, and the angry looking woman uncrossed her arms to hit the play button on the CD player.

"Linden Lea Soprano Track." A stale monotone voice announced the start of the music, which I'd heard many times before, because I'd been practicing with the CD for weeks. I thought my entrance was strong and all of the judges immediately started writing. What were they scribbling? Two phrases in, I realized I was more focused on the judges than I was on the song itself, so I tried to bring myself back to the music, thinking about the lyrics that I was singing and what they meant. I got through the song, but I could feel myself go flat on the last note. All I had to do was be in the top percentile of students. I didn't need to be perfect. I still had a shot.

Next came the sight-singing and I heard my mom's voice telling me to take my time and not to rush. I breezed through and was pretty sure I got a perfect score. I thanked the judges and exited the room, wishing the other girls in line good luck on my way to the auditorium where my mom would be waiting. Keeping an eye out for Adam Weinberg just in case he got there early, I spotted my mom sitting in the second row, reading a newspaper.

"Mom," I said, getting her attention as I walked briskly toward her.

"Nikki! How did it go?"

"It went okay. I think I was flat at the end and wasn't focusing enough on my breath but I think I did well on the sight-singing. I really hope it was good enough." I was still shaking.

"Why are you so hard on yourself?" she asked not waiting for an answer. "I hope you didn't get that from me. Did you do the best you could?"

"I think so."

"Then it was good enough." I gathered my things and we headed out to the car. "And you know, Nikki, if for whatever reason you don't make it into the choir this year, that is an important lesson to learn too. I know you'll be disappointed, but rejection is a big part of the field you want to go into and it's important to learn how to deal with it, and more importantly, to learn how to bounce back.

The following Tuesday afternoon, I got a phone call after school from my music teacher saying I was accepted. My mom was teaching at the time, but my dad was there to share the good news and congratulate me.

"Great job, Nik! Your dad always knew you'd get in."

Usually I appreciated his undying belief in me, but it also made him lose some credibility. How did he "always know I'd get in?" I didn't get in the year before. It would've been a very realistic outcome for me not to be accepted that year, too. I smiled at him. His eyes were wide and even his ears even seemed perked up, like an excited puppy.

"Thanks, Dad." I said, and left it at that. Growing up in a house full of secrets meant a life of second-guessing. It was enough to drive any person mad. I knew my mom felt it too, but in a different way.

The rest of that night at Rabbi Feldman's, I felt like prisoner in my own mind. I avoided making eye contact with my dad and my dad avoided making eye contact with my mom and my mom tried to make eye contact with everyone. My dad borrowed Dale's bulky phone charger to charge his phone, and eventually the storm let up and we all piled into our respective cars. My mom asked me to ride home with my father. I wasn't sure if it was because she wanted to be alone, or because she wanted to ensure my dad drove straight home.

My dad and I didn't talk much in the car, but he did try to revive the Twiddlebugs from *Sesame Street* that he used to do all of the time when I was little. He mainly did it when I was in the back-seat behind him; he'd make a fist and extend his pointer and middle fingers, kind of like bunny ears, only the fingers would remain fluid, and he'd make them talk in high-pitched voices and say they were the Twiddlebugs. Excitement took over whenever I saw the Twiddle-bugs, AKA my dad's hand, slowly climb over the top of the headrest of the passenger seat to check on how I was doing behind him. I hadn't heard from the Twiddlebugs in a good ten years, but all of a sudden, there they were next to me, hovering right over the automatic shift.

"Hi, Nikki!" my dad said in a high, squeaky voice.

"Dad, what are you doing?" I knew what he was doing. Regardless, that night we all got home at the same time.

MILE 10

I'm officially into the double digits. These are good double digits to be into. The following are a list of bad double digits to be into: Ten cookies in bed after a long day (PLD), ten drinks in one night (PLD), ten hours of hot yoga while hungover from the ten drinks in one night (double PLD). So far I haven't had to stop once, other than to grab water, and I don't intend to stop. I'm running this thing until the end. No walking, no detours, no nothing. Just ahead of me I see a woman I remember standing at the starting line with her husband. He must've run off, leaving her behind. I wonder whether she feels bad that she can't keep up or relieved that she doesn't have to. I'm still going at a pretty slow pace, but there do miraculously seem to be some people who are even slower and still behind me. The lone woman just ahead of me slows down to a walk and I eventually pass her, making a right on what appears to be a bike path of sorts. The road gets narrower and turns towards what looks to be a small forest. Nine miles down and I don't feel like total death, so that's a win. I'm going to be okay. The trees are finally shading me and my skin feels cool again, but this time sticky. I taste the salt around my outer lips and think about how my body is covered in dry sweat. How is my dad going to react when I cross the finish line? What am I going to say to him?

–Providence Marathon, 2011.

After a long week of binge drinking Diet Coke, stress-eating penne alla vodka, and taking midterms, I was fried. Sophomore year of college wasn't as easy as I thought it would be for a musical theatre major, but I'd managed to maintain a pretty high GPA (never mind that it could easily have been attributed to how well I did in tap class, African Dance, and American Sign Language). That year I was living in an NYU dorm on Broome Street, which made taking the Chinatown bus from Manhattan back to Boston for the holidays extremely convenient. Unfortunately, I was on the 6 o'clock bus that night, prime time for traffic, the day before Thanksgiving, no less.

I was a frequent customer of the Chinatown bus. It's safe to say I kept them in business, until they mysteriously shut down many years later, luckily after I'd graduated to trains and planes and rental cars—in other words, anything but the Chinatown bus. I'd gone back and forth so many times that by sophomore year I had enough points to get a free Chinatown bus water bottle if I wanted to. The

Dry Run

Chinatown bus eventually became kind of like an ex-boyfriend who went off of social media. We stopped speaking, but do have many memories together. Now, in my thirties, I don't hear much about the Chinatown bus anymore, but occasionally we'll pass each other on the highway, and we're cordial.

My favorite memory together was during my freshman year of college, when I was left behind, along with most of the other passengers, at a McDonald's off of I-95. There were two identical buses, since Fung Wah was clearly trying to do volume, and the driver from the previous bus accidentally got onto my bus and drove off into the sunset. I had three orders of fries that day. The first because that's what you should do when you have the opportunity to be at a rest stop. The second, to comfort myself after panicking over the thought that the bus had left with all of my possessions, and the third because I was bored, since all of my possessions except for my wallet were on the bus. Later that summer, during the Fourth of July weekend, the driver got so lost that my father had to get on the phone with him to give him directions. That went well.

That ride to Boston the night before Thanksgiving was long, dark, and for the most part, silent. I felt very much like Paul Revere only with a bus instead of a horse, going to Boston instead of from, and with no one to warn that the British were coming—because they weren't. Occasionally I'd hear a high-pitched female voice through the static of the driver's two-way radio, but the voice wasn't really loud enough to disrupt anyone from their sleep. I only heard it because I was up. It was almost like sleeping in New York City. After a few months, the sirens and the screeching of taxi cab breaks weren't enough to disturb my sleep. Instead it was my silent thoughts that kept me awake. Thoughts of not being talented enough to be at NYU, thoughts of missing my long-distance boyfriend, thoughts of whether or not I'd passed my Music History exam. At nineteen, I cared a lot about a lot of things.

The midnight ride was almost complete and I'd exhausted the November *Star Magazine* crossword, listened to the *Into the Woods* soundtrack twice, and watched one episode of *24*. There wasn't anything really left to do but sit there and let my mind wander. The bus was hot and smelled like leftover McDonald's. Luckily, there were very few cars on the road that late; most of the traffic we hit was in Connecticut. Whenever someone mentioned that they were from

Connecticut, I thought, "You're from that long state I have to suffer through on my way from New York City to Boston." I remember being excited to go home that weekend and not only see Suzie, but also my boyfriend at the time, Rob. We'd met the summer prior doing a production of *Godspell*; he was the lighting designer. How cliché. He was my first boyfriend, he was tall, dark, and handsome, and I loved knowing he was lighting me when I sang "Bless the Lord." I remember thinking it was quite the summer romance, and of course I finally lost my virginity during a production of *Godspell*. Our connection was so strong, we decided to try to make it work long-distance once I had to go back to NYC. Lost in my fantasy of Rob, the community theatre lighting guy, I realized that my dad still hadn't responded to the text I'd sent him about forty-five minutes ago when we'd turned onto the Mass Pike.

When I went to check my phone again, it buzzed in my hand right on cue and I suspected that it was my mother calling to ask for an ETA. Annoyed because that was the fifth time she'd either called or texted in the past two hours, I ignored the call; my backstory would be that I was sleeping. I'd get home when I got home and my mother didn't need to know my location at all times. What she needed to do was learn to relax. After all, my dad was the one picking me up, and he hadn't even texted me once.

The overhead lights turned on abruptly and I realized we were driving up the ramp to the bus terminal at South Station, at last. I gathered my backpack and duffle bag as quickly as possible and shuffled to the front of the bus.

I stepped off into the frigid air and could see my breath. After grabbing my suitcase from under the bus, I made my way to the terminal. My dad, who was sporting a black plastic-looking coat that was reminiscent of some sort of cutting-edge trendy trash bag, was waiting patiently near where I entered the building. I was secretly excited to see both of my parents. I missed them a lot when I was away at school, and even though I complained about her non-stop, my mom and I did talk on the phone daily.

"Dad, what are you wearing?" I asked before even saying a proper hello.

"Hi, Nik! That bus sure took forever!" He rolled his eyes, our classic "we're in cahoots" gesture and we laughed.

"No, but seriously Dad. What are you wearing?"

"It's the new hot look. It's good stuff."

"Of course it is," I told him. I heard Justin Timberlake's "Sexy Back" playing and realized it was coming from my dad's phone. It was his ringtone. Typical.

"We're on our way," he answered. He didn't even have to ask why she was calling. He turned his phone off and looked at me. "Mom is going nuts. 'Where were you? When, are you coming home? Have you heard from Nikki?' She needs to chill the F out!"

"Seriously. I feel bad I've been ignoring all of her texts, but, like, I'll be home when I'm home."

"Exactly." My dad looked good. He seemed to be his chipper old self; maybe he was just happy to see me.

We made our way to the parking lot and I climbed into the front seat of the good old Rodeo that by this point seemed indestructible, as my dad loaded my luggage into the trunk. I turned the radio to Top 40 as we backed out of the parking space. We pulled up to the gate to exit the lot and the parking attendant motioned for my dad to roll down his window. He had to have been in his late teens with a nametag that read "Paul."

"Your ticket, Sir?" he demanded, reeking of exhaustion, his ears prominently sticking out from his head, bearing a striking resemblance to Ross Perot. Dad opened his wallet, looked inside, then started fishing in his pockets.

"Hmm," he said to Paul. "I don't seem to have my ticket. How much do I owe you?"

"Dad," I said, "You haven't even been here a full hour. You're not going to bother to look just a little bit harder?" I checked the glove compartment and the area near the gear shift.

"Nope, I don't think I have it."

"That will be twenty-five dollars," Paul said, like he was about to drift off to sleep right there in the booth. My dad handed him a debit card and paid full price. The gate rose and we drove away.

"Mom will be pissed you lost the ticket," I said.

"Mom's not here and it was an accident, Nik."

"I know. I'm just saying." I wished my mom didn't freak out so much over little things. She used to only get upset over big things, but lately the slightest thing seemed like a production. We used to have so much fun, like when we did theatre productions together. And we still do have fun, she's just always so anxious. Sometimes I wish I'd known her before she had me. She used to travel all of the time and would tell me to never take even a domestic flight without my passport, because you never knew when a spontaneous opportunity to leave the country might arise. That was the woman who raised me. Then something changed, because that was not the woman who was now obsessively texting me asking when I'd be home.

"Are we doing still doing the Turkey Trot tomorrow morning?" I asked. As much as I pretended to hate it, I'd come to love the Turkey Trot and looked forward to it each year. I didn't care about my time or PR or anything like that, but it was nice to have something to do with my dad and it felt good to work off Thanksgiving dinner ahead of time. Everyone in the musical theatre department at NYU was so skinny, skinnier than I was, and I ran on the treadmill every single day. I didn't enjoy it, but it was something I'd just always done since going to college, like brushing my teeth. I wasn't fast, but running four miles a day made me feel deserving of a cookie. It was allegedly how my dad stayed so skinny all of those years. At that point, he didn't run many races, but still went on a run at least twice a week.

"Yup!" he said. "Turkey Trot. Gobble gobble gobble."

As far as I knew, and to this day as far as I know, that Thanksgiving pretty much marked the seven year anniversary of his sobriety and I was proud of him. Without saying anything I turned up the radio and of course Justin Timberlake was singing. My dad bounced up and down, grinning, while I sat back, fantasizing about mom's meatballs and spaghetti. That had become the signature dish she prepared every time I came home for a visit.

Speeding up Route 1 North, we didn't talk much. I'd always appreciated that my father was comfortable in silence, especially after long bus rides. He knew that when I gave him one word answers to his questions that I was not in the mood to chat and he respected that. Not wanting to strike out, he never asked more than two, and if I wasn't receptive he'd back off. We were approaching the exit for 128 and it was dark. There weren't very many other cars on the road, aside from a few sparse red taillights in the distance. My body felt a sudden impulse and I surprised myself when my hand involuntarily grabbed the arm rest attached to the passenger door. I thought I felt the car swerve ever so slightly, first to the left and then to the right, just enough for my body to notice. The motion of the car

Dry Run

didn't seem to alarm my father and he calmly turned the wheel to the right. We seemed awfully close to the guard rail on the right side of the road. The moment was fleeting and once we were on 128, he moved into the passing lane, and I tried to make the pit in my stomach dissolve. I recognized that pit. I'd only experienced it one other time, when I'd walked in on the man in my father's bedroom years ago, but the sensation was unforgettable. The subtle swerving happened so fast that I started to question if it actually happened at all. His eyesight had gotten worse with age and maybe he just didn't see the exit in time.

"You alright, Dad?"

"I'm great, Nik. Dad is so happy to have you home."

Several minutes later, I was relieved when we turned off the highway, but was confused when about five minutes from our house, my dad turned into the parking lot of a Richdale.

Like a true musical theatre major I said, "Why are we stopping, Dad? I have to pee like crazy. I might actually die." I didn't really have to go to the bathroom but that pit stop seemed unnecessary and weird.

"I just need to get the paper."

"You need it right now? At eleven thirty at night? Doesn't a new one come out in a few hours?" I sounded like my mother and immediately stopped talking.

"Yes," he answered. He left the car running so I wouldn't get cold and scampered into Richdale. Two minutes later he came back with a folded newspaper and a brown paper bag.

"What's that?" I asked.

"Just remembered we're out of Diet Coke." He put the paper bag in the trunk along with the newspaper. A few moments later we pulled into the garage.

"I'll get your suitcase out of the trunk," he offered. "I need to go check on the bunnies and make sure their water hasn't frozen. Go in and start eating, Nik!"

Ever since I was a kid, my dad and I had co-parented pet bunny rabbits. The first two were named Thumper and Pinky, and then we had Clover and Nugget. We'd since moved onto Daisy and Violet, named after the twins from the musical *Side Show*. The bunnies seemed to have come and gone in pairs. My mother hated animals so I was only ever allowed to have pets that lived outside, aside from my Turtle, Tara, who my mother disposed of while I was away on a field trip my junior year of high school. She said Tara the turtle made the living room smell during piano lessons so she set it free in a nice pond on the next street over. Incidentally, Tara was a tortoise, a land lubber.

Dad lingered in the garage to grab my suitcase while I lugged my duffle and backpack inside. The second I walked through the door I was greeted by my mother, jumping up and down and talking a million miles a minute about how petrified she was that we were never going to get home. That made no sense to me. She started twirling that curl hanging just below her left ear.

"Nikki! You look so pretty!" mom told me.

"Thanks, Mom." I was glad she thought so. I'd been straightening my hair lately and had recently gotten some lighter brown highlights to make my color a little softer. The horrible bangs I'd experimented with over the summer had grown out, thank God. I tried to force a smile, but I didn't feel much like smiling and I sensed she could tell.

"I've missed you! Have you missed me? Are you excited to see me?" My dad came inside, said he was tired from the drive, and went to bed almost immediately.

"Yes mom, sorry I'm just super tired."

"Oooohhhh," she said in her classic half whiney, half playful tone. I finished eating and announced that I was exhausted and would probably head to bed. I brought my empty plate to the kitchen sink and opened the fridge, pretending to look for something else to eat, standard behavior on my part. There were still two six-packs of Diet Coke in the fridge, one with all six cans and the other with five. I was pretty sure my dad had gone straight to bed, without opening the fridge. Was I crazy? "Okay, I'm going to bed too," my mom decided. "Don't forget to turn the lights out when you're done cleaning up. I'm so happy you're home!"

I ran the kitchen sink and scrubbed my plate with soap and hot water. At the other end of the house, I heard the door to my parents' bedroom shut behind my mother's clunky, uneven footsteps. Mom was never graceful. It was part of her charm.

My heart was beating out of my chest as I made my way to the garage door. Maybe he'd hid the alleged soda in the car. The front passenger side door to his car wasn't locked and I carefully opened it and climbed in, just like Dick Wolf would have wanted me to. There was no evidence in the front.

Now channeling Robert Goren, I slithered between the two front seats and into the back. The only things I spotted were an old banana peel and a Jack Higgins novel with some bent pages. I rolled myself over the back of the seats and into the trunk, squatted, and looked around still seeing nothing to prove what I knew in my gut to be true. It was so cold out there that I debated going back inside and ignoring the situation altogether. Also, if I didn't find the evidence, maybe it wasn't true.

The beer had to have been outside. When my dad and I first got home he'd checked on the bunnies, and then as far as I knew went into the house, dropped the newspaper on the kitchen counter, and went straight to bed, empty-handed. I headed to the driveway to examine the surrounding area. Thankfully, the outside lights illuminated a path close to the perimeter of the house, so I took a few steps down the driveway and found myself next to the rock garden sitting just to the left of the pavement. That had always been dad's favorite garden to "plant;" he changed the rock formation each spring. The area surrounding the rocks was covered with dead leaves and branches. Dad loved gardening and it always looked beautiful in the summertime.

Where else could he have possibly gone? The bunnies. He'd gone to check on the bunnies. I tiptoed down around the back of the house so as to not startle Daisy and Violet, shivering as I went; opening the door to grab my coat from inside the house would've made too much noise. Violet heard me coming toward the hutch and ruffled around in her little house. The wind was blowing and I couldn't help but feel a little scared because the bunny cage was at the edge of the woods. Who knew what could be out there.

The wind rustled the few stubborn leaves still on the trees. When I got to the cage, Violet's water bottle was frozen solid. Daisy's was empty. Through the wired bottom of the cage, I saw something shiny on the ground. I reached down to a pile of frozen rabbit shit and picked up an empty can. The green label read 'Heineken,' and my mind instantly flashed to seven years ago when Gerald pulled two cans of Heineken out of my dad's running bag at rehab. In many ways, that moment at the bunny cage was when it all started for me.

My heart was beating so low and so strong, I felt it drop to the ground. My gut was twisting. The wind was blowing. It was cold. Did my mom know about this? Had my parents been keeping it from me? Should I tell my mom? Should I just confront my dad? What if I told my mom and she couldn't handle it? What if I didn't tell anyone and my dad got into an accident because he was driving drunk and it was my fault because I didn't say anything to anyone? What if I told my mom and she threw my dad out of the house and he drank himself to death? How would Jack Higgins write my character's next move in this story? My mind felt like a maximum-security prison, my thoughts all prisoners, shouting over one another, all unable to escape.

Something moved in the woods and I got scared and immediately ran back around to the front of the house and went inside. Still clutching the beer can, I ruminated over what to do with it. I had to keep it as evidence. In an attempt to drown out my fear, I turned on the television and temporarily stashed the beer can in my bag. I needed to at least hide it until I knew what to do. I was going to throw up. It was times like those that I wished I'd had a sibling. I sat on the sofa, trapped, tortured, and alone. I thought about texting Rob, but wasn't sure what he'd be able to do, and I didn't want to ruin one of the few times I got to see him with this situation. He was my escape. I heard familiar indelicate footsteps coming toward the living room, unexpectedly, given that it was now well past midnight.

"Nikki?" mom says. "Are you still awake? I thought you were going to bed.".

"Hey, mom. I just needed some time to chill out before bed. I thought you were asleep."

"I couldn't sleep. I just took a sedative so hopefully that will kick in soon."

"Hopefully."

"Do you want some company?"

"Not really," I told her, my words, curt and apathetic. I felt guilty. Why was I so angry? Who was I angry at? Did my mom know what I knew and was deliberately keeping it from me or had he successfully kept it from her? Was I just as angry at her as I was at him, for making me live with this enormous secret?

"I'll sit with you if you want," she volunteered a second time.

"Mom, please don't take this the wrong way, but I'm super tired. I've had a really long trip and just need to be by myself right now so that I can decompress before I pass out. I'll see you tomorrow after Dad and I get back from the Turkey Trot." I still sounded harsh but I didn't know how else to react. I needed to shut her out.

"Ooooh," she sighed. She told me she loved me and went back to her bedroom. I thought about texting Suzie or one of my college friends for advice, but, seven years later, I still didn't want to be in big trouble. Those words still haunted me. I didn't want to disappoint anyone and I also didn't want to say the wrong thing. If my dad drank only one beer, maybe the issue wasn't as bad as it could've been. I wished I could account for the other five cans. Maybe if I could find them I could throw them out and prevent him from drinking more. That way, I'd never have to tell anyone, including my mother. My eyes darted around the living room, unsure of where to settle.

There were several family photos decorating the mantle, pictures of the three of us dating back to the mid-eighties and a few eight-by-tens of my dad running marathons. One photograph in particular stood out. My dad was wearing a tight yellow shirt, one size too small, and a pair of inappropriately short gray shorts. There wasn't an ounce of fat on his body and his hair was slicked back with sweat and wind. I checked behind the frame in search of a Heineken. Nothing. There was another photo of me when I was six years old eating a hot dog in St. Kitts, the Club Med vacation where my father entered a "Sexy Legs" contest and won. Sexiest legs at Club Med, February 1990—now that was something to be proud of. He was in the background of the photo wearing short green shorts and a tank top, giving the camera a thumbs-up. My mom must've taken the picture.

There was a third photo of my dad and I standing side by side at the beginning of the Cape Cod Canal, where he used to take me running as a little girl. I don't remember who took the photo, but I remember the day it was taken. It was a summer weekend when I was around nine years old and my dad had taken me on a run. In the picture, I'm wearing red mesh shorts and an oversized white T-shirt, my hair is French braided, and I'm squinting while smiling because the sun is in my eyes. Dad is staring straight at the camera and isn't smiling; he often treated photo opportunities as serious glamor shots. His hair was brown and cut in the style of a mop top, he almost looked like he had walked off one of The Monkeys album covers. His arms were folded in front of him. The sun was so hot that morning, and while I had every intention of running like a grown-up would, I quickly tired out after about a half of a mile. Dad kept going and I let him go, because I didn't want to ruin his run or hold him back. After that run he took me to get ice cream and said that a half of a mile was better than zero miles, but that I really need to try to run faster. At that point, I half tuned him out because I had ice cream and was happy.

Behind the television seemed to be the next logical place to hide something. I checked, but all I found was dust and wires. My attention went back to the couch, specifically where my father always sat to eat goldfish crackers and drink Diet Coke while watching TV. I moved the cushion to see what was underneath. I couldn't look directly at what I saw, but even out of the corner of my eye I knew it was a half empty bottle of wine.

Calling off the search, I stashed the bottle in my duffle next to the empty beer can, turned off the television, and went to my bedroom. I sat down on the floor and my eyes scanned the now faded Revolution soccer posters still taped to the wall. Back in my child-hood bedroom, I was overcome with a twisted feeling of déjà vu, not knowing what to do. I'd moved out of the house, but I didn't feel like I'd moved on with my life. I thought his problem would just disappear. Furthermore, I thought it had disappeared, but somewhere in my body, I knew it hadn't. I'd always known it hadn't. Maybe that's why I never talked to my mom about it; if it wasn't discussed, it wasn't true.

Completely at a loss, I managed to crawl into bed and laid awake for a few hours until my alarm went off at six o'clock, alerting me that it was time to get dressed for the Turkey Trot. My dad usually woke me for it, and I'd always yell at him, still half asleep. That year the alarm beat him, but I still thought it was odd that I didn't hear him milling about the house, fidgeting with the toaster, and counting down the minutes until he could wake me. I got up and walked across the hall, still in my pajamas, to my parents' bedroom and cracked open the door to find both of them sound asleep.

"Hey, Dad," I said, hoping not to disturb my mother. "Dad, it's time to get up for the Turkey Trot." No response. He was snoring. I walked to his side of the bed and lightly tapped his shoulder. "Dad," I said again. "Dad, let's get up!"

"What?" he muttered groggily.

Dry Run

"Dad it's the Turkey Trot. Shouldn't you get up?"

"No." The snoring commenced again.

"Okay," I said feeling rejected, and started to go back to my bedroom.

"Nikki," my mother's half-asleep startled voice stopped me.

"Yeah?"

"What are you doing? What time is it?" she asked.

"I was getting Dad up for the race, but it seems he's really tired this year so I'm just going to go back to bed."

"Oh," she said. "He's getting older, Nik," completely disregarding the fact that he was right there next to her. It was almost like he wasn't. She drifted back to sleep and I envied her. The room was completely dark except for the red light of my dad's cell phone charging on his nightstand. I backed out of their room and into mine.

Plagued with anxiety and guilt, I tried to decide how to solve my father's problem. I wanted to protect my mother from it and also wasn't equipped to deal with her panic-stricken outburst if she discovered he'd been drinking. Maybe I could just go back to New York and pretend it never happened. All of a sudden, I had an idea. I climbed out of my bed and went back into my parents' bedroom where they were both asleep. I grabbed my dad's cell phone, hit the contacts button, and scrolled to the Ms. Thinking of the mantra, "What would Jesus Do?" I copied Mitch's number onto a piece of paper and went back into my bedroom. Mitch was my father's closest friend, he would surely know what to do. He probably already knew about my dad's issues so I told myself I wouldn't be violating the pact I'd made with my mom. Chances were that he was up preparing for the Turkey Trot himself. I dialed his number from the landline in my bedroom. Unfortunately, my parents had the second phone line eliminated when I moved to New York, but the actual phone was still in my room so Mitch should've recognized the caller ID. There was no answer. I didn't leave a message.

MILE 11

My feet hit the ground. Left, right, left, right, left, right. Trying to stay light on them, I make a conscious effort to make sure I'm running on the balls of my feet instead of just slamming them against the ground. During Turkey Trots especially, or when we'd run the Canal, Dad would always tell me not to hit my feet so heavily. It's better technique and it's healthier for your joints if you run light. When I was younger I used to pound my feet even harder when he'd give me this advice, simply because I could get away with it. It always made him roll his eyes, while he tried hard not to smile, and that would always delight me. The irony here is that in the grand scheme of life, ultimately my dad got away with a lot more than I did, yet I'd continue to punish myself. Whenever my dad relapsed, I'd hold onto such resentment and start to hate myself. A slight burst of energy propels me forward about ten feet and then I slow down again.

- Providence Marathon, 2011.

For the first time in eight years I wasn't running the Turkey Trot. The silver lining there was that for the first time in eight years I was able to see the start of the Macy's Thanksgiving Day Parade, great news for a show-tune savant like myself. The cast of *Thoroughly Modern Millie* was singing the title song from the top of a small float. My dad was in his room sleeping and I was sitting in the kitchen, trying to decide what to do with the beer can and wine bottle still hidden in my bag. My mother started to make her signature breakfast, scrambled eggs and whole wheat toast. I was watching the parade from the kitchen so that I could keep my mom company while she cooked, and ultimately, so that I could be closer to the food. She was adding some pepper to the skim milk and egg concoction when the phone rang. She kept stirring the eggs with one hand and grabbed the cordless phone with the other.

"Oh, hi, Mitch…Happy Thanksgiving to you too!" I was struck by how cheerful my mom sounded, given this morning's events. She listened to Mitch. "That's strange, he's still asleep… no, he was too tried to run this year. He's getting old, Mitch," she laughed in a way that sounded almost forced. It always struck me how unapologetically and quickly she mentioned my dad's challenges when it came to aging, when I wasn't sure there had really been any tangible ones. "Thanks for checking in. I'll double check with him." She pressed the off button on the phone with her pointer finger and set it down on the table.

"Mitch said he got a call from our house this morning," she said, still staring at the phone.

"You mean Dad's friend, Jesus?" I asked, trying to deflect with humor so that I could buy myself some time to figure out how I'd explain the call. "Why is that odd?" I asked, knowing full well why it was strange.

"He said he got a call from our house number this morning, but I certainly didn't call him and Dad's still asleep. I haven't talked to Mitch in at least two or three years. Maybe he made a mistake." I sat there at the kitchen table, unsure of what to do. Picking at my cuticles seemed like a good temporary solution, then I got up and went to the cabinet above the counter and began pulling out plates to set a Thanksgiving breakfast table for two since Dad seemed to be sleeping in.

It was a beautiful day and the sun was shining right through the kitchen window. I stared out that window at the woods in the backyard and it looked like a movie set, completely untouched by any form of life, aside from Prescott, the next door neighbor's cocker spaniel, running around. All of our summer lawn furniture was still on the back deck. Apparently no one had the time or energy to move the furniture into the garage to preserve it for next year. Dad probably figured he'd just buy new furniture, and Mom surely thought that if she didn't look at it, it didn't exist.

My mom poured the egg concoction into the frying pan and took a spatula to it before the eggs had even had a chance to solidify. She grabbed the handle of the pan, lifted it on and off the burner, swirling the eggs around and stabbing at them with the spatula. I was worried she was going to burn herself and I caught myself off-guard when I blurted out, uncontrollably, "I called Mitch, Mom." She dropped the pan back on the burner, letting go of the handle, and turned towards me.

"Why would you call Mitch?" she asked half baffled and half laughing. "How did you even get his number?"

"I got it from Dad's cell phone," I answered.

"Why would you call him?" The eggs sizzled and she continued moving them around with the spatula, hitting the pan harder, but leaving it on the stove.

"I called Mitch because I didn't know who else to call." At that point I'd said too much to not continue what I was trying to say. I could see in my mom's eyes, which I was trying to avoid, that she knew exactly what I was going to tell her. "I think Dad's drinking again." There. I'd said it. My work here was done.

"Nikki, what makes you think that?" she asked. "He goes to AA every single day. He's been sober for seven years." Her voice got louder and more authoritative with each word. I wanted to agree with her and drop it, but I'd already said too much to backpedal. At that point, I wouldn't have escaped her inevitable interrogation anyway.

"Mom, I didn't want to say anything until I was sure, but last night I found beer cans under the bunny cage and a half empty bottle of wine under the sofa cushion." We were both quiet. The silence lasted a long time. The eggs were still sizzling and a thin layer of smoke started to rise above the pan. "I have the bottles in my room if you want to see them." I felt like such a tattletale, like a mean girl in the eighth grade snitching on her friend for smoking pot at a party. Only I was a narc, throwing my dad under the bus. My mom didn't cry like I expected her too. She stood stone-still and mute for a few long seconds while the eggs continued to burn and I continued to set the breakfast table. Without saying a word, she turned her back to me and ran to the other end of the house much faster than I would've moved in the Turkey Trot. The crash of her bedroom door shook the house.

"How could you?" she yelled through a flood of tears, as I tried my hardest to focus on a cast of hyped up singers and dancers performing "You Can't Stop the Beat" at the parade. The eggs, which had officially been left unattended, kept smoking and I rushed to grab the spatula that my mom had left resting in the pan. I was able to salvage most of them; I like my eggs well-done anyway, though there were some burnt chunks. My mother's yelling subsided and she emerged from the bedroom as if nothing were different. We ate our half-burnt eggs while gazing at the pristine woods and tattered lawn furniture.

"I love you, Nik," She broke the silence first. "You know that, right?"

"I love you too, Mom. But I will say, these eggs are not the best."

"At least they're just eggs."

Unsure of what to do, I decided to go for a run after breakfast. I usually avoided running right after eating, but I needed to get out of that house and clear my head. Desperate to be in a place where the only person I had to deal with was myself, I quickly threw on thermal pants, two sweatshirts, and one of my dad's winter hats that I found in the closet.

Trying not to pound too hard on the pavement, jogging lightly down our street, thoughts flooded my brain as I began my own Turkey Trot. My hands froze quickly and I wished I'd brought gloves with me, but something about the sharp, tingling pain in my hands kept me focused and present. What was going to happen to my dad? What could I do to help? A part of me also just felt shell-shocked and numb, like I couldn't believe that after seven years it was happening again. Also, had it been happening recently and my parents had just agreed to keep it from me? Was that possible?

I'd only planned on doing a few laps around the neighborhood. I tried my best to avoid patches of ice on the ground and let my mind wander, trying to think of things other than what was waiting for me at home. I thought of my friend Eric, who was also in my musical theatre program at NYU, also from Massachusetts. We'd met freshman year at orientation while in line for seconds at the buffet at the dining hall inside the Rubin dormitory. He was this dreamy boy from Newton, Massachusetts, and a Jew! At the time, I was single (obviously) and I started inviting Eric to my dorm room on Tuesday nights to watch *American Idol*. I'd strategically place dirty laundry on my desk chair so that he would be forced to sit close to me on the twin bed while we watched Ryan Seacrest, whom I'd always had a crush on. Every week my heart sank when he moved my dirty laundry from the chair to the foot of my bed. After five weeks of this, I realized that Eric also had a crush on Ryan Seacrest. When he officially told me he was gay, though I was disappointed that I wouldn't be having my first sexual experience anytime soon (this was pre-Rob), I did feel like it was a rite of passage. I was officially living the perfect musical theatre college life. Got my tap shoes, my headshots, and my first official gay best friend—I was ready to go!

We'd started going to the gym together and created this ritual where we'd both run three to four miles on treadmills next to each other, at ten minute mile paces, and high-five each other after every mile. That high-five signifying the completion of a mile always made me feel like I was checking something off of a list, which was help-ful on the days when I felt like I was in a holding pattern, not really accomplishing anything. My dad must've felt so satisfied after thir-ty-two marathons, and I wondered if he'd found the answers he was looking for. What was happening back at my house? I imagined it was something along the lines of my mom cleaning the kitchen and my dad at least pretending to be asleep. I could've called someone other than Mitch. I could've called a friend for help. Nineteen years old and I was still scared of getting into big trouble. It was my fault I'd chosen to obey my mother, and I should hold myself accountable. My dad chose to drink around the time I was coming home for a visit. Was he not excited to see me? At the time I hadn't yet developed the mechanism to understand that it wasn't all about me. After about ten minutes of running around the block, letting thoughts run in and out of my head, I gave myself my own high-five, having checked one mile off of the list, and headed back the way I came.

Later that day, my mom and I went to Thanksgiving dinner at Aunt Moira and Uncle Dale's house in Newton and left my father behind. Mom told our family that Dad had the flu. Aunt Moira told us how sorry she felt for him. Not only was he sick on Thanksgiving, his favorite holiday, he was sick the weekend I was home to visit. My mom echoed Aunt Moira's sentiments, like any loyal wife would, and I didn't say anything. Why was she protecting him? Why hadn't we told anyone that my dad was a drunk? Cara, Jackie, and I caught up on boys and Cara told us all about life after college and how I should try to stay in college for as long as possible. She'd won Homecoming Queen at Syracuse last year on a dare, and it sounded like her adult life was far less exciting than her reign at school.

After a few hours of gluttony, laughter, and lies, my mom and I went home. Before going inside, I checked on the bunnies to make sure they had enough water, while my exhausted mother crawled into bed next to my father, whose snoring rattled the house. I fell asleep, relieved that with Dad asleep, there wouldn't be any more drama until morning. Tremendous guilt trapped my body, like an evil villain holding a helpless maiden, when I realized I couldn't wait to go back to New York. I'd really turned a new corner, given that growing up I always got so homesick and just wanted to be with my parents. Throughout my middle school summers, I came home early from two summer camps. To be fair, one just plain sucked and the kids made fun of my colored sweat suits (obviously with tapered pants) and over-the-top soccer obsession. And the other camp was at an all French-speaking farm in the middle of Canada, where my only companion was a four-year-old mentally challenged child named Jean-Claude, since he was the only one who couldn't really speak the language, either. I was not set up for success in either scenario. If my dad were drinking then, I probably would have stayed at camp.

I woke up the following morning to my mother's loud voice on the phone.

"I miss you too, Charlotte. I'm so upset. I'm just sick to my stomach. No, you don't need to come. I think I'm going to visit him and then take Nikki shopping. I'm sorry we have to cancel. I know Nikki was really looking forward to seeing the girls."

I soon learned that I'd miraculously slept through all of the prior night's events, probably because I was so tired from not sleeping the night before. No one tried to wake me either. I don't think I've slept soundly through the night since. Around two in the morning, my father had fallen on his way to the bathroom. My mother, who was never *really* asleep, leapt out of bed when she heard the crash (at least the way she told it). Something was wrong with his legs. She called 911, an ambulance came, and he was carried out of our house on a stretcher. Apparently, she'd gone with him to the hospital, then came home to try to get some more rest, once things were under control.

On that Black Friday of 2003 we didn't attend our annual brunch. My dad was having his stomach pumped to get the remaining alcohol out of his system. He was at Beverly Hospital, just ten minutes from our house. I accompanied my mother to visit him because she made me, but I didn't want her to go alone anyway. When we got there, before even entering his room, she immediately hurried off to find his doctor to get some information, leaving me alone.

I recognized the man in the hospital bed. He was the same man who had crawled across my father's bed naked seven years ago. His uncombed blond hair and frosted tips had turned grey. I wasn't sure whether it was from alcohol poisoning or if he just really needed his roots touched up, probably both. His silver man bracelets had been replaced by a hospital band around his left wrist. His face was saggy and he had wrinkles that I didn't remember being there yesterday. Drooping cheeks distorted his complacent expression and

I'd never seen a pair of eyes look so sad. They weren't looking at anything, really. It seemed they were only open because there was no point in closing them.

My mother was outside the room talking to the doctor. I stood beside the hospital bed, completely still. The only thing I could think to do was to break into the pudding sitting on his leftover lunch tray. I didn't even like pudding, but my options were to stand there with nothing to say to my father, or to do absolutely anything else. Do something. Eat the pudding. I slowly reached for his untouched lunch tray on the bedside table, and glanced at him briefly to gauge his reaction. When I got no response, my hand inched closer to the cup of vanilla pudding. My dad didn't comment on my behavior and continued staring, catatonic, at the wall. My mother was hysterical outside, but I wasn't. I had pudding. I stood there, looking at my father, at the spot right below his eyes, because I couldn't look directly at them. It was hard to see someone I loved in so much pain, and it was even more difficult when deep down I also felt like he deserved to be in that pain. There was a tinge of satisfaction and a touch of vengeance that made me hate myself. It was easier to hate myself than it was to hate him.

"I really screwed up, Nik," he said, just as I made contact with the pudding.

"Over the past few hours I've done some real soul-searching, and I promise this will never happen again." I didn't answer. I focused on the pudding, intentionally taking my sweet time opening the cup. I turned it around a few times to make sure I had peeled the foil top off of the correct side. I put the spoon down, as if juggling both the spoon and the pudding was an impossible task.

"How's school going?" he asked. I willed my attention deeper into the pudding.

"Good," I answered.

"I know we haven't really had a chance to catch up this Thanksgiving. Mom says you're still dating Rob…"

"Yup." I cut him off after two questions, knowing he wouldn't go for a strike out, irritated by his effort to make small talk when he was lying in a hospital bed. It was a disturbing feeling, looking at someone helpless when I felt helpless myself, despite being in the more advantageous position. Oh my God what else could I do with that pudding? I wished there had been a more involved snack available but I worked with what I had. I experimented with how much pudding I could get onto the spoon and how flat I could make it before it entered my mouth. I was also pissed that he'd asked about Rob. Was that really what was on his mind, my love life? I was supposed to see Rob that night and had yet to tell him about this part of my life. I almost didn't want him to know; I didn't want him to think of me as a victim. And, to be fair, my dad's drinking hadn't really been an issue again until last night. I also didn't want Rob to know the heinous emotions I was capable of feeling towards the man who'd raised me or to think I had "Daddy issues," because I didn't. I glanced up for a moment, not to see my father's expression, but to see if I could quickly locate another activity or snack since I was almost at the end of the pudding. Coming up empty, I started taking as tiny bites as possible. I could play that game for a long time.

A nurse entered the room, my mother trailing behind her, and I caught the tail-end of their conversation.

"Years of alcohol damage have resulted in just one drink having a severely negative effect on your husband's neuropathy," the nurse explained to my mother, while I lurked in the corner clutching an almost empty pudding container. "Just one drink will interfere with his nervous system and cause extreme problems with equilibrium." I stared at the nurse's nametag, Cindy. Cindy helped my dad out of bed and into a walker. He clutched the handlebars, but his arms were so weak they bent at the elbow and his torso sagged. His legs, the best legs at Club Med 1990, looked like toothpicks under the hospital gown. His feet looked wilted in his short socks. How was this the same man who had run thirty-two marathons? How was this even the same man who picked me up from South Station just forty-eight hours ago? It was like he'd aged twenty years overnight. I would've given anything for a lost parking ticket to be our biggest problem. He struggled with the walker, his knees and elbows trembling.

"Dad is not good, Nikki," my mom said to me quietly, letting my dad and Cindy move ahead of us, out of his room and into the hallway, where there was more space to walk. Unshed tears welled in my mom's eyes. I watched her as she watched her husband's brittle body struggle to shuffle down the hall with the assistance of his nurse. "The doctor said that if he ever has alcohol in his system again, there's a chance he won't make it."

"Well that really sucks," I said without looking at her. I didn't know what she wanted me to say. It also seemed a bit dramatic to me at the time.

"The doctor said he's lucky to be alive," she continued, almost like she was trying to elicit more of a reaction from me. All I could get out was, "Sorry, Mom. It really sucks."

"I just don't understand."

"Yeah. It's pretty messed up," I said. My dad reached the end of the hospital corridor and slowly turned around to begin inching his way back towards us.

MILE 12

The bike path that I've been running on for a few miles now starts to become steeper. Not ideal. I'm actually now climbing more than I'm running. That's an exaggeration. Whenever I'm faced with a hill, I like to run really fast so I can gain the proper amount of momentum to get through it as easily as possible and also so the torture will be over quicker. Now that I'm about halfway into this long, steady hill with slightly less of an incline than Cat Hill in Central Park, I catch up to a row of bikers. They're moving along at a snail's pace, taking up the entire path, making it impossible to pass them, and it slows me down. I understand that the bike path is for bikers, but this is a marathon. There aren't supposed to be bikers. Are these people really that stupid or inconsiderate? What idiots. There's that short fuse again. There are a few spectators camped along the path and I start giving them looks that say, "Can you believe these fucking bikers?" My attempt to gain empathy from strangers so that my feelings are validated fails. I don't think anyone actually sees my over-the-top, annoyed, and dumbfounded facial expressions, but it feels good to make them. My right calf still hurts, especially on the incline, and I'm hungry. I've been running for about two hours. Why am I doing this to myself?

— Providence Marathon, 2011.

The walls of the room were white and the couch was a deep burgundy, not the plush brown leather couch I'd imagined. Dr. Miller had straight blond hair that fell just below her collarbone. Her black rimmed glasses made her look smart and extremely attractive. I sat there, staring at the floor, unsure of what to expect. Was she going to speak first? Was I supposed to start? The life-threatening silence was lasting slightly longer than I wanted.

There was a clock on the wall above my head. I couldn't see it, but I could hear the ticks each second; somehow I managed to have a hundred different thoughts between each tick. Was Dr. Miller tired? Did Dr. Miller think I was pretty? What did Dr. Miller do when she got off of work? What was I going to eat for dinner? Did Dr. Miller think I was boring? What would my parents think if they knew I was there? Would they be upset I hadn't told them I came to therapy? Would they be disappointed that I was in therapy? My brain fired off thoughts rapidly and uncontrollably, like one of those sparklers on the Fourth of July. Something had to come out of my mouth before my head exploded, but I didn't even know why I'd come to therapy in the first place so what could I possibly say?

That wasn't true. I knew why I was there.

I was there because the week prior, when I overheard two girls in my music theory class talking about how NYU offered students ten free therapy sessions per year, I felt a giant sense of relief. I was there because I'd just left my father in a hospital room, unable to walk, and when I looked at him a part of me felt vindicated. And, I'd abandoned my mother to deal with it on her own. She was stuck with the pain and responsibility, but I could just flee back to New York because I certainly couldn't miss class. So I just up and left and was taking musical theatre classes on my parents' dime and eating meal plans they paid for while they were most likely at the Beverly Hospital, eating hospital food and not speaking to one another.

Sadness lived in my chest and it had for a while. I didn't know where to run. That's not right, I wasn't even sad, I was guilty. And why did my dad seemed to drink whenever he knew I was coming home? At least, that's how it felt. It seemed so unfair to me that I had an escape and my mom didn't.

I'd tried to take my college professor's advice and throw my emotions into my acting. But the problem was that while performing gave me the power to create an alternative universe and fuel my real emotions into a storyline that was usually fabricated, it also made it hard to come back to real life. When I was on stage, even if it was just for two minutes, I treasured every second when I could speak my truth and not worry about judgement because it was all masked by the character I was playing. But sometimes, when I left the stage, I desperately wanted to yell, "That wasn't an act! That was me! That was real!"

Dr. Miller was staring at me and I felt stupid for coming to therapy. I'd always been a straight-A student and had it all together. I'd be so embarrassed if anyone found out. I didn't even want to tell my mother because I was sure she'd feel bad that she couldn't help and advise me herself. But deep down, I knew this was something I had to deal with on my own.

So many people had told me that college would be the best four years of my life and parts of it genuinely were great. But parts of it were not. The night before I'd left for Thanksgiving break, my musical theatre friends and I went out to Suzie's. It was our favorite Chinese restaurant not because of the sub-par chicken lo mein, but because the wait staff never asked to see our ID. My favorite drink to order was "The Affair," not because it tasted good, but because it was fun to say: "I'd love an Affair, please." I'd had one too many Affairs that night and had tremendous remorse the next morning. Eric and Martin had asked me to help them finish their Scorpion bowl. I'd had about four Affairs and recalled taking Martin's straw and sucking in what was left and all I could think was, wow my dad would be so disappointed in me for not learning from his mistakes. Or maybe I was disappointed in him. Everyone around me was laughing. Martin was high-fiving the waiter and Eric was focused on me. The lights were bright and I started feeling nauseous. Did I have a drinking problem? All my friends were drinking just as much as I was, but their dads weren't alcoholics so maybe I was different. I remember leaving my debit card with Martin, standing up, and running to the bathroom, where I vomited twice, rinsed out my mouth, popped two mints, and returned to the dinner table like it never happened.

But wasn't that what kids were supposed to do in college? I wanted to tell Dr. Miller all of that but I didn't even know how or where to start. I wanted to tell her that that morning, while dragging my body to the practice rooms on the ninth floor of 35 West 4th Street where I practiced both piano and singing for two hours, I walked extra slowly when crossing the street so that if a car or a bus was meant to hit me, it would mean that it was meant to be and that I deserved it.

I was afraid to tell Dr. Miller because I was scared she'd just tell me that this was typical nineteen-year-old angst and that everyone went through it and that the only solution would be to grow up. Frightened that she'd tell me she read my file and that I should be thankful I didn't have real problems like an abusive uncle or having to drop out of college because of how expensive it was. Petrified she'd tell me that I didn't have the right to feel unhappy. I was scared I'd fail therapy.

My right foot tapped the floor and my left thumb compulsively massaged my right, very sweaty, palm. Dr. Miller was staring right into me when I looked up at her. She looked so calm and composed. I tried to match her, but my insides were screaming. Would my mom be mad if I told a therapist my dad was an alcoholic?

"Hi," I say, finally breaking the silence. "I really like your couch!" Why did I say that? I readjusted myself in my seat and touched the coarse upholstery again. "Nice fabric!" I said. God, I was such an idiot.

"It's nice to meet you, Nikki," she said in the most soothing yet even tone I'd ever heard. Ice, broken.

"You too," I replied with a smile on my face. I waited for her to continue or to ask me one of those cliché therapist questions I'd seen on television like, "Why are you here?" or "How does this make you feel?" but she didn't. I got it. The silence was a tactic. She wanted me to do the talking.

"I had no idea NYU offered free therapy sessions. This is such a great service."

"Yes," she replied, "it is."

"Yeah, I heard some girls in one of my classes talking about it. Very awesome."

"That's great that you were able to get that information. So, what brings you here today Nikki?" Success! I'd done it! I got her to crack first! I celebrated my small victory and then felt the back of my neck start to sweat.

"I've been feeling bad about some things I've done and thought that therapy might be a good way to talk some of this out." I was impressed by how articulate I sounded. There was no way I could keep up this charade. She asked that I start by telling her what specifically made me make an appointment, as in an inciting incident, and told me to put myself back in that moment. So I did. I took a deep breath and returned to three nights ago when I had had dinner with Eric.

Raindrops were beating steadily against my umbrella. Already ten minutes late to meet Eric for dinner, short breaths and long steps propelled me to Little Italy. My brain stammered when my phone's vibrations pulsed down my leg. Flustered, trying to juggle the umbrella, my Disc-Man, and my purse, my dorm room keys fell out when I accidentally dropped my purse onto the wet pavement. A gust of wind blew my umbrella inside out when I bent over to get my keys, and the relentless rain pummeled my head, ruining my straightened hair. "Fuck my life right now," was the phrase running through my head. I was so angry and wasn't sure at what exactly. The missed call was from my dad. I wasn't sorry I missed it; I was

Dry Run

annoyed that he caused me to drop my purse in a puddle and that my hair was wet and curly.

He must've been home from the hospital. There was no cell reception in his room, and he wouldn't have been able to call me unless he'd been released. My phone rang again almost immediately and I ignored it.

The third call came when I was two blocks closer to dinner. Against my better judgement, I answered.

"Hello?" I said, annoyed, pretending not to know who it was, as if Caller ID weren't a thing.

"Hey, Nik," Dad said, his voice wobbling and soft. We were both quiet.

"Do you need something?" I broke the silence. "I'm kind of busy."

"Nope. I just wanted you to know that I'm so sick to my stomach thinking about what I've done."

"Okay…"

"I got out of the hospital today and your mom drove me to sit by the beach so that I could do some soul-searching."

I said nothing. It was his responsibility to fill the silence, not mine. Also, what was soul-searching exactly?

"I did some soul-searching. A lot of searching, and I realized I've made a lot of mistakes. A lot of wrong turns." It was like my dad was trying to navigate that conversation using a broken GPS.

"Sorry, Dad. It's raining here. I can't really hear you." I could hear him just fine.

"Oh," his voice got softer and lower. "I was just saying that I've done a lot of soul-searching and I'm sick with myself. You and mom deserve so much better and Dad has really fucked up. I really suck. I'm so sorry."

"Okay."

"Did you have a good trip back to the city last night?"

"It was fine. Sorry, Dad, I'm running really late for dinner because you made me drop a bunch of things when you called." I immediately felt horrible, but also didn't feel like apologizing. I didn't owe him an apology and in some way, my attitude towards him felt warranted. But it also made me feel worse about myself, like I was kicking a horse that was already down.

"Okay. Have a good dinner, Nik."

"Bye Dad."

"Okay. Bye-bye."

After hanging up the phone I promptly threw my broken umbrella in a nearby trashcan. The jig was up. I was wet. I opened the door to Da Nico where Eric was sitting at a table in the back, texting someone or maybe playing Snake while he waited for me.

"Sorry I'm late," I said as I frantically sat down, letting my bag dry out on the ground. I took a sip of water. Eric looked so put together in his red plaid button-down shirt tucked into jeans.

"Get caught out there in the rain?" he asked, breaking into laughter. It was clearly his code for telling me I looked awful. "How was home?"

"Fine."

"Did you get a haircut, Niks? It does look great…you look just like *Liesel in The Sound of Music* when she comes in from meeting Rolf, soaking wet!" This was his attempt at making me feel better. It did not. The waiter brought us bread and I grabbed a piece before the basket could even touch the table.

"How are you?" I asked. "How was your break?" Even though I realized a romantic relationship with Eric was off the table, and I was technically still dating Rob, the community theatre lighting guy (who to be fair went on to have an extremely impressive and successful career in the lighting business), I still couldn't help gazing into Eric's eyes. I didn't want to be rescued, I wanted to be relieved. For a second his eyes distracted me from the stress of being late and the anxiety of what was going on at home.

"It was good. How about you? How are you parents?" I was prepared to answer anything but that question. He could have asked about the food or about my family in general, but he had to go and specifically ask about my parents. I forced a smile, as seven years of repressed emotions started fighting their way up from my gut to my chest. I tried to ignore it, but could feel them starting to flood my body and stop short in my throat. Clenching my throat, and feeling scared that I might lose control, I swallowed hard, attempting to force it all back down where it had stayed hidden.

"Fine," I said quickly in an octave lower and softer than my normal speaking voice.

"Are you sure?" he questioned. "Something doesn't sound fine."

I held my breath for a second and tried to think about anything but my father. Digging my nails into my right thigh, I hoped that if I could focus on that physical pain, it would distract me from the gathering, uncontrollable emotions. I was nineteen years old and should've been able to compose myself better than that.

"Yeah. Totally." My body was conditioned to not break promises. Trained to not break rules. My mother's haunting words replayed in my brain: If I find out you told anyone about this, you're going to be in big trouble. That was seven years ago. The waiter came over to share today's specials and presumably to take our order.

"Do you know what you'd like?" he asked us both in an Italian accent, and with a helpful smile.

"I know what I want. Nik, are you good to go or do you need another minute?"

"I'd like…" The back of my throat started to close up, a dam holding back a flood of tears. "I'm fine. Really," I said, trying to prepare Eric and the waiter for the eruption that I may not be able to prevent. The stream of tears broke through the dam mid-order.

"Penne alla vodka," I finally managed to eke out. The waiter grinned, showing his teeth, and transferred his weight back and forth between his two legs. Clearly not knowing what to do, he looked to Eric.

"We'll do a penne alla vodka and a baked ziti, and a bottle of Pinot Grigio." He knew it was my favorite, we clearly needed it, and we'd never been carded in Little Italy before.

The waiter hurried off and I sat there at the table across from Eric and began to sob. Big gulping sounds poured out of my mouth, interrupted only by gasps of air. I cried tears for the twelve-year-old girl who had to look up alcoholic in the dictionary because she was too afraid to ask. I cried more tears for the child whose father wasn't there to coach her soccer team during the play-offs, and for the girl who unintentionally smuggled beer into her father's rehab facility and readily accepted the blame. I cried for the thirteen-year-old girl who walked in on her father having some sort of withdrawal episode and faulted herself for not doing anything about it. I cried fifteen, sixteen, seventeen and eighteen-year-old tears for the child who remained silent, so scared of getting into trouble. I cried for the guilt I still felt for harboring resentment towards my parents when they loved me so unconditionally and had given me so much. Then I cried for the woman who suspected her father might be drinking again when he stopped at Richdale to buy beer and whose father later drank it and hid the empty cans in the bunny cage. I cried for the woman who had handled this alone until that moment, but simply couldn't do it anymore. The dam was broken. And in the process of releasing seven years of repressed emotion I knocked over my water glass.

I'm so sorry. I'm such a mess," I choked out between sniffles.

"Slow down. What's up?" Eric asked, concerned, reaching out for my hand.

"I'm so sorry," I squeaked out. "This is so embarrassing."

"Please, it's me you're talking to. Besides, when have you ever had any shame?" We laughed because if we didn't, I'd continue to cry.

"My dad is an alcoholic," I blurted out, just as a teenage bus boy came over to clean up the spilled water. "My God you have no idea how good it feels to get that out."

"Woah, woah. Slow down," Eric said. "How long has this been going on?"

"Since I was twelve. You're the first person I've told. My mom was so paranoid about anyone finding out and I haven't wanted to disrespect that but I can't do it anymore. Can you do me a favor and keep this between us?"

"Of course. Wait, start from the beginning…"

We sat in the restaurant for three hours with copious amounts of pasta, wine, and an order of meatballs that we placed forty-five minutes after the pasta was eaten. We then ordered two slices of Oreo cheesecake so that I could have an entire piece all to myself. He let me cry some more and listened. What a relief it was to be heard after seven years of silence. I'd been set free. I told him how angry I was at my dad and how I felt like I'd been awful to my mother and how I just didn't know how else to be. After we closed down the restaurant, Eric hugged me and put me in a cab. Something felt different. I had a sense of security, like everything was going to be okay, no matter what happened with my dad. I pulled my phone out of my purse and called Suzie.

Dr. Miller interrupted me for the first time: "So to be clear, that was the first time you've ever shared with anyone that your father struggles with alcohol addiction?" Her soothing voice brought me right out of the Italian restaurant and back to her room and the ugly couch.

"Yes."

"And how did that feel?"

All of a sudden, I was no longer alone.

MILE 13

It is unfathomable to me that I'm almost halfway there, and I wrestle between reveling in the fact that I've almost completed half of a marathon versus crying over, 'Oh my god I still have slightly more than half of a marathon left to go.' I was tired before, but now I'm really tired. There's a woman a few feet in front of me who I haven't seen before. I notice her blue shorts and immediately want them because they're loose-fitting and high cut, making them revealing yet not slutty, a very difficult combination to achieve. I down another gel shot, this one is orange. Orange is my dad's favorite color. The course has flattened out and finally, after this last mile of incline torture, the bikers in front of me pull over to the side of the road in single file. I run past them and realize that they're a group of mentally handicapped individuals whose leader is congratulating them for finishing a bike ride. I'm an asshole. My lips still taste like salt and the top of my head is starting to feel sore from the sun. It hadn't even occurred to me to put sunblock on the part in my hair. Maybe I deserve a sunburn.

– Providence Marathon 2011.

"No tuna fish!?!?!?'

My mother's anxious voice bellowed from inside the kitchen and across Buzzard's Bay. Vacationers and low-brow neighbors sitting on the beach turned their heads toward the corner cape house where my mother had taken umbrage with today's lunch. It was the July after my sophomore year of college and Dad was sober; he had been for about eight months. Sitting on the beach, I stared over the top of my magazine at my dad through my favorite pair of giant, cheap sunglasses with thick white frames and a scratch on the left lens. He was sitting quietly across from me in a beach chair digging his toes in the sand and reading the sports section of *The Boston Globe*, his arms and chest glistening from a layer of glittery tanning oil. Neither my mom nor I approved of my father's frequent trips to Planet Sun, but as my mom said, he was a sixty-two-year-old man— if he wanted to go tanning, he'd go tanning. After all, it was better that he be addicted to tanning beds than to beer and he got a tanning discount with his new gym membership. He had joined one in order to keep up certain physical therapy exercises.

"Hey!" my mother yelled to my father from the porch. "Didn't you pick up tuna last night?"

"Calm down!" my dad yelled back. "It's in the cabinet to the right above the sink."

"No it's not! It's not there!"

"It *is* there. Open your eyes."

"Okay, I must be stupid." My dad looked at me with his eyebrows raised, egging me on to share in his playful annoyance. "Can somebody help me *please*?" My mom wasn't amused.

"Mom!" I yelled at her. "It's in the cabinet to the right above the sink. I saw it earlier. It's not that hard to find."

"You know, between the two of you, you'd think I could get a little help here." Feeling culpable, and having made a New Year's resolution to be nicer to my mother, I got out of my beach chair and walked up the stairs to the porch where I stopped to towel off the sand from my feet as best I could.

After my grandparents died, my mother and her two siblings inherited the houses, otherwise known as Camp What-The-Fuck, which had since been shortened to CWTF.

Typically, no one showered at CWTF, unless it was an outdoor shower. A showerhead attached to the outside of each house was shielded by three fence walls—tall enough so nobody could see you naked (unless they stared directly in through a crack), but short enough so that it was in fact possible for a pesky family member or neighbor to engage you in conversation while you were naked. The most beautiful time to shower was just before sunset.

There was no air conditioning in either house, both were two stories, and each had a television receiving exactly one channel. Both houses were occupied by my extended family pretty much every summer weekend between Memorial Day and Labor Day, eating tuna fish for lunch every day, and having a massive cocktail hour every evening while my dad went to AA. At that cocktail hour, my loud, Jewish family drank too much Prosecco, ate too much Muenster cheese, and overused the expression, "Jesus Christ!"

The kitchen floors of CWTF were always a bit sandy (Grandma Thelma had done her best) and the walls were all too thin. Sometimes the floor leaked when it rained and there was an occasional spider on the ceiling. After bedtime, you could hear absolutely everything that happened outside, from neighbors going to the beach to drink, to summer flings going there to make out.

Once inside the kitchen, I found the tuna.

"Thanks, Nikki. I just didn't see it."

"No problem."

"Do you think three cans will be enough for everyone?" She asked me as if I were an authority on portions of tuna.

"I mean, who's eating? You, me, Dad, Charlotte, Donna, and Ray, right? Dale, Cara and Moira will probably do their own thing. Three cans will be fine." Dale and Moira were super into natural foods and things like tofu, and often ate separately.

"Thanks. That's all I need. A little help."

"Mom, it's lunch. It's not like the world is ending."

"Please don't be mean to me. I'm just trying to make sure everyone has a nice time." Cue underscoring. Out of nowhere our conversation had a soundtrack, as an adagio piano arrangement of "Grand Old Flag" came from the living room. Usually, Aunt Donna started practicing at seven in the morning before we were awake, but today it seemed she was starting late. Yesterday I was woken up by an all too forte and deliberate rendition of "Give My Regards to Broadway," and the morning before it had been "Eleanor Rigby." She was rehearsing it with an electronic metronome, a simulation woodblock with a piercingly high triangle dinging on every other beat. "Eleanor Rigby" was going to be an even tempo if it was the last thing Donna ever did. She'd recently started performing at a local assisted living center, in addition to a nursing home a few towns over from her.

While Aunt Donna serenaded Buzzard's Bay, mom and I made our plates and left the tuna, chips, and fruit that she'd cut up on the counter for the rest of the family to help themselves. I grabbed a Diet Coke from the fridge and reached into the freezer for my chocolate chip cookie. Grandma Thelma had always kept chocolate chip cookies in the freezer and no one had any intention of breaking that tradition. Besides, they were quite good frozen. Next to the ocean, my mom joined me at the table while Charlotte and Uncle Ray headed back inside to fix their lunches.

"Nikki, let me read you this passage!" my mother said to me excitedly as the wind blew open the pages of *Codependent No More*. There was a stack of self-help books on the chair next to her, each one with multiple bookmarks where she'd carefully noted pages she might want to return to. I could see she was ready to make lunch conversation as deep and as meaningful as possible. Her topic as of late had been not letting people steal her serenity.

"Mom, I'm kind of busy," I said, while eagerly making chip sandwiches out of my tuna. Ever since I was a little girl, I'd loved squishing my tuna fish between two Cape Cod Potato Chips and eating them like mini sandwiches. Something about it made the tuna taste saltier and less fishy. "A Grand Old Flag" started for the fourth time. My mother was very involved in another one of her Al-Anon books. She read while she ate. Last weekend it was *One Day at a Time*. The weekend before it was Echkart Tolle's, *A New Earth*. That weekend it was Melodie Beattie's *Codependent No More*.

"Nikki, come on," she plead. "You're eating tuna fish. You're not busy. Just let me share this with you."

I caught my dad's glance for a split-second when he got out of his chair and headed into the kitchen. He smirked and rolled his eyes at me. I didn't roll mine back. While I wasn't the biggest fan of my mom's self-help revelations, I got very protective and defended her when my father gave her a hard time for it. If it weren't for him, she wouldn't have been on that crusade, and if it weren't for her, he'd likely be dead. He walked by our table and made a quack like a duck whose beak was stapled shut, and I couldn't help but laugh. Sometimes his behavior was inexplicably strange, as if the older he got, the less it seemed he could interact with other humans and instead had to communicate with animal noises.

"Will you stop?" My mom said to him and slammed her book down, as if she could interpret his duck language. "Fine," she said before she got any sort of reply from him, "I'll keep it to myself." Mom picked the book back up and went back to highlighting selected sentences. "Charlotte will listen to my passages when she comes back. She'll appreciate them." Ever since Charlotte's husband decided to devote himself to Judaism, she often came to the cape by herself for summer weekends and was considered immediate family. I'd finally forgiven her for eating the crust on my cheesecake several years ago.

"Fine, Mom," I said a few seconds later, guiltily, "You can read them."

"No. You don't want to hear them."

She was right. I didn't. My mother went to at least six Al-Anon meetings a week by that time and every other word out of her mouth was "Al-Anon." A few months ago, she sent me a copy of *One Day at a Time* in the mail and told me that if I read one page each day she'd buy me a new pair of shoes. Bribery at its finest. Al-Anon had clearly saved her life and worked miracles in helping her cope with my father's addiction. But I didn't feel broken and therefore I didn't want to be fixed. Even if I *was* broken, maybe I just wanted to stay that way. At least for that time. Maybe I just wanted to take that journey alone, on my own and in my own way.

When I was home last Thanksgiving my mom tried to coax me to go to several Al-Anon meetings with her. "Nikki, I've got a great idea!" she'd say. "Let's go to the Cheesecake Factory and then hit up an Al-Anon meeting!" Or, "Let's get manicures and then swing by an Al-Anon meeting!" And of course, "I want to stop at an Al-Anon meeting on the way to our hair appointments. You can just come with me so we don't have to take two cars." In politics, when a sneaky politician is trying to ratify something by quietly slipping it onto another bill it's called a rider. I couldn't help but laugh remembering her old tactics. My mom would have been a terrible politician. I knew it came from a place of love, and I thought my resistance towards it had more to do with needing space in my relationship with her than it did with Al-Anon itself.

A few moments later, Charlotte joined us on the porch with her plate of tuna, chips, and fruit. Her hair was still in an immaculate black bob like it hadn't been touched since our brunch several years ago, and this time her nails were a shade of sheer pink. "A Grand Old Flag" began for the fifth time.

"What a lovely lunch," Charlotte said to my mom. "Oh, I see you're still highlighting your book." It became clear to me last year when my dad was in detox and I overheard my mom on the phone that she'd told Charlotte about my dad's disease. Of course I was relieved she'd been getting help and talking to friends, but why was she allowed to decide when to go public and I wasn't?

"Yes. We can talk about it when Nikki's not around. She doesn't like my books." It made me seethe when people referred to me in the third person when I was sitting right there.

"Mom. It's not that I don't like them. It's that when you preach passages to me it makes me uncomfortable. It's not for me, okay? I appreciate the fact that it works for you. It's not for me. Please can you just accept that?"

"You're just too young to appreciate it," she said and my blood started to boil. It felt condescending and like my mom was too overwhelmed with self-preservation to be able to see things outside of herself. I'd talked about this with Dr. Miller, but my free sessions quickly ran out.

"I'm going next door for a while." I was about to snap. It was something beyond what Al-Anon stood for that got under my skin. Did she even remember the vow of silence she imposed upon me? Now she was allowed to tell the world about my father, yet I was forced to stay quiet. She'd seemingly shared our struggles with some family members, but definitely not all, and since we didn't talk about it, it was difficult to know who knew what. And maybe it was my own fault for staying silent. Technically, it was my choice. Loyalty can be a dangerous thing.

The irony was that I'd taken my very first sip of alcohol in that very house. It was the summer right after my freshman year of high school, during my father's longest period of sobriety, on a Saturday night in August after my entire family had gone to sleep. Suzie came for a sleepover weekend and both of us wanted to experiment with the dark side. You know, be prepared for the high school parties that I never went to because I was too busy rehearsing for *West Side Story*. It was pitch black and the only thing we could hear on that hot sticky night were the toads that came out at night, jumping in the grass, and insects buzzing against screen doors. Suzie and I crept into the kitchen, opened my grandmother's liquor cabinet, and took a bottle of brown alcohol from the back. It looked pretty old and we poured ourselves shots in disposable paper cups. Suzie had heard that whenever you took a shot of alcohol you were supposed to chase it. Unaware that we were supposed to chase it with a more palatable liquid, we chased this mystery brown liquor with more palatable Pepperidge Farm goldfish. We giggled so hard that night, and while I hated the taste, my first sip of alcohol felt like some rite of passage. I also felt oddly satisfied, knowing I then had a secret to keep from my mother, one that would likely destroy her if it got out. At least, it seemed that way at the time.

I felt myself smirking at this memory as I stood up and took my paper plate next door, to see Aunt Moira and Uncle Dale who were sitting in beach chairs on the lawn overlooking the ocean. Cara couldn't have been far either. I was fuming from my mother's comment about me being too young to understand Al-Anon. Just because I didn't relate to her coping mechanism, I was made to feel inferior. I knew it was an innocent comment on her part, which was why I thought it best to just walk away.

Aunt Moira was sprawled out on a chaise lounge in front of the house, painting her nails bright red. Her toes were already a matching shade of red and they popped against her skinny white leggings. Originally from Canada, Moira used to be a speech pathologist at Salem State University, although she'd since retired. She also had psychic abilities and a very successful kinetic healing practice. She'd healed me a few times, but I'd never been able to tell if it was a supernatural gift or her incredible perspective on life. Either way, it seemed to work.

When I was younger I used to be afraid of Aunt Moira and her unapologetic demeanor. She was famous for asking deeply personal questions. That was a trait I'd grown to appreciate immensely over the years. She once asked a single friend of my mom's if she was a lesbian—within five minutes of meeting her. Another time, I overheard her asking her daughter, my cousin Cara, if she was having good sex. One piece of wisdom I'd taken from Aunt Moira: 'It never hurts to ask.'

Moira's fireball spirit blended in with the orange and yellow marigolds that lined the garden separating our lawn from the beach. In addition to frozen chocolate chip cookies, Grandma Thelma had started the tradition of planting marigolds along the beach, and argued that they were the only flower that would decorate the lawn and withstand the salt water. Over the years, my dad, the gardener, challenged this theory, testing out geraniums one year and daffodils the next. But sure enough, Grandma Thelma had been right.

"Hey, Nikki!" Aunt Moira said, "What's going on?" She'd lost hearing in her left ear so she often shouted when she spoke.

"My mom won't stop reading me passages from Al-Anon books so I decided to come hang out with you." Aunt Moira once asked me how I was doing with my dad's addiction, so I knew my mom had told her.

"Oh no. Your mom really loves her Al-Anon, doesn't she?"

"Yeah and I appreciate that it works for her but I'm so sick of having it shoved down my throat."

"Well, did you tell her that?"

"Yes. She wasn't pleased." I think what bothered me is that a lot of the time when she talked about it, she went on and on about how she'd tell stories about me at meetings and how she had the meeting members, which she referred to as the audience, in stiches laughing. I felt like she used Al-Anon as a chance to test out comedy routines for external validation and it drove me insane, especially when she was using me as material!

"Give you mother a break, Nikki. She's been through a lot and thank goodness she's found something like this to support her. I know it may seem excessive to you at times, but just try to be kind and patient. She loves you so much and your father hasn't been a walk in the park."

"Yeah. I know you're right. It's just so frustrating."

"I just don't know that your mother is capable of hearing you right now. I think she's still using all of her energy to cope and hold her life together. Your dad seems to be doing well this summer, eh?" The Canadian in her came out.

"I think so."

"Do you talk to him about how he's doing?"

"Not really."

"Grand Old Flag" stopped and Aunt Donna came clonking down the back steps and over to Moira and me. She was wearing bulky khaki shorts and a purple boating hat that shaded her face from the sun.

"What's happening over here?" She asked cheerfully.

"You're looking at it, Donna," Aunt Moira answered.

"Oh, how nice!" When she realized she wasn't missing anything exciting outside, she retreated back into the house and the metronome triangle started dinging every other beat again. Aunt Moira kept painting her toes and I looked over at my mom and Charlotte, who were still next door on the porch. I couldn't hear what they were saying, but my mom appeared to be reading passages from her book while Charlotte listened lovingly. My dad had returned to his beach chair down on the sand and held a plate of tuna on his lap. I dragged a chair into the sun in a spot between the two houses and pretended to take a nap. Aunt Donna started practicing "Eleanor Rigby." Eventually I didn't even hear the piano. I could only hear the lyric of the chorus in my mind.

Dry Run

MILE 14

I hold onto the guilt I felt from the biker mishap for about the first half of this mile, but what's the point? Heart's "Alone" is now playing. There's a man a few strides ahead of me to my right. I wonder what he's listening to. He looks like the kind of guy who'd be listening to Ben Folds or All American Rejects, rather than Kanye West. I can't keep up with his stride so I let him go. His speed is out of my control. I guess everyone is in this alone to begin with anyway. Even the husband and wife at the starting line separated. They'll meet at the end, all right, but they both need to run at their own pace. The sun is now hot and the chaffing under my arms has become more and more apparent, despite my best efforts to ignore it. The skin in between my legs starts to feel sore too, despite the cream I'd applied. I listen to my breath, which is faster than the beat of "Alone." Water. I would die for some water. I'm more than halfway. Now I'll start counting down instead of counting up. I'm halfway to my father.

—Providence Marathon 2011.

The sky was still pitch black at five-thirty in the morning when I shifted my purple NYU Alumni sweatshirt in my seat at Gate D-6, trying to get comfortable. I wished I'd dressed warmer for February, but I didn't want to be overheated stepping off of the plane in San Juan. Usually my parents and I flew together, but that year I was flying out of JFK and they'd becoming directly from Boston. Oddly, even leaving for vacation seemed dull and I felt like I should've been more excited than I was to be taking a few days off from the hustle of New York City. By that point, having graduated the previous May, I'd been done with school and a real working adult for just under eight months. Even the thought of a three-day break from my relatively new, anxiety-provoking job and taxing schedule should've felt more appealing.

The summer before my senior year of college, I scoured Craigslist looking for a job I could do for a few months and then quit; I'd made plans to travel for part of that May, and had a performing gig lined up for August. Getting a job for two months felt unnatural and completely against my nature, since the only thing I'd ever quit was soccer, and that was only because of the *Fiddler on the Roof* conflict. But one day I saw an online advertisement with the headline:

"Actors Make Great Telemarketers!" I auditioned for the job and got the part. And there was some validity to the ad. I did make a great telemarketer, but I had not been warned that I'd be a miserable one.

Every day, for eight hours a day, I was tasked with cold-calling attorneys at law firms in New York City, asking if they needed staffing services. After being given a list of names and numbers, I was expected to pick up the phone in my little secluded cubicle and sell to individuals who were sometimes twice my age and had three times my level of education. After two eight-hour days of people hanging up on me or telling me to lose their number, I'd decided to spice things up by delivering my opening line in various foreign accents. At least that way I was putting my college degree to good use, and I did actually make some headway with a potential customer while speaking in a British accent. After one week of torture, I decided I'd rather be poor than be hung up on all day. But when I tried to quit, the owner of the company said he'd never seen resilience and discipline like mine (let's not get carried away), insisted that I stay on board, and offered me a new role at the company. That's when I became a legal recruiter and took on the responsibility of head-hunting paralegals, legal secretaries, and document review attorneys. That May, I still went on my planned vacation to Spain with my new love interest at the time (Rob and I had come to an end), which wound up being a disaster, primarily because I viewed him as my mature and established future husband while he viewed me as a twenty-year-old side piece, then took time off to perform in a production of *Merrily We Roll Along*. When I graduated the following year, my boss offered me a full-time job at fifteen dollars an hour, with the caveat that I could leave and audition whenever I needed to and the understanding that if I booked a show, I'd leave for the duration of that contract without pay and still have my job waiting for me once the contract ended. For the past several months before that vacation to Puerto Rico, I'd been getting up at five in the morning at least three days per week so that I could be the first person in line at every open call in Manhattan, landing me at the office by ten-thirty if I was lucky; most auditions didn't actually start until nine or ten.

The way non-equity theatre auditions worked was that actors were seen in the order in which they arrived. Even if an audition started at ten, which most did, people started lining up as early as five-thirty in the morning to put their name on an unofficial list. Most of the studios weren't even open at that ungodly hour, so we'd camp out on the sidewalks of Manhattan in the pitch black, and sometimes, freezing cold. Some girls would do their makeup on the sidewalk, others would chit chat; I typically did the *AM New York* crossword. The actors were usually let inside about an hour before the audition, when the unofficial list was transferred to an official list, then we'd all scramble to get seats in front of the mirror so we could do our hair and put ourselves together, since most of us had just rolled out of bed in order to get in line earlier. I always shot to be in the first ten people because the sooner I auditioned, the sooner I could get to the office.

I'd gotten really good at my job. Though constantly fighting the insecurity that came with dealing with Harvard law graduates and the fear of them finding out their career was in the hands of a twenty-two-year-old musical theatre major, essentially a fraud, I'd managed to hone some helpful tactics. My favorite was that whenever a candidate called my direct line asking for me, I'd answer in a slightly higher tone of voice and say, "Nikki is in a big meeting right now. Can I take a message and have her get right back to you?" Needless to say, in theory, that Puerto Rican vacation was coming at a good time.

During college and high school I used to look forward to family trips and getting to spend some quality time with my parents, but at that point in my life, once Puerto Rico rolled around, the thought of the three of us sharing a hotel room made me feel claustrophobic. I'd spoken about this in therapy the week prior with Eleanor, the therapist I'd been seeing since graduating college. I'd told her that sharing a room with my parents made me feel uncomfortable and a little invasive, but since I was an only child, it didn't make sense for them to spend hundreds more dollars so that I could have my own room; I should be grateful that I was getting out to town for a bit. Eleanor said that my thoughts on the matter were valid and that she didn't think it was unusual that I felt that way. She suggested maybe making it a point to carve out some alone time for myself during the days, like taking a walk or going for a long swim. I loved Eleanor. She was my favorite of all my therapists primarily because she always gave me advice, which therapists are trained not to do. She also loved sharing confidential information about her other patients, which I also enjoyed. Eleanor had to have been around my mom's age and always looked hot. She was still blonde, skinny, and had definitely had work done. I saw her on-and-off all through my twenties, took a hiatus, and then returned to her in my early thirties when I found myself living with a man I was prepared to marry, who was showing signs of alcoholism.

A blast of cold air shot between the jet way and the plane as I boarded. Once I settled into seat 18A, I checked my phone and saw that I had a text from my mom. It read: Dad sick and coming tomorrow see you soon. My gut coiled around my intestines before I had time to process that information. I remembered what happened every other time my dad was "sick" and I hated that that was where my brain went. Even though he'd been sober for three years by that time, the muscle memory was impeccable. Would I ever trust him again? Would there ever be a time when the thought that he could have relapsed wouldn't cross my mind? Stay present. There was nothing I could do to help my parents from a plane. I battled to just be where I was and at that moment that was in seat 18A.

My flight landed at nine and I guessed that my mother would arrive—alone— after lunch. I stuffed my bag underneath the seat in front of me. A few minutes later I felt the plane take off and by the time we were in the air, I'd drifted off to sleep. When I opened my eyes, we were landing. After exiting the plane, I walked through the airport and followed signs that read: "To Cabs." Eventually I turned my phone back on and saw that I had three more texts from my mom. They all read: Call me. I called her.

"Hi, Nik!" she answered.

"Hey Mom, I just landed. Got your texts."

"How's the weather there? Is it beautiful?"

"What's up with Dad?" I cut right to the chase.

"He really isn't feeling well. He was throwing up all night. I just feel so bad for him. I called the airline and was able to pay a fee to get him on a flight that leaves tomorrow so he can at least still get a few days in the sun. Two nights will be a quick trip for him, but it's better than nothing and I know he was looking forward to this."

"Wow. Okay. Is he okay?" I asked.

"Yes, he's just got some sort of bug."

"Are you sure that's all it is?"

That's what I thought too, Nik, but he assures me it's just a bug. Besides, I would know." She knew what I was thinking and her

Dry Run

response was infuriating. Or was she right, should I also be giving my dad the benefit of the doubt? Was I being unfair?

"Okay Mom. Listen, I'm trying to get a cab to the hotel. I'll see you when you get here?"

"Can't wait, Nik! We'll have a fun mother-daughter night tonight. I love you! See you soon!" I hung up, baffled that she was so upbeat, almost manic.

Later that day, after a cab ride, a check-in, and a costume change, I found myself sitting by the pool at the Marriott in Puerto Rico, devouring a burger with ketchup and some waffle fries. I was sure to apply lots of sunscreen so that my face wouldn't become totally overtaken with freckles, the Irish in me. It was funny, Dad didn't really look Irish or Scottish—maybe because he'd spent so much of his life in tanning beds that he was just permanently tan—but I definitely inherited his Irish fair skin. I texted my mom to let her know where I was so that she could find me when she arrived, which should've been any minute. After another bite of my burger, I saw her coming towards me from the hotel lobby dressed in shorts, a t-shirt, and a baseball cap. She was carrying a summer tote, which I was sure was filled with self-help books. My phone rang.

"Nik, I'm here. I can't find you!" her eyes darted around so quickly it reminded me of that scene from *The Exorcist*; her head spun frantically, looking around everywhere except for where I was sitting. My mother had both the worst sense of direction and an astounding inability to follow them.

"Mom, walk to the bar by the pool. I'm right there. I can see you."

"Oooh," she said in a faux-annoyed and semi-confused tone. I stood up and waved and yelled "Mom!" as loud as possible. She saw me and rushed over to greet me with a giant and somewhat smothering hug.

"Oh you look so beautiful!"

"And smart?" I say hopefully, joking around.

"Yes so beautiful and smart."

"And funny?" I added.

"Yes, you're my beautiful, smart, funny daughter. Are you glad to see me?" I genuinely was. I was so excited to have a night with just my mom in Puerto Rico. We could talk about all of the things I wouldn't discuss in front of my dad like Owen, my boyfriend at the time, and Pinot Grigio. The waiter came back with my check and I handed him my debit card.

"Nikki, just charge it to the room," mom said.

"Don't worry about it." I didn't make a ton of money, especially since I'd just started my job full-time last May and had been missing hours to go on musical auditions, but I knew my mom paid for that entire vacation. She'd been single-handedly supporting the household since my dad fully retired the year before. I could pay for lunch. It made me feel good to pay for lunch. Afterwards, we headed for the beach where the sand was so hot that we had to keep our sandals on until we found a place to park ourselves.

At the edge of the water, there was a little girl who looked to be around five-years-old, splashing in the waves as they hit the white Puerto Rican sand. My chaise lounge was plush, and I pretended to read *Harry Potter and the Sorcerer's Stone.* But really, I couldn't stop watching that child, who was about to be swallowed up by a giant wave. She was laughing, unaware of the danger. Just before a wave broke on the shore, her dad swooped in and lifted her high in the air, as she giggled even more loudly. I could feel the pages of my book becoming sticky with salty air and I closed it for a minute. My mother was next to me, furiously writing in her book with a pen, underlining sentences from Eckhart Tolle's, *The Power of Now,* and checking her cell phone for a non-existent missed call after she turned each page.

"Any word from Dad?" I asked casually. It seemed like the right thing to say.

"Nope. But as Al-Anon would tell me, it's out of my control so I'm just going to stay present and enjoy the moment." I asked her how my father had been and she told me how she thought retiring had been such a relief for him and that work had been making him depressed. My dad had always made the lion's share of the household income. I was pretty sure he helped pay for my mom's two cancer surgeries and I knew he'd also supported her when she quit her full-time job to go to graduate school. What it must've been like for a generous person to no longer have the ability to be generous… at least with money. My mom told me that he'd been filling each day by going to two AA meetings, and searching Craigslist for other jobs to fill time during his retirement.

Dry Run

After a few more minutes of catching up, she turned back to *The Power of Now* while my heart fell apart a little at the thought of my dad sitting in front of the family computer by himself, skimming through ads on Craiglist. At least he hadn't given up all together. Anyone who was alive and still fighting in some capacity, whatever that may be, hadn't totally thrown in the towel. My dad didn't retire because he was old, he retired because for, whatever reason, he couldn't keep it together. Based on his most recent relapse, it also seemed like alcohol had done a number on his physical body. Through frequent physical therapy he'd managed to get his walking back, but according to my mom, he was still a little shaky on his feet.

"What have you been up to recently?" I changed the subject and tried to make a real effort to be kind to my mom. She told me about her piano students and that Sue Chang was getting ready to graduate. It also turned out that she'd started volunteering at a homeless shelter for women and had been teaching music to mothers and their children. My mom casually mentioned that this was an all Spanish-speaking homeless shelter, odd since I'd never known my mother to speak a word of Spanish. She'd never even taken me to see *Evita*. But it sounded like it was making her feel good, though she did express some concern around the fact that the shelter was having a hard time picking up on the music, and then told me the repertoire she'd selected included "Frere Jacques," "Music of the Night," and "John Jacob Jingleheimer Schmidt."

She looked at her phone again.

"Mom, for someone who's reading *The Power of Now*, you're checking your phone a lot." My tone sounded judgmental and apathetic.

"I know, Nikki, I just can't help it. I think it's very strange that I haven't heard from Dad all day. I know it's out of my control. I'm powerless. Al-Anon would tell me, "Let go and let God." I didn't respond. I was resentful of the Al-Anon mantras, but I thought it best to keep my feelings to myself. That was also the first time all day my mom had admitted that she was concerned for my father. She was starting to come down from her frenzied high, whether it was a result of her being wildly excited to be on vacation, or a mechanism to counter reality.

We spent the next few hours soaking up the sun and reading our books. Every twenty minutes or so, she got up and walked away to make a call. When she paced back and forth in front of the water, I noticed the silhouette of her right hand twirling that curl below her ear. She was either trying to reach my father, or getting a pep talk from an Al-Anon friend. Maybe she was doing both. For the first time, I felt relieved that she had the Al-Anon support system. It took some pressure off of me.

After a long day of travel, beach time, and no word from Dad, we ate an early Italian dinner. My mom loved Italian food and, no matter what country we were in, insisted on Italian every night. She was the person who ordered spaghetti at a steakhouse. After a glass of wine and an order of pasta in a pesto sauce, we were in our hotel room by eight, watching a rerun of *Law and Order.* Though it was odd not having Dad there, I certainly didn't miss his snoring.

The next afternoon we found ourselves in the same place on the beach as the day before, reading our respective literature, mine about a child wizard and hers about tools to keep you from losing your shit if your alcoholic husband doesn't show up to a family vacation. I snuck off and tried calling Dad myself, secretly, so my mom wouldn't know his absence was bothering me, too. When we didn't hear from him yesterday I hadn't ruled out the possibility that maybe his phone had died, but the calls weren't going directly to voicemail, and by that point it had been more than twenty-four hours.

"Hi, it's me, please leave a message." My brain couldn't help but jump to the worst-case scenario and I was suddenly overcome by empathy for my mom. How did she deal with that, day in and day out, wondering if he was going to make it home alive? All it took was one time behind the wheel of a car to accidentally kill someone, or himself for that matter, just one right turn that was a little too sharp, just a hair too close to the guard rail. What if my dad was dead? Why else wouldn't he be answering our calls? I drilled my feet into the sand and watched my fluorescent orange toe peek out through the tiny white and brown grains, curling my toes until they hurt and I couldn't see them anymore. Sometimes it was easier for me to assume the worst. At least that way I was fully prepared for the call that would eventually come, whether it was from my mom or from a police station. I turned back towards the ocean and saw my mom fidgeting with her book, turning pages faster than she could actually read them, yet trying everything in her power to take in the words on the pages and stay calm. To be frank, it sucked. Suddenly I was furious that my dad was ruining my vacation. His well-being and whereabouts were clearly all my mom and I could think about and it was infuriating. Maybe I needed to go for a run, clear my head a little,

Dry Run

or at least feel like I was doing something proactive. I walked back to my mom, dragging my feet through the sand to make the walk extra difficult for myself because for some reason I felt like it should be.

"Still no word from Dad?" I asked her, sitting back down in my beach chair nonchalantly. His flight should've landed two hours ago.

"Nope. But it's out of my control. I'm not going to let this ruin my vacation. All I can do is hope that his phone is dead or that he's so sick he checked himself into a hospital where he doesn't have service."

"Right," I said. "I'm proud of you, Mom. I'm really impressed with how well you're handling this." That was tremendously difficult for me to say, but I meant it.

"You're proud of me? You're proud of your mom?"

"Sure."

"Did I tell you I'm starting a program at Salem High School for kids with alcoholic parents?"

"Cool." I sounded disinterested, and in many ways, I was. It occurred to me that I rarely asked my mom anything about her life because one of the perks of a mom is that I get to talk to her about myself the entire time. And when I'm in a bad mood, it's accepted that she's the first person I'd call to take it out on. It's the unspoken mother-daughter rule. But in that particular scenario, it really pissed me of that she was creating a safe place for teenagers with alcoholic parents to have a place to go and talk, when I was forced to suffer in secrecy for ten years. Those kids got to miss class to talk about their problems, while I had been forbidden to open my mouth. Maybe that was her way of repenting, but the irony was intensely aggravating.

"You know," I blurted out, as if I were affected with Tourette's syndrome, "I didn't tell anyone about Dad until I went to college because the first time Dad drank, you told me that if I told anyone about his alcoholism I'd be in big trouble." It was the first time I'd ever addressed the issue with her directly.

"I know and I'm so sorry. I've thought about that at least once a day for a long time and it is one of my biggest regrets, but please understand where I was coming from. I taught in public schools for twenty-five years and I knew kids could be so mean. I watched so many students get bullied or made fun of or gossiped about. The last thing I wanted was for children at school to make fun of you, or make you feel shame."

"Fine. But it still sucked."

"Nikki, if I could take it back I would. That is one of my biggest mistakes I've ever made and had to live with." I could sense her getting defensive. I guess I didn't blame her. It wasn't like she could take it back.

"It's fine," I said curtly, because I didn't know whether I meant it, but I did know that she needed to hear it. More importantly, she deserved to hear it. We all made mistakes. Hers wasn't a malicious one. Was I supposed to hold it over her head for the rest of her life? Considering how much angst this had caused me over the last ten years, I found the conversation to be a little anticlimactic. I think that was partly because I didn't want to fight with her on that trip, but also, having experienced my father's antics first-hand over the last ten years, it was hard to truly be angry with my mother. I was furious with her, but the amount of compassion I had for her was tremendous and growing, despite the fact that it was difficult for me to show or communicate.

"It's funny," she said interrupting my train of thought, "Your dad and I used to love drinking on vacation together. I just thought we were social drinkers and that it was normal when he would come home from work with a bottle of wine and a six-pack of beer every night. I'd always join him for a glass or two of wine, but then I'd stop. After the wine, he'd continue with a few cans of beer, and it never occurred to me that he had a problem with alcohol because he was so high-functioning. He ran at least sixty miles per week, his law practice was thriving, and he'd run thirty-two marathons at approximately six and a half minute miles. Then one Wednesday morning in October, I got the call that changed my life. It was nine-thirty and he told me he was drinking. That was the morning of the evening I had you stay at Suzie's."

I'd never asked what exactly had happened that morning. It was possible I never wanted to know. It was the emotions I was left with, so in many ways the actual incident seemed irrelevant. And talking about my father's alcohol addiction with either of my parents was never a favorite activity of mine. Whatever happened that morning wouldn't change the outcome, so I guess it never really mattered to me or occurred to me to ask. I had all the information I needed.

We sat there quietly for a few long seconds and I wondered if this was a foreshadowing of future family vacations with just my

Dry Run

mom and me. I scanned the beach for the little girl happily splashing in the tide yesterday, but she and her father were nowhere to be seen. The waves were ebbing to and from the shoreline. I thought about how on all of our previous family vacations, my dad was always the first one to jump into the water. When I was little I wanted to grow up and be just like him, because he was the only adult I knew who went swimming in the ocean, regardless of how cold it was. My mom never went swimming and I had it in my brain that only kids and my dad ever went in the water. If I could just be like him, maybe I'd never grow old. One day, while playing freeze-tag with him in the ocean at CWTF, I made a promise to my eight-year-old self that every time I had the luxury of being near the ocean, I would also go in the water, for as long as I was alive.

I put down *Harry Potter* and ran for the ocean, diving right into a wave as the lukewarm water pounded my muscles. The current was so strong that I hesitated to stray too far from shore. After my dip, I returned to my mom's side and laid down to dry off.

"Well, since your dad's clearly not coming, what do you say we go to the casino and spend his portion of the vacation money on blackjack and alcohol?" my mother suggested. I was impressed that she hadn't tried to book an earlier flight home and I was determined to show her a good time. Her cheek bones lifted in excitement, though her eyes looked droopy and helpless.

"I think that's a great idea." Part of me wondered if we should've sent someone to check on my father, which seemed like an obvious choice, but my mom would be home the day after tomorrow and my guess was that she didn't want to involve others in our family affairs. Also, it would've been at least an hour drive for Charlotte or any of our immediate family who knew about dad. It almost would've made more sense to call the police, but, for whatever reason, my mom didn't seem to be trending in that direction, so I didn't push it.

"You know, as worried as I am about Dad, he did this to himself and I'm grateful for this special time with you. Normally I wouldn't book a vacation for just the two of us because I'd be too scared to leave him on his own, but this is happening for a reason and I'm not going to let this ruin our time together. We may not get this again for a long time."

"I hope you're right, Mom." We packed up our dirty beach towels, brushed the sand off of our beach bags, and went back to the hotel.

MILE 15

It's such a strange sensation, running with other people, yet at the same time, running alone. Everyone is on their own path, with their unique set of struggles. There's a man just ahead of me whom I've seen a few times out on the course. He's a bit overweight, and is wearing a bright yellow T-shirt that says "AIDS AWARENESS" in all black capital letters. I wonder if he's running for charity, or to achieve some sort of weight loss goal, or maybe both. Then again, who knows. I bet no one would guess just by looking at me that I'm trying to save my alcoholic father. No one would guess by looking at me that I need to understand why someone would put themselves through this amount of pain for four hours. Yet we're all experiencing the same pain, though we're feeling it differently from one another. For the first, time today, my body is starting to feel truly exhausted. I wish I had my dad's walker so that I could wheel myself to the finish line. Am I running this race just to run it? Or will it actually have meaning? God, I hope it has an impact. Please don't let this be for nothing.

—Providence Marathon, 2011.

I was sitting in the back seat of a New York City taxi cab that had taken too long to hail, during rush hour, and it was raining hard. My flight back from Puerto Rico was delayed and I'd finally made it back to NYC after eleven hours of travel. All I wanted to do was crawl into bed and turn on the DVRed episode of *24* I'd missed while I was away.

I turned off Taxi TV because it made me nauseous and I had a headache. My cell phone vibrated and I adjusted myself so I could pull the phone out my back pocket. *MOM* flashed across the screen and even thought I already knew who the call would be from, my chest started pounding when I saw that it was her. I let the call go to voicemail and put the phone back in my pocket and sat on it. Her flight had left Puerto Rico around the same time as mine so she'd be arriving at our house just about now.

We stopped at a red light and the endless row of red tail-lights ahead made me want to pull my hair out. The helpless agony of being stuck in New York City traffic reminded me of how little control I had over certain aspects of my life. Maybe I should start going to Al-Anon meetings. My cell started vibrating again and I tried to ignore it, but as we continued to inch up First Avenue, my phone vibrated a third time, indicating that I had a voicemail.

"Nikki," my mother's trembling voice spoke and I couldn't tell if it was her voice cracking or the reception going in and out. "I found Dad when I got home…on the kitchen floor." Silence and phone static. "He seems to have hurt himself pretty badly. I don't know how long he's been here. An ambulance came. Please call me. I love you. I'm so sorry."

My first instinct was to delete the message and put the phone back in my pocket, so I did. Part of me couldn't believe she'd left that information in a voicemail, but the other part of me was relieved that she did, so I didn't have to react or respond in a comforting way. I mean, what was I supposed to do with that? That voicemail made me feel like I shouldn't have been in Puerto Rico enjoying myself, and like I could have done something to stop my father from drinking, all at the very same time. I just wanted to stop the overwhelming thoughts. Make them stop.

"Are you having a good night?" I asked the driver, cheerfully.

"What?"

"Are you having a good night, Sir?"

"Yes."

"Good! I'm so glad." All of a sudden the traffic cleared up. Must've been an accident. We were hitting all green lights and immediately I wished we were still stuck at a red one, delaying the inevitable. Just as soon as I wanted to be trapped, I was abruptly freed, and soon enough we pulled over in front of my apartment on the Upper East Side. I slid out of the back seat, pulling my luggage with me. Standing there on the corner of Seventy-Second and Second, all I felt was numbness. My father was in the hospital because he'd been lying blacked out on our kitchen floor for anywhere up to seventy-two hours and I felt nothing. What kind of person did that make me?

I headed upstairs to my apartment and found it empty. I'd forgotten that my college best girlfriend and post-college roommate, Analise, had spent the week in New Jersey with her family and wouldn't be back until Monday. I thought about calling my boyfriend, but he too was out of town that weekend and I didn't want to bother him while he was with his family. I also didn't really feel like talking, to anyone. The thought of returning my mom's phone call out of pure obligation did cross my mind. Instead, I shot her a text that said, "Got your message. Will call later," so that she didn't put out an Amber Alert. I lugged my bags into my bedroom, went to my closet, pulled out a pair of jeans and a sexy black top, threw on a pair of heels and some red lipstick, grabbed my pea coat, and left.

There was a bar a few blocks from my apartment called Bounce that I'd passed many times, though I'd only ever been inside once when I had to use the bathroom. Loud club dance music and flashing disco lights were not my scene. Bounce was usually crawling with girls sporting fake tans and bad dye jobs and dudes wearing way too much Axe body spray. It was a Friday night around nine so the streets of the Upper East Side were rather tame. I flashed the bouncer my ID and since it was early enough, was able to get a seat at the bar. I slung my pea coat over the back of my chair and ordered a beer, even though I didn't like the taste. A Bud Light to be exact, since it was the only beer I actually knew beside Heineken; I was never a beer drinker. The bartender brought me a glass full to the brim and I handed him my credit card. "Keep it open," I told him. I'd never actually started a tab before and it felt powerful. The bartender was fairly attractive and looked to be about thirty with a giant black tattoo of an eagle around his left arm. He must've been from Philly.

I didn't like my beer but kept drinking anyway, forcing myself to finish it. After I did, my stomach felt bloated. Vodka would be next. My stomach wouldn't be able to handle another beer and I knew my dad drank vodka too. I ordered a vodka cranberry, sucked it down, then ordered another. The bartender was becoming increasingly more attractive. The music got louder and the lights got brighter. Bounce was getting crowded as people in their early to mid-twenties started to compete for the bartender's attention, and the conversation around me was drowned out by Panic at the Disco's, "The Only Difference between Martyrdom & Suicide is Press Coverage." A guy trying to order a drink squeezed in next to me and bumped my elbow, spilling my drink. He apologized.

"Don't worry about it," I told him. "It's fine." His pants were too tight and there was gel in his hair; I assumed he was from New Jersey. I ordered a fourth drink and checked my phone to see that I had five missed calls from Mom. I turned it off. The sexy, tattooed bartender came back and poured me a shot of brown liquor. "Drink this. You'll like it," he said. "On the house." I had no idea what it was, but I figured my dad had probably done some shots in his day, so I took it. I wanted to know what made someone lose control. I needed to understand what made someone drink to the point where they blacked out on their kitchen floor and missed a flight to Puerto Rico. Something about taking that sip of the mystery drink felt vindicating and vengeful at the same time. In some ways getting hammered felt like a way to get back at my father in a "look what you made me do" sort of sense. It also felt like a way to punish my mother, though I wasn't sure what for.

Life was happening around me. A group of girls were at one end of the bar whispering about something and I watched a man wearing a tight white t-shirt and gold chain resting on his chest hair slap one of them on the ass. The girl laughed and smacked him back on the shoulder. The bartender was chatting it up with one of his buddies, probably a regular, at the opposite end of the bar. I sat alone, bloated and empty.

In front of me, above the rows of liquor, was a streaky mirror in which I could vaguely see my reflection. My hair looked a little disheveled and my red lipstick had worn off, most of it left on the rims of empty glasses. The music was so loud I could feel the beat of the bass in my chest. The disco lights stopped and for the most part the bar was dark. I couldn't see clearly enough to look my reflection in the eye, but I could see enough. My eyes were glossed over, like the space behind them was empty. My cheeks were motionless and my shoulders slumped. If I could have closed my eyes and disappeared, I would have. The last thing I remembered from that night was ordering another drink.

The next thing I knew my alarm clock was urging me to wake up for my regular Saturday morning kick-boxing class. I took a very heavy swing toward the clock. My head felt like it was getting pounded by a Mac truck over and over again. Why wouldn't it just run over me? I finally made contact with the clock and it stopped echoing through my sinuses. The sun streamed through my window, piercing my eyes so sharply that for a second I thought I was dying.

I managed to roll out of bed, overcome by the tsunami about to erupt from my bladder. Tripping over my shoe, I fell into the doorframe of my bedroom on the way to the bathroom. With the help of the wall, I was able to guide my heavy body to the bathroom, where I saw my wool pea coat in the sink, half-covered in vomit. I sat down on the toilet and stared at the wall, unable to move. For a while I stayed put, mustering up the strength to journey back to bed. Though the alcohol had worn off, the complacency from last night had not. I had no desire to move. What would have been the point? I felt just as empty in my bed as I did sitting on the toilet, and at least on the toilet, I wouldn't have to go through the trouble of getting to the toilet again if I had to pee.

My head felt like an empty shell, as thoughts came and went as they pleased, making it clear that they had the power. "You're such a bitch." "You can't even call your own mother back." "What a terrible daughter you are." "What a waste of space you are. Your own father is in the hospital and you don't even care." "Why did you drink yourself sick last night? Do you know how disappointed you mother would be if she knew? You betrayed her." The voices grew louder and my heart grow weaker and I didn't have the strength to fight back. "I'm sorry," was the only response I had. "I'm sorry. I'm sorry. No, I'm sorry. I'm really sorry. Sorry." I still played the game, only now that I was older I didn't need the board.

My alarm clock started screaming at me again from the bedroom. I must've accidentally hit the snooze button before. Fuck my life. Why was this happening? I grabbed the bathroom door and pulled myself up, using the wall as a crutch to get back to my room. I just needed the noise to stop.

Dry Run

MILE 16

The course turns again, leaving the forest behind, and now running parallel to the Atlantic Ocean. The air changes, and being so close to the water inspires me to take an extra big breath to take in the sea. So often in life I forget to breathe. I never actually think about my breath unless I'm out of it—out of breath, that is. It's funny the places your mind goes when you have so much time to do nothing but think. Oceans always remind me of my father but I'm thinking this maybe isn't the most opportune time to take a dip. I wonder how far along my dad would be if he were running right now, if he could run right now. He was so fast, I was never able to catch up to him ever, until the day that changed. Until the day, I passed him. My calf starts cramping up again. I probably have about two hours or so left, which isn't that long. It's basically the length of a good rom-com or the season finale of "24." In just two hours this will be over. I try to channel my dad and keep going.

—Providence Marathon, 2011.

Historically, the biggest con to having a summer birthday was always having to forgo the classroom cupcake scenario that took place every time a student had a birthday during the school year. The biggest pro had always been getting to have a birthday celebration at CWTF. When July 11th rolled around, whatever weekend I was at the Cape that was in a close enough proximity, my mother would, without fail, present me with a cake that usually had a validating message on it. One year my cake read, "Happy Birthday to my funny daughter." Another year it read, "Happy Birthday to my favorite daughter." It was also always a blessing when these cakes actually made it to the dining room table. One year she accidentally dropped it on the floor, and another year my dad took a giant slice the day before the celebration, somehow not realizing it was for my birthday.

When my twenty-third birthday rolled around, as per usual, I was celebrating at CWTF, only my dad wasn't there. Feeling bloated from the two giant slices of birthday cake that had miraculously made it into my mouth, I sat on a low branch of my favorite childhood climbing tree. I'd always loved that particular tree because it was located at the back side of one of the houses, and if you positioned yourself just right, you could see into one of the outdoor showers. Though I had zero desire to see any of my family members naked, knowing I had the ability to peep did make me feel powerful and a little mischievous. An under-tempo version of "Misty" was starting for the third time, muffling the sound of my mother asking everyone, "Where's Nikki? Has anyone seen Nikki?"

Fifteen years ago, that tree would've been the first place my mother would've thought to look for me, but now she'd be shocked to learn that I could still climb trees, let alone fit on that branch. I knew I was safe for a while, as long as I could tolerate overhearing her flip out over her "missing" daughter. She was especially on edge that day; her husband had disappeared just a month prior.

He was able to stay sober for a few months after the Puerto Rico episode, but in June my mother found empty beer bottles hidden around CWTF. One was behind the washing machine, another was hidden among Grandma Thelma's marigolds. That relapse wasn't like the others, it pushed my mom over the edge. She threatened to throw him out of the house, and for the first time in my life, I wasn't sure whether or not he'd come back. I'd never heard words so cogent from her, and I'd never heard phrases so evil from him. The day after their version of the Civil War, Dad took his car, which my mother had been paying the lease on, and disappeared for a week. He surfaced at a hotel in Danvers where he'd been drinking, racking up credit card debt, and not returning anyone's phone calls.

"You're the reason I drink." That's what he told my mother when he finally took her call. I wanted him dead. Feeling protective over my mother and angry for all she'd struggled with, I wanted him dead. Just for a second. After nearly a week of him seeking refuge at the Marriot, she threatened to leave him. It was then that he saw no other option than to comply with her demands. He checked himself into the Gosnold Rehab facility on Cape Cod.

There was a little garden in a wooden barrel that I could spy from my haven in the tree. It was always Dad's favorite garden because it was just *his*. When he wasn't around, no one else took care of it. Uncle Dale would mow the lawn, and Uncle Ray helped with most of the other gardens, but that barrel was covered with dead geraniums and it seemed to me that it was only a matter of time before it was all dirt. The truth was I missed him not being there that summer.

When I was a little girl and demanded an audience (let's be honest, I often still do), he used to watch me climb that very tree. I'd coax him away from his station at the grill where he'd routinely burn hot dogs, so he could watch me pull myself up all the way to the first large branch. He'd give me a standing ovation every time. One summer he hung a rope from one of the branches so I could swing back and forth like the acrobats in the Big Apple Circus. That rope broke during Hurricane Edward in 1996. The frayed end was still wrapped around the branch.

"Calm down! She'll be fine! She's an adult!" Aunt Moira shrieked, over the sound of Aunt Donna's piano. The breeze combed through my hair, and my hands smelled like ocean and tree bark. The rustling of the leaves in the wind soothed me. The door to one house slammed as my mother dashed over to the other.

"Ray, have you seen Nikki?" she asked. Before he could answer, Charlotte's car pulled into the driveway and she emerged carrying what appeared to be several different types of cheese, and a few bottles of Prosecco.

"Well, hello," she said in a perky and grand voice, to no one in particular, assuming someone would answer. "I come bearing gifts." She had clearly just done a grocery run.

"Charlotte!" Aunt Moira yelled excitedly from her lawn chair, situated in a spot behind the houses right where the sun was hitting. "Thank God!" Can we please get this woman some Prosecco?" she demanded, referring to my mom. "Get over here!" she continued to yell in the direction of my mother, "Charlotte has a present for you!"

"Oh thank you, I'm all set."

"Come on," Aunt Moira encouraged, "Have a drink. Your husband is in rehab, not you. Let's celebrate your life and have a drink. Either that or we can smoke a joint." Mom laughed for the first time all day. The women pushed three lawn chairs together in the five o'clock sun.

"When's he coming home, next weekend?" Charlotte asked my mom. I heard the pop of one of the bottles of Prosecco.

"Yes. Next weekend."

"How do you think he's doing?"

"You know, I spoke with him today and he sounds like he's doing well. The whole thing hasn't been easy for him but his walking does seem to be getting better." I remembered hearing what nurse Cindy had said several years ago, as I clung to a half-empty pudding container for dear life, words that didn't make sense to me at the time: *Years of alcohol damage have resulted in just one drink having a severely negative impact on your husband's neuropathy, just one drink will interfere with his nervous system and cause extreme problems with equilibrium.* "They have a physical therapist working with him twice a day to help with the neuropathy. I think he's made some really good friends there, too. He told me that earlier today a bunch of the patients played baseball and divided themselves into two different teams. It was the Recovering Drug Addicts versus the Recovering Alcoholics." Charlotte spit out her Prosecco and my mom gasped for air.

"You're both nuts," Aunt Moira yelled, joining in.

"What is the age range of men in rehab? Maybe he can meet a nice single guy for Nikki," Charlotte suggested. I stopped smiling. "Misty" stopped too, and a rigid, forte "My Romance" came from the piano inside the house. Deciding to join the crew, I quietly climbed down from my tree, taking in the ocean as I descended.

"Well there's the birthday girl!" Moira said, greeting me while raising a glass and standing up from her chair. I so wished my cousins were there, but Jackie was traveling and Cara had a wedding.

"Nikki! Where have you been? My mother ran up to me desperately opening her arms and I reciprocated with a "hands-off" hug, the kind where you act like you're hugging someone but actually just pat the sides of their back. I brushed her off as fast as possible and pulled up my own chair.

"So what's the latest?" Moira asked. "Who are you shtooping?"

It was never Moira's brashness that I found shocking, it was the fact that she had zero filter regardless of who was in her presence.

"Moira, you can't ask her that," Charlotte jumped to my defense. "Her mother is right here. So, Nikki, who are you shtooping?"" All three of them laughed like buzzed hyenas. I joined out of embarrassment; I was also slightly depressed that the real answer was no one. I had a feeling that everyone in my family thought I was promiscuous because I went out on so many dates and had a portfolio of ridiculous stories, some of which did happen to revolve around sex. I shared them simply because they were too entertaining to keep to myself. I was a performer, after all. And I liked to be authentic. I'd started to build a performance brand based on saying what I was pretty sure everyone else was thinking, but was afraid to verbalize. But the truth about my dating status at that time was I hadn't been out with anyone since Owen had dumped me a few months earlier.

"Nikki, where have you been?" my mother asked me again, after the laughter over my non-existent sex life wore off. "I've been looking all over for you and calling your name."

"Sorry, I didn't hear you," I lied.

"Where were you?"

"Mom, calm down, I just needed some alone time."

"But where?"

"Does it really matter?"

"I guess not. Are you having a good birthday?"

"I am." Moira and Charlotte started planning the menu for the evening's barbeque while my mother zeroed in on me. "How are you doing?" I asked her simply to break the silence.

"I'm fine. I've been looking for you because I really wanted to talk to you."

"Okay. What's up?"

"Can I talk to you privately for a moment?" At that exact second, Charlotte and Aunt Moira exchanged an I-don't-want-to-be-involved look. I was annoyed that my mom found whatever it was on her mind —which I was sure wasn't urgent—and needed to speak with me at that very moment when I'd much rather be socializing with the group.

"Sure," I answered, wanting to avoid conflict and drama. My mother got up from her chair and lead me to the corner house.

"I talked to Dad today. He said to wish you happy birthday."

"Okay." I was relieved she brought him up because I was certainly not prepared to ask.

"He's doing really well, Nikki. He's excited to come home. I think this time he's really kicked the drinking. I haven't heard him sound this good in a long time."

"Cool."

"He gave me a letter to give to you. It was an assignment from one of his groups at rehab. It's for both of us but he really wanted you to read it."

"If it's so important why can't he just tell me?"

"Nikki, you know communication has never been his strong point." I said nothing. My mom took the letter, written on yellow legal pad paper, out of an envelope and handed it to me.

"You want me to read this right now?" I asked.

"Read it when you want. I'm going back over next door to join the others for the rest of cocktail hour."

"Thanks, I'll come over in a minute."

"Okay. Are you alright?"

"Yes, Mom. I'm fine. I just want to be left alone.

Tension hung in the air when my mother left. I was sure my impassive attitude hurt her feelings but I just couldn't help it. The whole situation with my dad really brought out the worst in me, a side of myself I really abhor.

Watching through the window as my mom walked back over to Moira and Charlotte, I pulled the note out of the envelope and unfolded it. My dad's handwriting has always been terrible. His words were slanted and half-printed, half-scribbled.

Dear Family, the letter began. *I'm sorry…I never drank in high school or law school, a little at Syracuse. In my working life, alcoholism just seemed to take off. I slowly fell into a dark place. For so long, I thought I was leading a good normal life. I became very depressed at times, not wanting to get out of bed. Sneaking beer and vodka became all-important. I put so much energy into sneaking alcohol. Didn't everyone do it?*

Around the same time that both of my parents passed away, my wife was diagnosed with breast cancer. Trips to my wife's doctor really scared me and the recent death of my father hurt me badly. Everything was happening at once. I dealt with this by drinking, even in the morning: Scotch for breakfast. I was self-medicating. My thought was that alcohol would make me feel better but it just made everything worse. At that time, I felt my life could have been over. Why go on? I drank on and worked on my father's estate. I should not have been the lawyer for my father's estate, as it was very painful. After a trip to rehab I did manage to stay sober for many years before this relapse.

Many years sober but so what, I thought. Actually, I wasn't thinking. I have no specific memory of taking that first drink after years of sobriety. It just happened and felt good. I just did it. It felt good and I just kept doing it. I still eventually found myself alone hugging a vodka bottle in the Marriot Hotel. Being a drunk didn't affect my work for a long time. I was a good lawyer. I was up at 7:00 every morning to take Nikki to school. At some point, I became overwhelmed with the disease of alcoholism. My recollection is vague as to the timing. I was always sneaking, hiding booze, and lying. Even though it was life-threatening, I drank on.

The first thing I would think of in the morning was where I would have my first drink of the day, not that it could kill me. One morning, I called my wife at work. She was teaching music at Revere Public High School at the time. I cried out desperately for help and needed to tell her that

I had a huge drinking problem and had lost control of my life. Alcohol was my demon. It consumed me and I truly felt it had taken over my life. I was depressed.

Even though I experienced a few bouts of sobriety each one was short lived. I was living in a fog. I never realized what I was doing to myself and I was clueless as to what I was doing to my wife and daughter. My marriage, and my relationship with my daughter became fractured. I drank on. The alcohol was all controlling. It turned my life and family upside down. One rehab blended into another in a blur. When I finished a rehab, my only concern was who knew about it. Now I don't care who knows. I want people to know. I am feeling very badly about myself and I think this is a way of punishing myself.

The rest of the letter was more of the same, one apology after another. It was nothing I hadn't heard before.

Why was it so important to him that I needed to read that? Towards the end there was a line that read, "*I deserve what has happened to me. I've brought it upon myself. My wife and daughter would probably be better off if I died.*" I threw the paper down on the floor in a fit of anger and refused to read the rest. I had zero tolerance for his self-loathing. I wouldn't allow him to have self-pity. He didn't get the privilege of being self-deprecating. I went over to the staircase in the living room and kicked the bottom step as hard as I could; my foot immediately started throbbing inside my sneaker. I took a deep breath and stood there for a moment, taking in the pain. The yellow paper glared at me from the floor, and I limped over to pick it up. I folded it back up, copying the exact creases my dad had made and put it back in its envelope. I shook out my foot, put the envelope on the dining room table, and went outside to return to drinks with my family as if nothing happened.

"Happy Birthday, Nikki." Uncle Dale pulled up a chair to join cocktail hour festivities. "My Romance" still underscored my life.

"Thanks, Uncle Dale," I answered. I grabbed a handful of cheese puffs and poured myself a small glass of Prosecco.

About a month later, CWTF was getting ready to close. By that time, my dad had been home from Gosnold for about five weeks and seemed to be doing okay, but we didn't speak much. I guess we didn't really have much to say to each other. He'd recite scores of Red Sox games and I'd respond with a polite "cool" or "that's too bad." Also, by that time, I was more interested in the Patriots pre-season games than baseball.

That particular morning in late August, the clock above the stove read seven-fifteen, but I wasn't tired. After lying awake in bed for several minutes, I threw on shorts and a t-shirt and took my old car to the Cape Cod Canal to go for a run. As I passed through the living room on the way to the front door, I saw Aunt Donna playing her electronic keyboard. She was wearing giant headphones so that she didn't wake anyone, but you could still hear the keys clicking. I scanned the sheet music as I passed by and saw that she was learning to play "The Saints Go Marching In." Making as little noise as possible, I snuck out the back door.

It was too early for the neighbors' children to be up and the sun was shining and the grass was just wet enough that the dew stuck to my ankles. I made my way towards my old friend, the black Subaru Outback with its broken cassette player that only played Act II of *The Scarlett Pimpernel*, and noticed that my dad's car was missing. He'd been filling his summer days with AA meetings and Cape Cod League baseball games, but I wasn't sure where he would be at that early hour.

I slid into the driver's seat of my Outback and fired her up. Justin Timberlake's "Sexy Back" was playing on the radio and I rolled my eyes because that was still my father's cell phone ring tone. Within minutes, I arrived at the Cape Cod Canal, the famous man-made waterway that connected Cape Cod Bay in the north with Buzzard's Bay in the south. It was roughly seven miles long and had an eight-foot wide strip of flat concrete that ran alongside the water.

It was funny, I really didn't enjoy the act of running, but it was one of those things my body had just been conditioned to do pretty much my entire life. If a day passed when I didn't do it, I felt a void, or rather, a sense of unproductivity. It occurred to me that throughout my life, whether it was a good thing or a bad thing, running had really been the one constant.

My dad and I used to run along the Canal all the time when I was a kid. He'd always joke that it was my training for the Turkey Trot. I pulled into a parking spot. Looking through the windshield at a man in cut-off shorts and a white sleeveless tank top that only covered half of his gut, I smiled. The man looked to be in his late fifties, with pale skin and a faded armband tattoo. There was a woman next to him in an even shorter pair of jean shorts, with long, fried blond hair. My dad and I had always been fans of the denizens at the Cape Cod Canal. I could be twenty pounds overweight and would still be the most athletic, not to mention the youngest, person to set foot on the strip. I also might've always been one of the only runners to have both a college degree but, more importantly, all of my teeth. There was also mismatched Boston sports gear to boot, seniors running in a Patriots jersey with a Red Sox hat.

Safely tucking my keys under the front seat, I left the back door open and made my way to the starting point. Gravel churned beneath my sneakers as I walked across the parking lot. After leaning down to tie my shoe, I cued my iPod (finally) to my running playlist of summer pop tunes.

The sun shone brightly but it wasn't hot enough yet to make the run difficult. I wanted to do five miles that morning so I made it a point to start off slowly. I passed an older man walking with his fishing pole and a younger couple trying to navigate roller blades. When I was little, my dad and I would run the Canal side by side and he'd always try to make me go faster than I could. I'd fake shin splints or some sort of ambiguous sports injury so that I wouldn't feel pressure to keep up with him. Truthfully, I hated running with him; running had ultimately always been a race against myself. I was my own fiercest competitor, and I wanted to keep it that way.

My pace was slow but steady. A sail boat passed by me in the opposite direction, and I waved back to the three passengers who waved at me. I could hear them laughing but couldn't hear what they were saying. On the other side from me there was a row of motor homes where fishermen and their families had camped out. An older couple sat in a pair of lawn chairs overlooking the water, both wearing Red Sox hats.

About twenty feet ahead of me I saw the silhouette of a man outlined by a thick ray of sun. He was barely jogging and I soon closed the gap between us to about ten feet. He wore the wardrobe of an adolescent, neon yellow shorts falling just below his wilting ass cheeks, and a bright blue tank top that clung to his brittle frame. His hair was bleached dry from the sun. And then I realized it was my dad. I was surprised he was out on the Canal at all, considering part of his treatment at Gosnold was learning how to walk again. He was running so slowly that I could probably have walked and still managed to keep up with him. He stopped for a moment to rest and I jogged in place, afraid to pass him. I was really looking forward to getting in a good run that morning, but the thought of passing my father pained me. Sadness snuck up on me; it was so difficult seeing my father's body break down like that. Then again, it wasn't my fault he relapsed. He did that to himself. Why should my workout suffer because he drank himself to his own deterioration? I could feel my adrenaline rising, kick-started by anger, as Dad started running again. I played out the different scenarios that could go down. Maybe he'd be so far into his own running zone that I could run past him and he wouldn't even notice. Perhaps I could become so entrenched in my zone that I could pretend not to see him and get away with it. Or, maybe I could camouflage myself within another pack of townies and he truly wouldn't be able to find me when I ran by him. The more I thought about it, given the current crowd, the third idea probably wasn't a realistic option.

Fifteen years ago my father was running marathons and I couldn't keep up with him. But on that dreadful and beautiful August morning, with the sun shining and the breeze blowing, his daughter was about to outrun him, and it wasn't because she was fast. I didn't want him to hurt. I didn't want to cause him anymore embarrassment or pain, and I'd hate to cause him further shame. His back muscles tightened as he breathed heavily. Winded, he stopped again, that time resting his hands on his knees and facing the ocean. I seized the opportunity, turned up my music, and ran. I ran fast and I ran hard. I needed that moment to be over. Anxiety ran with me and I worried about how my actions would affect him, feeling anger that he did that to himself, regret for shutting him out, and pain and frustration and love. Just as I passed him, he looked up at me. I pretended not to see him. He may have called out to me, I didn't really know. I let the guilt drive me instead of letting it weigh on me.

I had to pass him. I had to do it. Eventually I finished my five miles and returned to my car. My father was nowhere in sight. When I got back in the car my entire body stung with the mounting heat of sunbaked air. When I got home my dad's car was still not in the driveway. It was almost nine and I joined my mom and Charlotte who were having coffee on the porch.

"Where'd you go, Nik?" Mom asked.

"Oh, I just went to the Canal for a little run."

"Great! How far did you go?" I often forgot that my mom too was a runner before she had me.

"I just did five miles."

"Good for you. Did you see Dad?"

"No. I didn't see him." I lied. "Was he there?"

"He was earlier. He had an AA meeting over the Bourne Bridge. He's been going to the earlier meeting so he can drive one of his friends from Gosnold who relapsed, his wife threw him out on the street. Your father has been picking him up at the Bourne Bridge every Saturday morning for the past month and driving him to this AA meeting, then dropping him back off on his way home."

"Cool. Are there bagels in the house?"

"Yup. They're right on the counter. Charlotte brought them. Yum."

I moved inside, poured myself a glass of orange juice and put a poppy seed bagel in the toaster. Through the kitchen window, I saw my dad's car pull into the driveway. I made myself busy as he walked through the kitchen door.

"Hey, Nikki," he said.

"Hey, Dad."

"I saw you running on the Canal today. Good stuff." I looked at his face and felt surprised. His eyes were beaming and he couldn't have looked prouder. "You're really getting fast. Someday you'll run a marathon, but you'll never be as fast as your dad."

"Dad, I assure you, I'll never run a marathon."

"After you've run a marathon, you'll feel unstoppable." His thought was cut off by the sound of the toaster dinging. He grabbed the sports section of *The Boston Globe* which was sitting on the counter next to my bagel station and made his way through the living room to the porch. He teetered off balance just a little bit and used the wall for support. I spread cream cheese on my bagel and then headed next door to see Cara and Ted.

MILE 17

My underarms feel like they've been burned by an iron leaving my skin raw and bloody. I guess I have no choice but to stick it out and luckily I have a pretty high tolerance for pain. I imagine my dad does too, because I think I get it from him. He must've endured so much pain over the course of thirty-two marathons. He still suffers pain, I'm sure, when he thinks about how he's messed up his life. I can't fathom how hard someone needs to be pushed before they self-destruct, but I also can't comprehend how someone could run thirty-two marathons. Maybe my Dad is addicted to pain. Maybe pain is actually the safer option for him. I chose running this race over simply having a conversation with my father so that means on some level I must prefer pain too. It's safer and easier to be in pain than to have, but feel undeserving of happiness. I'm spent, I'm sweating, my underarms hurt like a motherfucker, I'm panting like a senior citizen dog and I just want to die. I would literally give anything for this race to be over. 9.2 left. At least I can now start counting down in the single digits, which mentally seems more palatable. Tired. Dead. I'm starting to slip away.
—Providence Marathon, 2011.

The gym was crowded that December night. There was always a large demographic of bros working out after work, and there was always at least one whose grunts from lifting weights could be heard over the buzzing of the cardio machines. I'd strategically positioned my towel to cover the dashboard of my treadmill so that anyone walking by wouldn't be able to see the clock and know when I'd exceeded the thirty-minute time limit enforced during peak hours. I usually ran in the early mornings when there weren't any time limitations, but that particular morning I'd slept in. The fan on my treadmill was turned on high because the gym always tended to be overheated during frigid weather. Cold air blew into my face making breathing a little challenging, but the rest of my body was overheated and I needed to get air from somewhere.

Running on autopilot, my finger hit the arrow pointing upwards on the panel in front of me increasing my speed from 6.0 to 6.1. Dad always said he hated the monotony of running on treadmills, but I liked the fact that I could control my speed. Ever since my senior year of college, I'd run a minimum of four miles a day, five days a week, at at least a ten-minute mile pace. It was strange; it felt like some unusual cruel form of punishment. But I'd found that over the past year and a half, since graduating college really, those forty minutes of physical pain were far less torturous than the hours of negative self-talk that happened when I didn't run, or even worse, when I didn't make it four miles. One of the most tragic feelings in the world to me was not being able to do what you'd previously proven to be capable of. "You're lazy, you're going to get fat, you're useless, you're a waste." The voices in my head raced next to me, and I ran harder, hoping to leave them in the dust. I couldn't get off the treadmill until they were quiet.

The lone grunter's audible exhale echoed across the weight section of the room every time he successfully completed a squat. It was unclear whether he was seeking attention and just wanted everyone to know how hard he was working, or whether it was a genuinely involuntary response. The machines were all a-buzz and the mirror in front of me was starting to fog up.

Sometimes my entire life felt like I was on a treadmill, an endless strip of rubber that kept circling around and around where you couldn't fall below the minimum speed. If I hit five auditions per week, that was twenty per month and hopefully I'd at least get five call-backs out of those twenty auditions. Same thing with my job. If I called fifty candidates per day, I was bound to get at least twenty of them on the phone. At least ten of those should be open to exploring a new job opportunity, and maybe five of those ten would be in the right salary range and possess the appropriate qualifications. And then there was my dating life. If I set up three Internet dates per week, that was twelve new men per month, which was one hundred-forty-four per year; you'd think one of them was bound to be husband material. I also lived in fear that I was always just average, but that working three times as hard as everyone else was what separated me from my competitors. I conditioned myself to go through the motions to avoid beating myself up for not working hard enough if I didn't get results. But in the end, results were results.

Glancing down and moving my towel aside to peak at my distance, I saw that I'd successfully completed a mile. After giving myself a high-five, I hit the up arrow again until the red number that indicated speed read 6.2. Ever since my ex-boyfriend Owen told me that running anything slower than a ten-minute mile was a waste of time, I'd never let my speed drop below 6.0. Four miles at a minimum ten-minute mile pace. That's as low as the bar would ever go, otherwise I'd failed. I often wondered why I was so afraid of failure. I mean really, how bad could it be? The answer I always came back to was: pretty bad. I couldn't let myself down. And more importantly, as an only child, I was all my parents had. If I fell below four miles at 6.0, they had no one else to pin their hopes on. It was all riding on me. I never quite figured out where that pressure came from because my parents certainly never imposed it on me, but it was the only way I'd ever known how to operate. My entire life I'd always found it peculiar when Aunt Moira asked me how I had enough hours in the day to do what I did, or when Charlotte told me last year at Black Friday Brunch that she always admired how I shot for the stars. The irony was that I never thought of myself as someone who shot for the stars; I worked my face off out of a paralyzing fear that I'd fall below them. I was at a distance 1.0 and I bumped my speed up to 6.3. Distance and speed, the only things in my life I could control.

The grunting stopped, leaving just the aggressive buzzing of machines humming throughout the room. There were still a few people in line for the treadmills and I looked around to evaluate whether anyone else seemed to be winding down their runs, so that I could potentially get away with exceeding thirty minutes. My dad was doing well. We still didn't talk much, but I did think about him a lot. There just wasn't really much to talk about. My mom kept me updated on the important things and I was sure she did the same for him. After a summer of my dad in rehab, my only solution was to throw myself into auditions, since booking a show seemed like the only solution to my problems. If I could just work hard enough land a contract that would allow me to do nothing but sing and dance for a year, I wouldn't have to worry about my depressing job, I'd have a legitimate excuse for not being able to find a boyfriend, and I likely wouldn't be able to go home for the holidays. Getting cast in a show was going to be my ticket out, and the first week of that December, it had finally happened. Distance: 1.5. Speed: 6.4.

It was a Tuesday when I got the call that changed my twenty-three-year-old-life and found out I was cast in a touring production of the musical version of *Dr. Dolittle*, where I'd be starring in eight shows a week as a singing parrot. I didn't remember a morning before that call when I slept past six because I'd been auditioning every day. In fact, a few weeks earlier, I'd sat on a stoop on Twenty-Fifth street between Seventh and Eighth Avenues and called my mom scream-crying that I was a failure and was going to quit NYC and move back home to the Boston area. I'd gone on twenty-five consecutive auditions and had just gotten cut from the one call-back I'd had, for the national tour of *Hair*. There was an improvisational dance section and I completely bombed. They cut ten out of twenty girls and I was one of them. All of a sudden, not being accepted into District Chorus my sophomore year of high school felt completely insignificant. Distance: 2.0. Speed: 6.5.

That night of my *Hair* fiasco, I ran my usual four miles to save myself from feeling like a loser, then went home, ready to throw in the towel. I'd told Analise I didn't want to go to the open casting call for a children's tour of *Dr. Dolittle* the next morning and that it felt like a waste of time. She told me that I should go and that she thought it would actually make me feel better to get back on the horse. Taking her advice, I got up at five the next morning, stood outside in line for two hours, sat around inside for two more hours, then sang. The following week, I had a call-back after which I got a phone call from the casting director not only offering me a role, but also giving me my Equity card. That meant that I could join the actor's union and not have to wait on line at open calls, and would have the luxury of scheduling my auditions the day of, so I could run out and do them on a lunch break instead of having to get up so early. I accepted on the spot. My ticket to freedom had been granted. I was sad to leave Analise and Eric, who had been steadfast friends through all of my struggles, but it would only be for six months and I was excited to embark on that new chapter of my life. What a great start to January. 2008: The year of new beginnings.

I was able to sublet my room to a close friend from home whom Analise knew and liked. Eleanor said that she'd like to continue phone sessions with me while I was away. During our last appointment, she'd suggested I explore medication; she was concerned that I was clinically depressed, especially given that both of my parents were on antidepressants. I told her it would have to wait five months until I returned from my tour. And besides, at the time, I'd rather have felt the drastic highs and low lows than felt just fine all of the time. Fine was average, and I thought the worst thing I could ever be was average. That show was what I needed. It was going to solve all of my problems because I'd be so happy doing what I loved that nothing else would matter. I just had to get through Christmas with my family and then I'd start rehearsals the next day. Distance: 2.5. Speed: 6.6. I gave myself my ritual end-of-mile high-five.

The woman running on the treadmill next to me slowed down to a walk, meaning one of the three people in line would be able to get on. I just needed to hang onto that treadmill for one more mile. The neckline of my grey t-shirt was soaked in sweat, and I took a giant swig of water from the bottle sitting in my cup holder. My mind continued to wander. Maybe I'd even meet a boyfriend on tour. The possibilities were endless and I was thrilled to learn that I'd be the only female cast member. The past six months up until that point had been a series of poor Internet dates. The most promising was a third date I'd had a few weeks earlier; I'd decided to cook us dinner. Before Steve came up to my apartment, he asked if we could take a walk along the East River, where he informed me that he'd actually decided to get back together with his ex-girlfriend and that that would be our last "date." I returned to my apartment and ate the three-course meal I'd spent the day preparing, by candlelight, with Analise. I'd made her least favorite dish, which I referred to as chicken in a cranberry glaze. It had been marinating in our fridge for the past twenty-four hours. She referred to that dish as vom chicken, because she thought it was disgusting, and felt it bore a striking resemblance to vomit. Distance: 3.0. Speed: 6.7.

Last week I'd gone on a date with a gentleman who I'd vetoed because he insisted that for our second date he come over to my apartment and give me a cooking lesson. While the salmon was great, the song he played on the guitar that he brought over, was not. After lying through my teeth, giving him a glowing review of the opening number from his original piece, *Duane Reade: The Musical!* I decided to end it. And that past weekend, I'd had my first ever one-night-stand. I should've known better that the screen name "Dr. Hottie" was bad news, but since I never trusted my instincts, I ignored them. The next morning, I vividly recall "Dr. Hottie" getting out of bed with my maroon sheet wrapped around his waist. He took a long look out the window facing Seventy-Second Street, looked back at me lying in bed, and then looked back out the window and uttered, "I can't wait to move back to Israel. There's nothing for me here." I never heard from him again. Shocking. Distance: 3.5. Speed: 6.8.

Sometimes I wondered why I continued to go on so many dates when I'd had so little success. A part of me loved the stories, and like everyone else, I guess I was also holding out hope that if

Dry Run

I went on enough of them, I'd eventually find "The One." Just like after enough auditions, I eventually booked a show; it was all about volume. Analise, who'd had the same boyfriend since high school, asked me if I thought I intentionally pursued men who were so ridiculous that they'd never work out, so that I wouldn't be disappointed if it didn't *actually* work out. She was in graduate school to become a therapist and loved to come up with theories about my tragic dating life. Sometimes I thought it was just New York City and the crazies who lived there, nothing more. I just wanted to leave town for a while and escape all of the noise. The cold calls, the dates, the vom chickens. I was glad Eleanor was willing to do phone sessions.

Less than a half of a mile left. I could do it. The sweat dripped off of my forehead and onto the tray below treadmill's display panel. Something about seeing my sweat in front of me made me feel accomplished and validated. It was physical proof that I'd done something with my time. I started to feel short of breath and my calves were on fire, but I wouldn't drop the speed. I was going to suffer through. That was my prerogative.

Distance: 4.0. Speed: 6.8. I gave myself a high-five. I was done for the day.

MILE 18

I'm super exhausted, and not the I'm-tired-and-could-really-use-a-rest kind of exhausted, but the if-I-don't-stop-soon-I-literally-might-die kind of exhausted. Tension is building in my quads and my joints start to be inflicted by a dull pain. An ex-boyfriend once told me that when your sweat is cold it means that you're burning calories. I touch my stomach for a temperature gage and it is in fact cold, in case there was any debate over whether or not I was burning some calories at this point. The course has leveled out and I'm running by a giant field that reminds me of the fields my dad and I would pass on our way to the Turkey Trot. It's odd to me that my dad always says he loves flat roads when over the course of his life he could never seem to stay level. He never had much of a taste for steadiness. More of an interest in speed, I guess. Attempting to revel in temporary monotony of the course, I shake my shoulders and let out an exhale. I'm four miles away from the longest training run I've ever completed. I can't quit now. Not at Mile 18. You fucking keep going. You do not stop. Stopping is not in your DNA. I feel the urge to cry and let out a gasp or two. Breaking point. Keep going. I can do this.

−Providence Marathon 2011.

There are those moments we all experience when we wake up and think, oh God, what did I do? For me, that moment was in the Summer of 2008 when I woke up spooning a half-eaten bag of fries on the empty seat next to me on the bus. What was I thinking? How had I not eaten the entire bag? When the bright cabin lights turned on, I stuffed a few of the remaining fries in my mouth and prepared for my arrival in Boston. It was a Friday in early June and I'd agreed to go home for a family reunion being hosted by some relatives on my mom's side that, to be honest, I wasn't aware existed until I'd received the invitation. Though I was a little skeptical when I learned that the party venue was an Assisted Living Center off of Route 3, my cousins and I had decided to make a CWTF weekend out of it. I'd put in extra hours at the office that day since I'd had a lot of musical auditions that week, so I was arriving at South Station later than I would've liked. The *Dr. Dolittle* tour had been amazing, how could it not have been? Six months of driving on open highways cross-country pulling one-nighters, staying in subpar hotels,

Dry Run

performing for audiences, running on half-broken treadmills, and just living. But since the show closed last month, I was back to square one. Luckily my job at the legal recruiting firm was still secure and I showed up at nine o'clock the Monday morning immediately after my return to NYC. Everything was just as I'd left it. The auditions, the cold calling, the endless Internet dates, the depression. It was all there waiting for me. My escape plan worked, I just didn't realize that it was so temporary.

With the aftertaste of French fries lingering in my mouth, I turned on my phone, and sure enough, a series of text messages rushed in. Three were from my mother, one was a second date request from a gentleman who had taken me to a bar at the Port Authority last week and asked me for five dollars to cover the cost of my glass of happy hour wine, and one was from my dad. It read: Roo is here.

Somewhere over the course of the past three months, my father had developed the persona of a kangaroo. I was unclear exactly how it had come about but he constantly referred to himself as "The Roo" and spoke in third person. Though I guess he'd always spoken in third person, the tense just all of a sudden had a character to accompany it.

Perhaps he'd developed that habit while at rehab, or maybe he'd just always been that weird. Sometimes when he called himself "Roo," he did this odd gesture with his hands where he'd bend them at the knuckles and pretend that they were paws while simultaneously scrunching up his face. Regardless, it was so bizarre that it always made me laugh. Maybe it was a way he felt comfortable communicating because he didn't have to use real words. Or, maybe it was simply a way of keeping the mood light, I truly didn't know. But he seemed to become "Roo" only when communicating with me. It was our thing, maybe it had replaced the eye roll. And the crazy thing was, I addressed him as "Roo" and did the Roo paws back. Yes, I thought it was odd that he'd developed that alter-ego of a marsupial at age sixty-five, but if he was sober, I was willing to let it slide.

When I got off the bus, "Roo" was standing at the gate to greet me, wearing a flamboyant coral long-sleeve top, a pair of plaid shorts, and a dog tag necklace. His hair was grey and his skin looked damaged from the sun (or the tanning beds, more likely), but he seemed happy. As far as I knew, he'd remained sober since his stint in rehab the summer before.

"Hi, Nik!" he said with half-open arms.

"Hey, Dad!" I said avoiding a hug and patting him on the head instead. If he wanted to act like an animal, I'd treat him like one. He lifted my bag even though I could see it was a strain for him to carry. His arm with my bag trembled ever so slightly and hung much lower than the other arm. I thought about offering to carry my own bag, but also didn't want him to feel bad, to feel like he wasn't capable. He was my dad, after all. Once in the car, I reached for the knob to adjust the radio and my hand grazed a banana peel draped over the cup holder. I wished he'd keep a cleaner car; it seemed like such a simple thing to throw out a banana peel, he could've even tossed it out the window.

"Ticket, please," the parking attendant said in a gruff voice as we pulled out of the lot, holding his hand out lethargically. "The Roo" fished through his wallet and then looked under the banana peel. Next, he checked his pockets and rifled through the glove compartment.

"What happens if I don't have my ticket?" I had a strong sense of déjà vu.

"You pay full price. Twenty-eight dollars." Suddenly and unexpectedly feeling defensive, I leaned over, looked through the open window, and raised my voice, "He has to pay full price even if he was only here for fifteen minutes?"

"No ticket, full price." The dreary parking attendant clearly wasn't interested in negotiating. Why were all South Station employees always so depressed? My dad opened his wallet to reveal a five dollar bill, then continued to search his pockets, under the front seat, and again in the glove compartment. I couldn't figure out if my dad was just irresponsible and had misplaced the parking ticket, or if he couldn't remember where he put it.

"We take credit cards," the attendant chimed in. I pulled out my wallet and came to Roo's rescue because I knew he didn't have any credit cards. Last year his spending had escalated, and, with some strong coaxing from my mother, my father agreed to cancel all of his credit cards. It seemed so controlling to me at the time, but I'd come to understand why she did it. I handed my dad my credit card and insisted he take it. He ignored me, wouldn't look me in the eye, and kept rummaging around the same places he'd already checked. The car behind us honked.

Dry Run

"How did I lose the ticket? I just had it. I'm such a bad Roo." His voice got a little higher, and I reached over him and handed my Visa to the despondent parking attendant.

"Thanks, Nik. I promise I'll pay you back." The shame in his low and timid voice was prevalent. "I'll write you a check." We drove out of Boston not saying anything to each other. Once we turned onto the highway, the awkwardness of the lost parking ticket receded and we interacted normally again.

"Did Mom tell you I got a job?"

"No, she didn't." I thought it odd that my mom hadn't mentioned that, especially since she and I spoke every day. After hunting on Craigslist for nearly fifteen months, he finally got hired as a mall security guard. I wasn't sure how to react. My father defended criminals as a lawyer for thirty years and I couldn't really picture him breaking up a fight outside of Claire's over a pair of stolen earrings. He went on to tell me that he got to be at the mall every day and just sat in his car and read books because no one actually stole anything. His words got faster and his tone got higher when he talked about the uniform he got to wear, which was all black and looked like one of Jack Bauer's outfits.

"Great…"

"We find out our assignments at the beginning of each week. I was only called in once this week but I'm hoping to get some more hours next week. I love my AA friends too. Harriet and Sal. I'm doing really well."

"Nice."

I wanted to be happy for him, but the truth was it was difficult for me to see him like that. It was like he was working so hard to illustrate how he'd turned his life around, and more importantly, he was trying to show me that he was happy, which made me think he wasn't. His voice gave away his desire for my approval, and it pained me that I couldn't find it within myself to give it to him. Maybe I was afraid to be happy for him, assuming that we'd both be disappointed the next time he relapsed. I wanted more for him, but at the end of the day, what more could he want for himself at that point in his life other than to stay sober? It was a hard battle that I didn't understand. I wished I could've filled him in on my life, but I felt stunted. When someone has put themselves on the brink of death so many times, it's challenging to let that person back in. It was simpler to just talk about Red Sox scores. I couldn't lose what I'd already lost.

"Now I just have to figure out what to get your mom for her birthday," Dad said. He was trying to be open and talk about his life with me, and I was giving him very little back. My one-word answers must've made him feel like every time he tried to stand up, I deliberately pushed him down. My brain thought empathy, but my body spat out apathy. Something about keeping my distance felt safer, even though it also made me hate myself. "You're a terrible daughter. You're heartless. You're a bitch." That was what the voices in my head were saying.

As we drove past the Westgate Mall en route to CWTF, I thought about my dad being a mall security guard. The powerful defense attorney turned alcoholic turned mall security guard with no credit card sat beside me behind the wheel, grinning as if he had no recollection of his former self.

By the time we arrived at CWTF it was almost midnight. Sure enough, even at that hour, a slow pianissimo version of "Memory" resonated across the property, this time with no metronome. I snuck past Aunt Donna and scurried up to the bedroom. Dad followed, relying heavily on the banister. Miraculously, my mom was asleep. I was excited to see her in the morning when I woke up; the family reunion wasn't until Sunday, so I'd get to enjoy a day with just my close family.

The next morning, I woke up to a few drops of water falling on my head. I looked up to discover that the roof was leaking and assumed that it must be raining outside. My watch said it was eleven. I don't think I'd slept that late since I'd blacked out drunk the night I returned from Puerto Rico. I could hear my parents chatting in the next room and I got up to say hello. Just before I got to the doorway of their bedroom, I heard my dad ask my mom to borrow forty dollars.

"What for?" my mom asked.

"It's raining and I was going to ask Nikki if she wanted to go to the movies." I turned around and headed down to the kitchen, not wanting my father to know I'd overheard him asking my mom for money. I could see Aunt Moira sitting next door under the porch awning, chatting with Cara and I went to say hi. I noticed a check on the counter as I passed through the kitchen. I looked closer and saw that it was made out to me, in my dad's handwriting. The amount was for thirty dollars and on the memo line, *Nikki Parking Ticket* was written in a scribble, slanted script. I was torn between taking the check to preserve my dad's dignity as a provider and ripping it up because I knew he probably needed the money. I put it in my pocket so he'd at least notice that I'd taken it, I would decide later whether or not to deposit it.

The last time I'd seen my dad's handwriting was in that same room, when my mother gave me the note he'd written at Gosnold. I was struck and dominated by a fear that he'd die thinking I hated him. I felt it right in my throat and put my hands around my neck to make sure my glands weren't physically swelling. What if he relapsed again or one day just stopped fighting because he felt there was no way to ever win back our relationship? What if he felt so discouraged by my inability to recognize how hard he'd been working to stay alive that I ultimately killed him?

There was a notebook in the drawer next to the fridge and I ripped out a page. The next several minutes were spent filling a sheet of white paper with words that were hard to find. At least words written down were better than ones left unsaid. More than anything, I just wanted to feel some sense of resolution. Since I didn't have the courage to speak to him in person, I decided to do what he did to me and wrote it down instead. I had to say something. "I admire your perseverance. I think your dedication to AA is amazing. I love you," were a few of the phrases I used. Vulnerability was not my strength, but I could at least get some phrases that modeled inspiration down on paper, God forbid anything were to happen to him. I folded it up and tucked it into the back pocket of my jean shorts for safety.

Later that afternoon, I knew my dad was asleep because his snoring shook the entire street. My mom said that he'd started taking more naps as of late; according to her, that was normal for people in their late sixties. The snoring echoed through the hallway as I climbed the stairs and the door to his bedroom creaked when I pushed it open. I tiptoed across the carpet to his bedside table, clutching the folded letter in my right hand and bent down to leave it on his nightstand. Then I stopped. What if he tried to talk to me about the letter after reading it? I wanted him to acknowledge what I wrote and then never say anything to me about it, ever.

Unable to leave the letter, I instead left the room and paused in the hallway to think. Inspired by the humming of a plane I heard flying over the house, I unfolded the note I'd written and refolded it into a paper airplane; it lightened the emotional weight for me. After molding a mediocre model of a 737, I reopened the door to my dad's room and prepared for take-off. Seatbacks and tray tables up!

Much to my dismay, the airplane flew about a foot before doing a one-eighty and drifting to the ground. I picked it up and tried again. The second time it flew about two feet but landed under the dresser. Picking up the plane a third time, I walked over and placed it on the carpet in the middle of the room where he was sure to find it when he woke up. Mission accomplished. I headed downstairs and joined cocktail hour next door.

MILE 19

Less than eight miles to go. I can do this. Inhale. I can. No one can take this from me. Exhale. I'm in control and this is a concrete situation where I can control the outcome. Inhale. The pain under my arms has become almost unbearable and I'm fairly confident there's blood, self-inflicted blood. You'd think someone might've warned me about underarm chaffing. I wonder if my dad had ever experienced it, I mean, he must've. I can't control the chaffing but I can control continuing to run despite the chaffing. Exhale. I can will myself to keep going despite my arduous mission. I fear that if I stop I won't be able to start again and I've almost made it to mile twenty. I can't quit now. And if I stop, I also don't know how I'll be able to start over with my dad. Also, if I stop now, the first eighteen miles will have been for nothing. I promised myself I'd run this whole thing even if it kills me and even if it also means going slowly. I'm not an elite enough of a runner to care about time. I literally just want to survive, like my dad. Sometimes it amazes me that he's still alive. Keep going. Nothing will stop me. Nothing can stop me. Go.

—Providence Marathon, 2011.

My throat was closing up and I thought I was dying. That's what I told Dr. Dend the pharmacologist, a colleague of Eleanor's, when she'd asked me to take her back to the incident I'd described to her on the phone. Her office smelled like a library, bookshelves full of old books aged like wine, decorated the walls. Dr. Dend had short dark hair and wore a beautiful gold cross necklace that I kept fixating on, like a baby mesmerized by a shiny object. She asked me to put myself back in the moment when I thought my life was over and instructed me to recount it to her in as much detail as I could remember.

For a split-second I considered asking my cab driver to take me to the nearest emergency room, but then I think of how silly I'd look if nothing was actually wrong with me. It was a nice night out. The weather had just started to transition from summer to fall, and it had been the kind of day where short sleeves were okay during the afternoon, but a sweatshirt was necessary at night. My head was pounding and I kept trying to swallow, but my mouth was drying up and it felt like my air supply was about to be cut off. The red brake lights that flashed every time the car in front of us slowed down seemed extra bright, to the point where they blinded me through the windshield. Was this how I was supposed to die? Was this the end? My heart started racing, sprinting in hopes of freeing itself from my chest, and I tried to take some slow, deep breaths to slow my pulse beat. My left thumb was pressed against my right wrist trying to count the number of beats. I was headed up Ninth Avenue, trapped in bumper-to-bumper traffic, so it didn't look like my cab driver would even be able to get me to a hospital in time in the event that I were dying. I'd have to run there, and how could I run if I couldn't breathe?

Had I eaten something that day that didn't agree with me? I'd had the split pea soup with turkey that I always had at lunch. Was it possible that the turkey was undercooked or infected by some weird disease? Was there an unusual ingredient in the macadamia nut cookie I'd had for dessert? Was I having an allergic reaction? Had I developed a nut allergy? After another deep breath, which caused my heart to pound even more rapidly, I touched my throat with my hands. It didn't seem to be getting bigger, but I could no longer swallow. My saliva had vanished, leaving my mouth a barren desert. How could my throat feel like it was swelling on the inside, but seem perfectly normal when I touched it from the outside? Was I losing my mind?

My hands tingled and my entire being was plagued by the terror that I was about to take in my final gasp of air. Was I having a heart at-tack? My impulse was to text someone, maybe Analise or Eric, or maybe even Suzie or Megan, because I just wanted someone to know what was going on with me so that I wasn't alone, but every single atom of my body was focused on staying alive. The fear that I wouldn't be able to calm myself down just made the wheels in my brain spin more out of control and my windpipe was rapidly shrinking. I didn't want to die. Sometimes I did, but right then I didn't. Not like that, in the back of a taxi cab in Hell's Kitchen.

My cab driver said something but I couldn't put an iota of energy into hearing his words. Instead I clutched the sweat pants that I'd thrown on over my leotard and tights after dance class and just tried to breathe. The pants were soft. Focus on the nice feeling of the pants. I touched my neck again and it still didn't feel like it was swelling from the outside. Next I examined my left arm, since I remembered hearing somewhere that when you're about to have a heart attack or a stroke, you sometimes experience a dull pain in the left arm. My left arm felt fine. Completely immobilized in the back of that cab I prayed to God to not let me die.

Dr. Dend sat there and listened as I explained my seemingly inexplicable near death incident. My face felt hot and I could feel sweat gathering under my armpits when she asked me if I often felt stressed or experienced high levels of anxiety. I told her that my life was no more stressful than anyone else's. I'd recently started a new job and was a little worried about having to start over and prove myself, but that was traditional stress that most people encountered at some point in their lives. At least, people who were lucky enough to have a job. Who was I to complain? And my new job was very similar to my last one in that I was still responsible for finding candidates and placing them in jobs in the legal industry. The big difference was that at my previous company I was recruiting mainly paralegals and legal secretaries, and now I was working with a newer industry called eDiscovery, placing people who handled data during the litigation process. My new boss said that I could still have all of the flexibility I needed for auditions, as long as I was hitting my numbers. More money, more pressure. Without breaking eye contact, Dr. Dend scribbled a few notes down on her pad. She remained silent, so I continued rambling.

Without thinking, I started telling her about the incident at work the week prior when I'd CCed my boss on an email and he called me out on a typo; I was convinced he was going to fire me and I'd be living on the streets and then have to move home to Boston. Seconds after that conversation about the typo, I found myself on the office bathroom floor, sobbing and hyperventilating. I could barely breathe. I thought about calling 911, but I couldn't stop thinking of how embarrassed I'd be if I was cured by the time the EMTs arrived, and I was eventually able to calm myself down. The voices in my head filled the entire building: "You're a fraud with a lousy theatre degree. You can't even type a basic email. Everyone in the office thinks you're bad at your job." I was surprised I hadn't been fired yet. That typo suddenly became a catastrophe and the epicenter of my work productivity.

Dr. Dend continued staring at me, without saying a word, so I did what I do best and talked about myself some more. I confided in her that I'd thought that when I returned from tour I'd book another show straightaway, but it turned out having my Equity card had put me in a pool of stronger talent and I was competing against people who had five Broadway shows under their belt. The voices in my head started talking again and eventually crescendoed to shouting. "You can't sing. You're a lousy actress. You only booked that show because you were the right size for the costume." They were so loud, a part of me wondered if Dr. Dend could hear them. She scribbled something in her notebook, this time breaking eye contact, and then looked back up at me. Her office was nice and it was a real one, unlike Eleanor's, who saw patients in the living room of her Upper East Side apartment. Dr. Dend looked to be around the same age as Eleanor, mid-fifties, and I wondered if they met in college or perhaps at some sort of therapist seminar. Neither she nor Eleanor wore wedding rings.

"Have you been sleeping, Nikki?" she asked me. Her voice was soothing and calm, like a mom offering to make a cup of hot tea, a quality that my mom lacked. Something about her was comforting and I wished Dr. Dend would make me a cup of tea even thought I really didn't like the taste of tea. I told her I usually slept six hours a night, but always woke up exhausted, even after the rare occasions I slept for ten. My mom always had sleeping issues and I felt like most people in their twenties did too. I never had a problem falling asleep, it was staying asleep that was the issue. And when I couldn't fall back to sleep it was usually because my mind was racing with thoughts like: "You're going to get fired if you don't hit your sales quota this week, you didn't get called back for that audition today, what if you never book another show? That guy you went on a date with last Saturday never called you again." Every path I'd started felt like a slammed door. Dr. Dend wrote down something else, her pen moving almost as rapidly as the words running through my mind.

"Nikki, have you ever thought about ending your life?" No one had ever asked me that question so directly.

"Of course not," the words flew out of my mouth, sounding almost defensive, like I was offended she'd asked, even though I wasn't really offended. "I just spent the last five minutes telling you about how I was in the back of a taxi cab dying of some unknown food allergy and all I wanted to do was get home alive so I could have Chinese takeout!" She stared at me for a long time. My pulse throbbed throughout my entire body and Dr. Dend sat there silently in her red V-neck sweater. I stared down at the oatmeal carpet and I knew she was looking at me. I could feel her eyes on me; she was waiting for me to talk.

"Sometimes I'll walk slowly through traffic and think that if I get hit by a car, then that's what was meant to happen and that it wouldn't be the worst thing. Or if I slipped in front of the train by accident it was simply fate affirming that my thoughts were valid and that it was time for things to end. And once in a while I think that if I accidentally fell asleep in my bathtub and drowned, it wouldn't be so bad, but I've never actually tried to drown myself." I assumed everyone had those thoughts. We were all human.

Dr. Dend's pupils got smaller and her eyes fixated on me intently, her neck stuck out and her straight torso leaned forward. I felt seen and naked. I'd never told anyone about my thoughts of death, partly because I'd assumed everyone either had them or was scared of them, or that they would think that I was a freak or get unnecessarily nervous and worried about me. I'd been feeling deeply sad for a while. But sometimes life was sad. I still went to work every day and made my cold calls and got to my auditions and ran my four miles. I wouldn't have been able to do all of that if I had a real problem.

That said, if I was being honest, some days I didn't wear clean underwear partly because I didn't think I deserved it and also because I didn't have the energy to put them on. The only thing that filled the empty feeling in my body was takeout, chocolate chip cookies, or Diet Coke; while I'd put on a little weight, running had kept most of it off. Sometimes it was a glass of wine that filled the void, but really, I was afraid of drinking too much, with all of the baggage attached to alcohol. When I drank, I usually just felt worse about myself. I didn't want to talk to my friends about my solemn moods and feelings of hopelessness because I didn't want to bring them down and make it their problem. But I did just feel so deeply lugubrious, like I didn't matter. I also didn't want my friends to stop hanging out with me because I was self-centered and depressing. Luckily, I had a college degree in putting up a front. In fact, the only times I felt I could truly be myself without fear of being judged was when I got to sing a song about a character who was sad or struggling, because that wasn't bringing anyone down—that was a performance. The moments of my life that I spent on stage in front of an audience were some of the only moments in my life where I felt zero anxiety and like I could truly be myself. It was always funny to me, that performing or public speaking, things that gave such a large part of the Earth's population the most anxiety, was a safe haven for me, like a childhood tree house.

Nothing excited me. It was a struggle to get out of bed in the morning but I did it because it was all I knew how to do. It was like my body knew it had to run on autopilot so that when my mind snapped out of whatever it was going through, I wouldn't be behind. It was like my brain had erased any recognition of happiness.

But I wouldn't have been able to function the way I was if I were depressed. I was making it through the motions, that had to count for something. I wondered if this was how my dad felt after his parents died, when my mom said he was depressed.

What made processing my feelings difficult was that when I looked at how good my life was on paper, I felt like I didn't have the right to feel upset or depressed. I didn't deserve to revel in pain because there were so many people out there who had it so much worse than I did. Even if I did think about suicide, it was only because my standards were too high and I was terrified I'd never meet them. I didn't think anyone, including Dr. Dend, could ever understand what it was like to be inside my head. "You're ugly. Your singing is flat. You're not making enough cold calls. You run too slow. You're not funny. You're stupid. No one will ever want to date you. You're a terrible daughter. You're a failure." It was the cruelest radio station ever, but the only one that always came in clearly.

Dr. Dend asked me about my family history with depression. I told her that both my mother and father had been taking antidepressants for a while. I didn't know the specifics.

"What makes you feel good?" she asked. The first thing that came to mind was when people laughed at my stories. I started telling Dr. Dend the story about the time two weeks earlier when I'd caught my hair on fire on a first date, exaggerating the size of the flames for comedic effect. Was I so desperate that I was begging my pharmacologist for a laugh? The second thing I thought about was the feeling got after I completed a hard run. That was a rush and a sense of accomplishment. It was something concrete I could point to and say, "See, you're not a loser you just ran four miles." And the third thing that came to mind was being able to sit down at a piano and play.

She told me that my thoughts, which she referred to as suicidal ideations, weren't normal. And that my panic attacks were a result of catastrophic thinking, which was a symptom of depression. She said that most people didn't, in fact, consistently wake up exhausted regardless of how much sleep they got. She asked me how long I'd been in talk therapy and I told her that I'd been seeing someone since my sophomore year of college, around four years. She asked if I'd ever considered medication and I told her absolutely not because I didn't want to gain weight, I didn't want to lose my ability to act, and I didn't want to pay for them. I also didn't want to be dependent on a drug for the rest of my life. But when she told

Dry Run

me, "You don't have to live like this," I started to reconsider. I didn't have to live like that.

Dr. Dend wrote me two prescriptions that day, one to help me sleep, the other for an antidepressant. She suggested that what I experienced in the cab that night was a panic attack, and given the information I'd provided, she felt strongly that I'd gotten so good at controlling my anxiety and depression during the day that it was manifesting itself in the form of panic attacks that were happening in my sleep, fueling nightmares, explaining why I'd wake up exhausted regardless of how many hours of sleep I got. I took the prescription slips and figured I could decide later whether or not to fill them.

What if the medicine changed me? What if I lost my ability to cry? What if the dosages were wrong and my body didn't react well? Dr. Dend said that the medicine would help give me some perspective and she believed that the drugs would help balance out some chemicals that would help my brain function on a more rational level. I'd never felt so alone and completely petrified. Did she think I was crazy? Was I insane? Would my parents be disappointed if they found out I was prescribed antidepressants and sleeping pills? Was I disappointed in myself? I'd grown so accustomed to that slice of darkness in me, what if I wasn't myself once that darkness was taken away? What would happen if the medications only revealed that I was driven by pain? What if I was a freak? The buzzer rang, transporting me back to the office that smelled like a library, and I imagined that meant that her next patient was waiting outside. After thanking her for her time I threw my tote bag full of sheet music over my shoulder, fluffed my curly hair to ensure that it had maintained its proper level of volume, and left, heading back downtown to my office.

MILE 20

The infamous runners wall is something I've heard about many times but never really understood until possibly now. My feet don't totally have feeling, the part on the top of my head still hurts. It actually really hurts. It hurts a lot, but who the hell aside from balding men thinks to put suntan lotion on their head? Maybe my pigtails were not such a hot idea after all. My breasts are going strong. They are, in fact, the only part of me, that is currently going strong. How did my dad do this so many times? I can't comprehend it. My body reeks of discomfort, but sometimes it's good to be uncomfortable. Fatigued. I don't see any runners in front of me and I glance over my right shoulder to see if there are any behind. Right now it appears I'm alone. Running. Inhale. Exhale. Dead. I hope there are people behind me. Oh my God, what if I'm in last place. No. Honestly, as long as I finish this thing I don't care what place I'm in. I can't swallow and for a second I feel my throat start to close up, but when I grab my neck from the outside it doesn't feel swollen. Salt. Taste salt. Keep moving. Next water station. I feel nothing. And everything.

–Providence Marathon, 2011.

Rain thudded heavily onto my dad's car as we pulled into the parking lot of The First Church in Danvers, a not-so-minor pit stop on the way to South Station. My dad looked for a parking spot, as I wondered if that particular pit stop was a good idea.

After years of my dad going to two AA meetings a day, I'd decided to attend one with him; this was more for me than for him. I thought that maybe if I showed him some support, I'd feel less badly about the resentment I was hanging onto, or at least maybe it would make my anger a little less visible. I was nervous and uncomfortable, but this was important. Sometimes it's important to be uncomfortable. I'd suggested the idea to him that morning. The words had come out of my mouth before I really realized what I was offering, but I guess that was the definition of an instinct? By that time, I'd been on medication for a few months. The main difference I noticed was that things in general seemed less important, in a good way. And I knew the fact that I was able to feel the significance of going to that AA meant that it mattered. After doing a loop around the lot, Dad pulled into a parking spot, (which was actually two parking spots). Before I could decide whether or not to say something about his uneven parking job, he'd turned off the car and was reaching into the backseat for his umbrella, which was next to his cane. He grabbed the umbrella but left the cane.

"Your hair is going to need this more than mine," he said, handing me the umbrella. While I appreciated the gesture, my hair was in a frizzy top knot since the rest of my day was going to be spent on a bus. Though my dad's hair still looked worse. It was uncombed and straight and stiff, likely from the years of hair treatments. There was a small bald spot on the back of his head that was starting to show. The dash from the car to the church wasn't so bad, but I could feel the bottoms of my sweat pants getting wet as the weight of the rain dragged the hem down to the ground. Sitting in ankle-soaked pants from Boston to New York didn't thrill me, but what could I do? My dad opened the door to the church basement and I closed the umbrella before going inside. I didn't want any bad luck coming my way, and while I wasn't overly superstitious, I was careful enough to not bring an open umbrella indoors. My relationship to superstition was similar to my views on Judaism. I wasn't overly Jewish either, but while I wasn't out there building a Sukkah Hut, I did occasionally fast on Yom Kippur. I've never taken Communion, and never let a black cat cross my path, either.

My mom wasn't aware of our plans that morning, at least to my knowledge. I assumed she thought I was getting an earlier bus back to NYC. It was possible my dad told her about out planned excursion to AA; I didn't really know and had little interest in finding out. I didn't want to be grilled and put on the spot about my AA experience and made to feel guilty for not ever having given Al-Anon a chance.

We walked down two flights of grey stairs, slick with water that other people had tracked in from outside. The stairwell was dimly lit and haunted by an air of sadness, or maybe that was just my impression. We finally made it to the bottom of the staircase, which opened up into a room filled with roughly forty people; I was shocked by the size of the crowd. Before we could get very far, a man wearing a plaid red and black lumber jack-like button-down shirt and jeans greeted my dad.

"Hi," said plaid shirt guy in a husky voice. He must've been a smoker.

"Hi, Sal!" my dad replied.

"Is this Nikki?" He gestured to me.

"Yes! It is!"

"Hi, Nikki! It's nice to *finally* meet you!" Sal reached out to shake my hand.

"Nice to finally meet you too," I said by default.

"Your dad has told you about me?" Sal said.

"Yeah!" After about three seconds of Sal's strange, alarmed reaction, I remembered that AA stood for Alcoholics *Anonymous* so I tried to back pedal out of that conversation. "I mean I just know that he has friends in AA," I continued. "He didn't mention you specifically. I haven't actually heard so much about you in particular, as I have about all of you collectively, as an anonymous group."

"Well welcome!" Sal said after a tense, two-second pause. It was unclear to me whether he'd been serious or trying to deliver some weird AA joke. Regardless, he offered up some snacks, motioning to a table against the wall and AA's stock went up. There was a coffee maker (which I could've done without since I didn't drink coffee), some Styrofoam cups, and a plate of bagels and doughnuts. There was one chocolate doughnut left and I snagged it. I hadn't had a chocolate doughnut in years. My mom would never let me have them as a kid, but every now and then, Dad and I would sneak one in after a soccer practice.

"Over here!" a woman called from across the room, clearly trying to get my dad's attention. It seemed she'd saved us both seats among a row of metal folding chairs that were all facing "the stage."

Dad turned to me and said, "I'm the most popular Roo in AA." Feeling pretty confident he was the *only* Roo in AA, I rolled my eyes and we laughed. Following my dad's lead, we walked over to the woman, whose name I came to learn was Harriet, and took our seats. Harriet was an older, heavy-set woman whose grey hair had frizzed in the rain, and there were still some water droplets stuck to her glasses. Her hair was pulled into a low pony-tail and she told me how lovely it was to finally meet me and gave me a giant hug, engulfing me in her sweatshirt. She said my dad talked about me nonstop and that everyone was dying to meet me. I had no idea that I was such a Danvers AA celeb. Another woman introduced herself as Paula, and asked if I was the *famous* Nikki who did shows in New York and wanted to know how my acting career was going. I was completely taken by surprise; I had no idea my father even really followed my acting career those days. My proud mom liked to broadcast to the world every detail about every audition I went on, and I assumed she kept my dad up to date, but we never actually discussed it.

Alcoholics were so nice. Harriet chatted with my dad and Paula while the woman next to her eavesdropped with little subtlety. The whole room buzzed with chatter and every now and then I heard a "wicked awesome" pop out from the crowd. I'd expected to see a basement full of depressed introverts but instead I was surrounded by a room of mostly social butterflies who all seemed so excited to be there. Maybe they were just happy to see each other, or to not be alone. And the Boston-themed clothing on that rainy Sunday morning was out of control: Red Sox sweatshirts, Patriots sweat pants, Celtics hats, you name it.

I did notice a few people who kept to themselves, like the girl sitting five seats down to my left. She was wearing ripped jeans and a black tapered sweatshirt and her shoulder-length hair looked like it hadn't been brushed in a while, kind of like my dad's. The light from the ceiling caught her silver nose ring, making her stand out. Behind her, there was a man wearing a red Patriots hat, chowing down on a chocolate doughnut. There was something about his face and the way he was eating the doughnut that caught my attention. His eyes remained complacent, and he didn't seem to be enjoying the doughnut, but didn't seem to dislike it either. He was just eating it. I wanted him to be excited and loving the shit out of that doughnut. If that doughnut couldn't get him excited about life, then nothing could. I didn't recall ever seeing such an apathetic doughnut eater in my life. It made me think of how I felt a few months ago: hopeless, empty, trapped. Though finding the right dosage was tricky at first, antidepressants had really agreed with me over the past few months. They didn't solve my life, but I did feel like I'd gained an ability to realize when things weren't actually that important versus when they were. The bad wasn't the end of the world, and in turn, the good wasn't the answer to all of my problems. My life had stopped being a series of climaxes and had started being a pattern of manageable challenges with some nice afternoons sprinkled in. The highs weren't as high and the lows weren't as low, but I could still discern the two. For the first time in my life, I had perspective. And I still cried, I still got angry, I still experienced joy, I could really enjoy a doughnut. A few minutes later, my people-watching was interrupted by a woman with dark hair who looked to be in her late fifties standing up at the front of the room and speaking into a microphone.

"Okay everyone, we're going to begin." Her voice was lower than what I'd expect from such a skinny and frail-looking woman. Folks around the room took their seats and the sound of metal folding chairs clinked against the wooden floor as the damp, cold room was warmed by the congregation of recovering alcoholics. I looked over at my dad, as his eyes stared straight ahead. Harriet was smiling a warm smile, and Sal, who was still across the room manning the entrance, looked happy. The girl with the nose ring still appeared somber and shy, and doughnut man had finished eating. A few crumbs lingered on his grey moustache.

"I'd like to commence this meeting by awarding the sobriety chip," the dark-haired woman announced in a thick Boston accent. The man who ate the doughnut stood up, went to the front of the room, and took a small coin from the leader of the meeting. He'd been sober for six months, about the same amount of time I'd been on medication. I started to wonder if my dad had any of those chips and what happened to them when he broke his sobriety. The room applauded, and everyone started reciting in unison: *God grant me the serenity to accept the things I cannot change, the courage to change the things I can, and the wisdom to know the difference.* I sat there silently, the way I did when I was at a Catholic funeral and the mourners started singing a hymn I wasn't familiar with. The prayer ended and the frail female with the uncharacteristically low voice introduced the speaker for that day, a woman named Dawn.

Dawn made her way up to the front of the room. Her faded brown hair must've been a beautiful russet color before it was flat ironed to death. Her discolored skin looked like it had been plastered on her body and my guess was that she was probably ten years younger than she looked, which would've made her around forty-five. Dawn stood behind the podium and began telling the story of her life. How she'd slept with countless men and been thrown out on the street by her parents, time and time again after "drinking" and "drugging." I thought about the men I'd slept with. There hadn't been a ton, but there'd definitely been more than a few, and hearing Dawn talking about waking up next to men she didn't remember meeting the night before made me question why I had a tendency to go home with men sooner than I probably should. Was I just a typical New Yorker in my mid-twenties? Was I seeking some form of external validation? Was I trying to achieve something? Was I trying to be liked? I thought I was a pretty good judge of character, and though many of the men I'd dated had displayed questionable behavior, like pulling out W2s on a first date and asking me for career advice after learning that I was a head hunter, or showing up at my apartment in a cab at four in the morning asking me for cash to pay for said cab, I didn't think any of them were bad people at the core. I'd always assumed I'd never been good enough to keep them around. And for the first time in my life in that AA meeting, it dawned on me that I was more concerned about meeting other people's needs than I was about other people meeting mine.

Dawn talked about how, since that promiscuous and reckless time, she'd dedicated her entire life to staying sober. I was struck by her words, but I wasn't entirely sure why. It was a tragic story, but it was one I'd heard before. I'd seen it depicted in countless episodes of *Law and Order* and Lifetime specials. What hit me was how the entire room was hanging onto every syllable. They already knew Dawn's story because they were Dawn. In their own ways, they'd all been where she was and her words gave them the strength to continue fighting their own battles and to gain comfort in knowing that they too had a chance.

Dawn talked for an hour and the meeting concluded. I grabbed a poppy seed bagel for the road and my dad and I walked back up the staircase. We said goodbye to Harriet and Sal, who'd made it up the stairs before us and were standing in the parking lot. The rain had stopped. We got in the car and I turned on the radio to avoid any type of awkward silence that might've ensued. He turned the windshield wipers off after they scraped against the dry glass. A few minutes later we were on Route 1 driving towards Boston. After about twenty minutes of pure radio, Dad broke the silence by starting a conversation.

"Did you like my friends?"

"They were cool."

"I love my meetings."

"That's great, Dad."

"Harriet has a Grandson in NYC."

"Interesting. Dad, how many AA meetings do you go to each week?"

"Two each day."

"Right, but how many different meetings with different people?"

"Six."

"So you figure that's about three hundred people. My guess is at least half of those three hundred people have children or grand-children in NYC. That's one hundred fifty. Out of those one hundred fifty people at least half must be male. Take those seventy-five men, and probably thirty-seven of them are in my target age range. Out of those thirty-seven at least eighteen should be single. At least nine of those eighteen probably have zero criminal history, good jobs, and are maybe Jewish. Perhaps you should start talking me up at all of your AA meetings? Seems like an untapped market."

I had to make everything a joke, a trait I knew I'd inherited from my father. When you put both of us in the same car, we weren't capable of having a serious conversation. The truth was, I was moved by the meeting and for the first time since he started drinking, I was proud of my father. He was fighting, and in his own way he was running a marathon with his soul, since his legs could no longer carry him. He used a cane to help him around now, not all of the time but a lot of the time, on days when his walking was bad. His driving was allegedly fine, the issue was just his equilibrium. Mom had said he was going for more tests next week to see if maybe some of the heart or depression medications he was on might have been negatively impacting his neuropathy. But no one at AA seemed to judge him for it or notice it, really. He'd left his cane in the car and I'd noticed that he was slightly off-kilter without it. He was struggling and I could see that, but for the first time the struggle didn't look so ugly to me. I saw an odd beauty in it. When you collected a bunch of struggles and put them together in one room, the power and force was tremendous.

MILE 21

How's the twelve-year-old kid asshole doing I wonder. Does he think about me at every mile just like I think about him? Does he even know I exist? What's his actual name? Is he on Facebook? Is this weird? I'm losing my mind. Literally losing my mind. Less than six miles to go. I don't know what planet I'm on, I'm just running. Well, jogging actually if we're going to get technical. All I have to do is just finish this race. When I finish, I will not be rejected, my father will know he's loved and forgiven, our relationship will be rectified and all of my problems will be solved. Water. I need water. Why isn't there a water stop here? Do they just want people to die? Am I dying? What if I die of dehydration? What if I pass out from heat stroke? Running, well, jogging, speed-walking at a run. I've been running for almost four hours. Holy shit. Water. Swallow. Breathe.

—Providence Marathon, 2011.

"Excuse me, Miss! You dropped something!" As I dashed out of my building and onto Seventy-Second Street, a neighbor I'd never met before waved my breakfast bar in the air. I forced myself to turn around and put up a calm front as I walked back to the older gentleman, who was walking his grey toy poodle, and hurriedly but graciously took back my breakfast, which had fallen out of my bag and onto the ground. I needed to make it to Seventieth Street in the next two minutes to catch the next Second Avenue express bus downtown in order to be on time for work, though the odds were against me. It was nine-forty-two, there was no way I'd make it to the office by ten. There were maybe two mornings a year, on average, when I'd accidentally oversleep, having set my alarm for PM instead of AM, and that day was one of them.

I wished I'd worn flats and brought other shoes to change into, but that morning I couldn't be bothered. My feet pounded the pavement and I knew that every step I took was whittling away my heels, especially because I'm pigeon-toed. My body was moving so briskly that my skirt kept twisting around my waist so that the zipper that should've been in the back was by my navel. It was nearing October and probably one of the last bare-leg days of the year.

It was a beautiful day and everyone in Manhattan seemed to be outside and in my way. Second Avenue was lined with people dawdling, walking their dogs, or pushing strollers. Some were running home from their morning workouts, and the rest of us, who were obviously trying to get somewhere, dodged them as if they were potholes.

Fishing my cell out of my bag, I called my mom, a regular part of my heading to work routine. I got her voicemail. The bus stop was just two blocks ahead, but I felt like I'd never reach Seventieth Street. I heard the express bus behind me, its engine distinct. It passed me and I hitched my tote bag onto my shoulder and ran, groaning to let everyone within earshot know what a bad Wednesday morning I was having. That was standard behavior on my part, often times it relieved my anxiety when I alerted people that I was in a bad mood instead of just being in one. Suddenly, I stopped dead in my tracks when I saw a human body lying on the ground. The bus pulled away without me.

Having lived in New York City for ten or so years by that point, I'd seen a lot of bodies strewn about in my day, but something about that one was different. Maybe it was that he didn't actually look homeless. Shocked, I wondered if I was the only one who'd noticed the man on the ground. Everyone else was walking by as if they didn't see him. It was as if he were invisible to everyone but me. Maybe people were distracted by their phones, or in too much of a hurry, too jaded, or too self-involved to stop. Maybe they figured that the person was none of their business or not their problem and simply wanted to stay out of it. But that didn't mean he wasn't there.

He looked to be an elderly man, passed out in front of an apartment building door. He was on his back and his legs were twisted so that one knee was facing Second Avenue and the other was pointed at the sky. In his left hand was a set of keys and just above his right hand was a bottle of sorts, mostly shielded by a paper bag, but I could see that it was three-quarters empty. I desperately wanted to ignore and walk past him myself, like he didn't exist, but I couldn't. A fly buzzed around the man's head and I couldn't help but think that this man, whoever he was, could've been someone's father. He didn't look homeless, but he didn't look polished enough to be on his way to work. Under different circumstances that man could've been my father. His left ankle began to twitch against the concrete and I set my heavy bag down. I dialed 911.

"Hi. Yes, I'm calling from the corner of Seventy-First Street and Second Avenue. There's a man here who appears to have fallen and is now unconscious, right on the southeast side of the street. No I don't know who he is. Ten minutes? Okay, yes I can wait here. No I don't know his name. Maybe about sixty? Thanks."

It dawned on me that having agreed to wait for the ambulance to arrive meant that I was going to be very late for work. Perversely relieved that I at least had a solid excuse, I called my office to let my boss know my status. There was an awning attached the building next door and I moved under it, out of the sun, and leaned against the brick wall of the building, taking a few deep breaths and adjusting my skirt. A young woman close to my age stopped.

"What's going on?" she asked.

"I'm not really sure," I told her. He was just lying there so I called 911. The ambulance should be here soon."

"Okay, good. So at least someone is doing something."

"Yeah."

The girl walked away as if the man was my responsibility, though I supposed I'd made it so. A few minutes passed and I heard sirens coming from the north and looked to see the lights of the ambulance flashing. I was surprised by how slowly it was moving, trying to navigate its way through Second Avenue traffic. My cell phone rang.

"Hello?"

"Yeah, hi," a man responded with a very thick Brooklyn accent. "We got a call from this number. Something about a man down on Seventy-First Street?"

"Yes, that was me who called."

"Great. Where are you exactly, ma'am?"

"I'm wearing a black skirt and a white top (as if I were performing in a middle school choir concert), on the southeast corner of Seventy-First Street and Second Avenue." Faced the direction of the ambulance and waved.

"I see ya." He hung up. When the ambulance pulled over, two men got out. One of them walked up to me and introduced himself as Mike. Mike was hot and looked to be around thirty. Maybe I should be calling 911 more often. His calm demeanor and seeming lack of urgency were surprising. His partner took his time walking over to the man on the ground, then squatted down and poked him on the shoulder. The man on the ground emitted a deep groan. Mike went over to assist and I watched the two paramedics shake the man awake and help him to his feet. The man stumbled and couldn't form a coherent sentence.

"You smell that?" Mike said to his partner.

"Yeah. Must've had a lot to drink. Shit."

All I could think about was my father. I hoped some girl in Boston would have done this for him if it were ever needed. Now that the ambulance was there, folks stopped and stared. Probably because the man clearly had help, pedestrians stopped to experience the excitement and were no longer threatened by the possibility of responsibility. Mike and his partner started walking the man over to the ambulance but he dragged his feet in resistance.

"Sir, what's your name?" Mike asked him. The man groaned again and leaned on Mike's shoulder and together they headed in the direction of the ambulance. My brain flashed back to the image of my father inching a walker down the halls of Beverly Hospital right after I ate his vanilla pudding.

The EMTs were able to get the man to take a seat on the back ledge of the ambulance, but he couldn't seem to support himself so Mike sat next to him, propping him up. It was like a newborn baby who hadn't yet developed the strength to hold up his head. A few minutes later I was told they were taking the man to St. Vincent's Hospital; he had severe alcohol poisoning.

"Would you like to ride with him in the ambulance?" Mike asked me. I stood there looking into his life-saving blue eyes.

"What?"

"Would you like to ride with him in the ambulance?"

"No. That's okay. I wanted to make sure he was okay but I have no connection to him whatsoever."

"You did a good thing today. Most people don't call. This man potentially owes you his life. If he'd been out there much longer he could've been a goner."

"It was nothing. I should get to work. Thanks, Mike." I parted ways with my future EMT husband, figuring that he had my number from the emergency call if he ever wanted to reach out. I took a deep breath and I finished the final block to my original destination where I waited for the express bus to take me downtown.

Almost two hours late, I finally arrived at work and kept to myself for most of the day, not in the mood to talk. I felt proud that I might've been responsible for giving that man a second chance, but

I was deeply bothered when I thought of his hypothetical daughter and how she must feel. I was that hypothetical daughter, and for the first time, I actually felt sorry for myself, a luxurious sensation I didn't ever feel like I deserved. But something was different about that day. I actually felt a glimmer of compassion for myself.

The next morning, on my way to the office, I passed the same stop on Seventy-First and Second expecting to experience a moment of pride, a moment of feeling like I'd done some good in the world. Instead I looked down to see the same man from the day before in the same exact same position, one leg facing up, the other pointed at Second Avenue, with another bottle of vodka on the ground, just out of reach. What the hell? I did a double take to confirm it was the same man. And it was, indeed, the same man whose life I'd potentially saved and who had made me two hours late for work the day prior. How was he back there? Stunned, upset, and angry, I pretended not to notice him and kept walking.

MILE 22

For the greater part of this mile there've been a surplus of orange cones guiding the course and I can't seem to turn corners without hitting them. Just get there, no matter what is in the way. I pass a row of houses and a rogue group of teenagers dressed in black are cheering me on. Out of nowhere I start flailing my arms and cheering for myself like a crazy person. I even give one of them a high-five. "I'm running a fucking marathon!" I yell. They cheer back. I don't know what that was. I'm back inside my skin now and pretend that never happened. That was spastic. Spastic and yet fabulous. At this very moment, with no strings attached to life, I feel free to say, think, or do whatever I want which is amazing. I'm free. It's almost like the sensation I experience when I'm on stage. Only, I'm out of breath. My head is pounding. It occurs to me that I haven't had to go to the bathroom and I figure it's probably because I'm sweating so much. Maybe I'll just tell my dad I love him. Or, is it possible I won't have to say anything at all? Time is running out.

—Providence Marathon, 2011.

My phone was vibrating from inside my bag as I was getting my hair done in a dressing room at a gay bar in Hell's Kitchen. An incoming text message. Although I'd promised myself that I'd tune out all distractions, the suspense of that pending message is killing me. Christopher stuck a few more bobby pins in my hair and I discretely reached for my purse.

"Do you want me to get your phone?" asked Christopher, about to take a curling iron to the back of my head.

"How did you know?"

"I thought you were going to put that thing away and focus on your show!"

Christopher was a former cast member of *Dr. Dolittle.* While touring the country together for six months we became fast friends and one of the best things about him, aside from his wit and loyal friendship, was that he'd since become a professional hair stylist. We'd had a grand old time on tour. Since the only thing on our calendars were the actual shows, he'd spend hours giving me elaborate hairstyles that would match whatever town we were in. Applebee's in Leesburg, Virginia had never seen such an exquisite beehive.

"Who's the text from?" he asked in a playful tone, as if he thought it might be from a dude.

"It's from my mom."

"What does it say?"

"We're here." I sat there taking special notice of the word, we. She didn't say *I'm* here but *we're* here. That meant my dad had made it to New York City. I hadn't seen my parents since Christmas, six months ago.

"So your dad must be feeling better," Christopher suggested. Over the past several months my dad's walking had taken a turn for the worse. My mom said he used his cane daily and his doctors still said it was his neuropathy, and probably a combination of the effects of the alcoholism on top of thirty-two marathons, which taxed the body as well.

"I guess so!" I told Christopher.

After two years of auditioning with my Equity card in New York City, I'd booked little work aside from the occasional reading. It was unclear to me if it was my lack of experience, or my seasoned competition, or maybe even the economic crisis of 2008. Or worse, maybe I just wasn't good enough to play in the big leagues. Though I was getting call-backs for a small number of Broadway shows, I just hadn't been able to get cast. And it was hard. There were days, even on antidepressants, I came home in tears because nobody would let me do what I loved to do, which was simply to perform. I often thought of my mom's advice, about how there will always be people who are better than I am and there will always be people who I'm better than, but lately, I just felt like everyone else was better. No matter how many miles I ran per day, or how many deals I closed at work, or how many hours per week I spent in vocal lessons or in dance classes, I just couldn't book a show. And it wore on me. There were days I'd come home one hundred percent convinced that the only reason I got cast in *Dr. Dolittle* was because I fit the costume and that getting my Equity card was a total fluke. Or that the production of *Grease* I did right out of college was only because I'd gone to school with the director. There were sleepless nights, even with pills, when I'd lay awake wondering if I was delusional, thinking I could sing and that maybe I sounded better in my head than I did to anyone actually listening. I was questioning everything. Why were my friends booking Broadway but I wasn't? Was I untalented or is it possible I was just bad at auditioning (which wouldn't have been the worst thing)?

What was really difficult for me was that my ability to do what I was most passionate about in the entire world was completely at the mercy of others' judgement. Rejection is a tricky thing in the best of times, and while in the world of performance you need to program yourself to not take things personally —sometimes it *was* about fitting the costume or having the right hair color or voice type, for better or for worse —but it felt so personal because you often bore your soul for strangers in that audition room.

There was a morning several months earlier, around the time I was getting ready to go home for Christmas, when Martin, a friend from college, called me to catch up for the first time in years. After covering all major life updates such as living situations and day jobs, we laughed for a solid ten minutes as I regaled him with tales of my Internet dating life. These included the following: A story about a guy who told me he had a huge confession to make, which wound up being that he had an eighth-grade reading level, a gentleman who turned out to be looking for a swinging partner, and a man who showed up to our first date high, ordered a round of drinks, and ran out of the restaurant five minutes into the date, and stuck me with the tab, claiming he was "bugging out!" Martin pointed out that it seemed like landing a good date and an acting gig were equally challenging for me at the time, and that maybe I could combine the two. He suggested I write my own one-woman show on the topic and offered to direct it. He said I should invite casting directors and agents and it would give me a chance to perform, and maybe even get me seen by some industry.

So I spent the first part of 2010 writing my one-woman cabaret about Internet dating, was called *Matchmaker Matchmaker I'm Willing to Settle!* And I have to say it was the first thing in my life that I'd created, aside from my eleventh-grade history fair project entitled "Showboat the Musical: A Frontier in American History," that I was authentically proud of. (For the record, my Showboat project did win the district, regional, and state history fairs of 2001.) It was opening night of *Matchmaker…* and I was performing my show for the first time at The Laurie Beechman Theatre, a prominent cabaret club on the west side. I'd invited my mother to that performance months earlier. She'd always wanted me to do a one-woman show.

"Here, love. Let me touch up your lips." Christopher the hairdresser was dating Christopher the makeup artist, whom he'd met online shortly after we got back from our tour. They billed themselves as a styling duo and went by "The Christophers." The two of them buzzed around me, working seamlessly as a unit to perfect every curl and eyelash. One Christopher sprayed the back of my hair while the other took a pair of tweezers to make sure my fake eye lashes were perfectly in place, while I kept ruminating over that text. It wasn't that I'd expected my dad to miss my show, but the Beechman was technically in a club, which meant the show was in a bar. On top of that, there was a two-drink minimum. I supposed he could order two Diet Cokes.

Dad had been sober for almost three years and I was nervous about him being at a bar. I felt a little guilty I'd chosen to do my show there, but at the same time he didn't have to come, though I was glad he did. When my mom and I chatted the day before, she'd warned me that my dad's walking had gotten significantly worse, and his neuropathy was triggered when he walked long distances. That's why I'd never imagined he'd come to New York City. Though on the flip side, I couldn't picture my mom leaving him at home for a weekend, given Puerto Rico, and there was no way in hell she'd miss my show. There was a staircase that lead down to the theatre where my show was being held and I worried about how my dad would descend those stairs. What if he couldn't get down to the theatre and had to wait upstairs at the bar? What if he fell? What if the bartender accidentally served him alcohol? Luckily Christopher (makeup) interrupted my train of thought.

"All right. Christopher just wants to touch up your mascara but your hair is done!"

"Awesome. Thank you guys both so much."

"It's our pleasure. You know we love you," said Christopher (hair).

"Honey, let me just borrow your lashes for two more seconds," said Christopher (makeup). He then held a mirror in front of my face and for the first time in a long time I liked what I saw. I looked beautiful. I was excited to perform and even more thrilled that both of my parents were there. For a split-second I felt like I was back in that black and white checkered dress with the cherry on the breast pocket, only instead of singing a Disney song, I was about to sing a series of show tunes that revolved around my tragic sex life and Internet dating fiascos. Several of my friends who'd been privy to the material asked me if it was weird for me to be talking about my dating life in front of my parents and family members in general. The truth was that thought hadn't popped into my brain until other people put it there. But I didn't want to censor myself just because some of the material was uncomfortable, and to be clear, none of it was for shock value. It was all genuine and I was of the school of thought that if it was real, then it was okay.

A few minutes later, I was alone in a stairwell that lead to the stage and gradually started to panic. What if my jokes were too raunchy for my parents? I started to run through them all in my head. Usually in a production that someone else wrote, you might fret about a note that's difficult to hit or making sure you don't miss a dance step, or that the costume change went quickly enough. But I was using my words, my stories, and my song choices. That show had me written all over it. Vulnerability at its finest, and it hadn't occurred to me until the house was open that I should be scared. But I guess at the end of the day, I'd always strived to do what scared me. The house went dark and my accompanist was already on stage. Terror washed over me the second before the lights went up. What if the audience thinks I'm stupid? What if no one laughs? What if my stories *were* too personal? Would everyone see my knees shaking and be able to tell how nervous I was?

"And now The Laurie Beechman Theatre is proud to present, Nikki MacCallum!" The sheer volume of cheers both put me at ease and made me feel like I had expectations to live up to at the same time, and I smiled and stepped on stage. That next hour was one of the best of my life. It was my show and no one could interrupt. I'd created it and no one could touch me. I was telling these true stories and people were laughing. I felt understood and relatable, but more importantly I felt free. At the time, I had no idea what was in store for *Matchmaker...* and had I known, that hour might not have been as enjoyable as it was. That hour took me back to why I loved performing in the first place. I got to tell my stories in a dark theatre with people watching to make people laugh, hopefully make people feel less alone, and to me, that has always been and always will be the epitome of home.

In the first row, my mother must've been on at least her second glass of Prosecco. My father had a Diet Coke and was wearing a loud orange sweater that was hideous, but the candle on the table illuminated his proud smile. The room was filled with loving faces; even Suzie and Megan had taken the train from Boston to New York to come see me. As I took my final bow, the audience applauded, my mom leading the charge, and everyone stood up, except for my father, but I knew why. I energetically said my thank yous and exited the stage, heading up the stairs to the bar as quickly as possible, so I could have two drinks of my own. My mom was already there, standing right next to the entrance, and was first in line to give me a big hug.

"Nikki! That was wonderful! I'm so proud of you! I always knew you'd be great at cabaret. There are some cute men at this bar! Maybe you won't be single forever!"

"Mom, this is a gay bar."

"So what?"

"You're right. So, what?" We had a big laugh and I gave her another hands-off hug. I wanted to ask her where Dad was, but my friends and other family members who'd come to see the show were trying to get my attention.

"Hi, Nikki! Congratulations!" Charlotte gave me a hug; she'd also driven in from Boston. "By the way, I tried to fix you up with the bartender but it turned out he's gay, too. Jesus Christ. No wonder you're single. Everyone in this town is gay. Everyone at CWTF is unemployed. You really can't win." I laughed. I looked around the room and saw Suzie, Analise, Uncle Dale, Aunt Moira, and Ray and Donna. Everyone showed up. Eric signaled to me from the other end of the bar to offer me a drink.

My mom resurfaced after a quick lap around the room. "Hey, Nik!"

"Hey! Where's Dad?"

"He's fine. He's still in the theatre. I told you his walking hasn't been great and when he sits for long periods of time he just needs a few minutes before he's able to stand up."

"Is he okay?"

"Yes. He's fine. I just went to check on him. He snapped at me a little and I think he just wants to be left alone right now. Mind my own business! That's what Al-Anon keeps teaching me," she said with a laugh. I hadn't seen my mom that relaxed in a long time. I looked at her flipping her hair back, drinking a glass of wine, being the life of the party and I saw a glimpse of the woman I remembered from my childhood. The woman who at some point had been abducted and plagued by panic and worry.

"You're not worried?"

"Sure I am, but it's out of my control." I always loved the "it's out of my control" game.

"That's true." The Christophers attacked me with a giant group hug.

"Congratulations, Nikki! Hi, Mom! Are you so proud of your daughter?"

"Oh hi, Christopher and Christopher. I am!"

My mother was occupied by all of my friends, who've always adored her, and many of whom had gotten to spend significant amounts of time with her when visiting CWTF over the years. While she held court, I went to check on my dad.

The theatre was full of abandoned tables and chairs in front of the unlit stage. It was an empty house except for my father, whose back was to me as he sat there paralyzed, just staring at that empty stage.

I felt compelled to help him but he might've been embarrassed to have his daughter see him in that condition. I stood there for another moment, watching him not make the slightest movement or show the slightest intention of getting up, and then slipped away to find my mother in the next room. She was still at the bar chatting with all of my friends.

"Hey, Nik! I love your friends, I love New York! I'm so happy to be here." She was like an overstimulated puppy. The most secure bank vault in the entire world wouldn't have been able to contain her energy, and it was both overwhelming and amazing. A few minutes went by and I looked over to see my dad's silhouette, as he slowly used his cane to enter into the bar. He was looking at the ground, probably in an attempt to not draw attention to himself. He came over to me and made the Roo paws and I made them back.

"I'm a proud, proud Roo!" I petted him on the head and asked if he'd like me to get him a chair.

"No. I'm fine."

"Are you sure?"

"I like standing!" He took another step forward deeper into the bar area, reaching for a nearby stool for support.

Mom came bulldozing through the crowd towards her husband. "Let's get you a cab and go back to the hotel."

"I'm fine," he said.

"You can barely walk."

"Just leave me alone."

MILE 23

My pace has surely dropped to a sixteen-minute mile, not that I was ever really keeping track. Who gives a fuck. To my right I see a child on the sidewalk. She's running around carrying this big white balloon that says "CONGRATULATIONS" in big bold block letters. She clings to it, while skipping about in her little yellow and white checkered dress, which I kind of want to spill ketchup on. Oh, ketchup. What's going to happen when she lets go of the balloon? Where will it go? Will it float up so high in the atmosphere that it will cease to exist? Maybe it'll lose some air and fall to the ground. I feel high. I wish I were high. Misery. With every stride the skin in between my thighs is ripped apart. My body is on autopilot, like its immune to the pain. The scars will be worth it. The closer I get to the end of the marathon, the more it feels like I'm running away from something than I am running toward something. My body is being transported through space by legs that don't feel like mine. I'm so hot. I'm cold and I'm so cold from the breeze stroking my sweat under the sun, that I'm hot. I wonder if the cellulite I'm insecure about on my ass has tightened at all over the past five or so hours. All of a sudden, I hear an unmistakable "ooo" vowel accompanied by wind chimes. Donna Summer herself. "Last Dance" has arrived, three miles early. Is my time really that slow? You know what, I don't care. I will listen to "Last Dance" ten times if I have to and it will guide me through the end of this race.

—Providence Marathon, 2011.

Fourth of July weekend was always my favorite part of the summer because it was usually hot, it was a week before my birthday, (I'd be twenty-six the next week), and when it was over I still had most of July and all of August ahead of me. That July 4th in 2010 was particularly memorable because I'd taken a week off from work to vacation at CWTF and had invited Eric to join me.

I'd already returned from the kitchen with a frozen chocolate chip cookie and was enjoying the sun while attempting the crossword in the most recent issue of *Star* magazine. I'd always loved the *Star* magazine crossword and perpetually felt a need to defend it because there's a huge misconception that it's "trashy" or "easy" or "based on fluff." While it isn't *The New York Times*, completing the *Star* magazine crossword was something I did consider an accomplishment.

As I continued to wrack my brain for the answer to five across, Aunt Moira napped in her chair beside Charlotte, who was painting her nails pink, while Eric tinkered with the squirt gun we'd bought at Walmart the day before. My mother was sitting at her usual table on the porch reading the self-help book of the week, and Aunt Donna was eating a bagel drowned in butter. My father would be back from his AA meeting shortly; he'd been sober for a full three years at that time.

I tried to forget that earlier that morning, around two AM, I'd caught a glimpse of my father stumbling naked to the bathroom. It was odd that he was walking around without clothes on knowing Eric was staying with us; I figured he'd be a little more modest around guests. Last night he'd left the table halfway through dinner with a stomach bug. Maybe he was just getting old and not thinking straight.

"What time does Dad get back from his meeting?" I asked my mom.

"Oh, he's actually upstairs sleeping. He's still not feeling well. Poor thing."

"That's too bad. I hope he's feeling well enough to enjoy the fireworks later today."

"I'm sure he will be. Eric, tell me about your life." She directed her attention towards my best friend. "Are you dating anyone?" my mother asked him taking a break from *The Untethered Soul*.

"Well, there are a few men I see here and there."

"So that's a no." Mom cut him off and they both laughed.

A Diet Coke craving overcame me and I was hungry for another frozen chocolate chip cookie. Well, not necessarily hungry for one, but I felt like putting one in my mouth, so I got up and walked into the kitchen. On my way to gluttony, I ran into my dad who was slowly descending the stairs, relying heavily on the banister for support. I uttered a soft and noncommittal hello. Instead of engaging me in further conversation, he unsteadily and lethargically made his way out onto the porch, motioning to my mother to follow him around to the side of the house for a private conversation. He wasn't using his cane, which always infuriated my mother and me. To be fair, at that point, he truly didn't need it all of the time, but it was clear he hated using it. I could see them through the kitchen window and the way they were standing allowed me to see my mother's facial expression quite clearly. Her eyes got wide as they talked and her

Dry Run

forehead started to tense up, then my dad turned in the direction of his car. I stood there in the kitchen, at the window overlooking the driveway. He got in the car and backed out of the driveway. Feeling uneasy, I returned to the back porch to talk to my mom and get a status update.

Apparently, my dad had decided to go back to Hamilton for the day. Despite it being the Fourth of July, he felt an urgent need for some alone time and wanted to take care of the lawn and gardens back home. My suspicion rose and turned into anger. Not knowing what to do with it, I directed it at my mother.

"And he has to do that specifically on the Fourth of July?" I asked. My tone sounded harsh, it was like someone else was saying the words that were coming out of my mouth and I couldn't control the cutting sound. "I came down here to spend time with my family. It was just odd to me that he'd choose to leave today."

"Nikki, he'll be back tomorrow, and honestly, I don't know what else to tell you, He said he needed a break from everyone, which I can understand. I can't control him. I'm not his prison guard. He's a grown man and can make his own decisions. Also, you have Eric here. It's not like Dad would get to spend that much time with you anyway." She wasn't wrong, and maybe that was why her dig nipped at my gut, making me feel guilty, like it was my fault dad didn't think it was worth it to stick around. At least that's how I took it.

"Okay. I just think it's a little strange, Mom. Don't you?" I could hear myself getting defensive, my words sounded abrupt.

"Nikki, I just don't know what to tell you."

"How's he feeling?"

"I think he's still feeling under the weather."

"Okay, well I guess that's that."

"We'll still have a great time tonight!" Her pitch got higher, masking her subtle worry that was never so subtle to me.

It made me sad that Dad didn't think he'd be missed. Or maybe he knew he'd be missed, but chose to leave anyway. What was going on in his head? Maybe nothing. Maybe my fear that he'd relapsed and was going to drink himself silly at our house in Hamilton was a reality. That afternoon my mom started pounding chicken breasts in preparation for the big holiday barbeque. On my way to the bathroom, I caught a glimpse of her taking a mallet to the meat. Her back was to me and she was looking out the kitchen window more than she was focusing on the meat she was pulverizing. I was worried she was hitting it a little too hard, but I didn't want to interrupt whatever she was working out on that poor dead bird.

In the evening, after our legendary cocktail hour, Uncle Ray took my father's usual place at the grill. We all gathered the paper flatware strewn about the dining room table and Aunt Donna serenaded us with a grand and patriotic rendition of "Grand Old Flag." It was nice to see her repertoire had expanded. Moira and Dale spent most of the dinner debating whether or not to get ice cream once they finished eating, and after the meal we all retreated to the porch to watch fireworks light up Buzzard's Bay. Everyone at CWTF was asleep by ten after a long day in the sun and too much food and fun.

The next day my father didn't answer his cell, taunting me with an eerie sense of déjà vu. He made contact for the first time around six-thirty that night when he pulled into the driveway. I was taking an outdoor shower at the time. My parents couldn't see me but I knew I'd hear everything they were about to say.

"Why haven't you been returning my calls? I thought you were dead!" My mom attacked him before he could even get out of the car. I'm glad she said it so I didn't have to.

"Calm down. I lost my phone," he retorted in a voice that was biting and unkind.

"You *lost* your phone?" Her voice was getting higher and her breathing more audible.

"Yes." He nearly shouted, which was completely out of character for the soft spoken and docile man that was my father.

"You couldn't call me from the house and tell me that?" Her words beat him harder than she had beat yesterday's chicken.

"Jesus, I lost it after I left the house today." That didn't make sense to me— he wasn't answering last night —but my mother didn't seem to think of that.

"Where did you lose it?" She touched her forehead and it was hard to tell whether she was blocking what was left of the sun from her eyes or simply reacting to him.

"Don't worry. We'll just buy another one."

"Where did you lose your phone?"

"For the last time, calm down. I wasn't feeling well on my way down here so I pulled into a parking lot at a Burger King to use the restroom and I left my phone in the front seat. I accidentally forgot to roll the windows up and some kid must've reached in and stolen it." He sounded more assertive and annoyed with each word, his volume crescendoed. I could see through the crack in the fence in the shower that he was looking around, probably trying to spot an escape route from the jaws of accountability.

"Who would do that?"

"I don't know."

"Maybe if we call it a few times the person will pick up."

"Maybe," my father said, raising his eyebrows and creating more wrinkles in his forehead. He looked past my mother out at the ocean.

I conditioned my hair a second time to occupy myself in that shower for as long as possible. After my parents went into the house, I turned off the water. Eric and I went out for seafood and my parents were asleep when we returned.

The next morning my mom asked if she and I could go for a walk on the beach for some mother-daughter bonding time. I rolled my eyes but I went because I knew it meant a lot to her, though something about the word "bond" made me uncomfortable.

"How's Dad doing?" I asked when we were a good three hundred meters or so away from the houses. I didn't really want to have that conversation, but what I hated even more than conversations with my mother about my father's alcoholism or self-help conquests was small talk.

"He's still got the flu or something, threw up last night before bed. You should really go and talk to him, Nik. I think that would make him feel better."

"You really think he's sick?" I asked, trying to gage how far in denial she was before pushing the issue further.

"What's that supposed to mean?"

"You don't think it's weird he left on the Fourth of July and lost his phone?"

"No, I don't think it's weird. He needed a break from everyone yesterday," she sounded defensive, "What was I supposed to tell him? No, you can't go? He's a grown man and I feel like I've already taken so much away from him. Are you and Eric having fun?" It wasn't like my mom to totally avoid an issue. But I guessed ultimately I wanted to dance around it just as much as she did, so I told her about Eric and my latest trip to the drug store.

A part of me wanted to come out and say it—that it was crystal clear to me that Dad had undoubtedly relapsed. But I hesitated because my mom's denial seemed so fierce that I didn't know if I could pierce it. And in a way I felt like it was my job to protect her from the panic and fear. Perhaps I should've considered speaking to my father directly and not even involve my mother. I needed to think about it. When we returned to the porch after our walk, my mother got a call on her cell phone. She immediately answered.

"Hello? Yes, this is my husband's phone! You're where? You found it where? Off of route 495? Grove Street? The Cabin? Are you open today? If I come in the next few hours will you be there? You're a pizza place? Great, and what's your name? Lisa." My mom was practically shouting and completely unaware of the loud volume of her voice.

"Someone found Dad's phone!" She yelled manically as if she was announcing the results of a sporting event. She ran into the house and I could hear her feet banging with every step. "Are you awake?!" she yelled to my dad as she charged up the stairs.

I looked at Charlotte who was quietly reading her issue of *The National Enquirer.*

"I guess someone found the phone!" she said. We looked at each other, our laughter breaking even more tension than I initially realized existed. I pulled out my phone and looked up The Cabin. It was in fact in Middleboro, on Grove Street. The bar was open every day from noon until midnight. I thought about pulling my mom aside and mentioning that small detail to her, but she just seemed like she was on a manic train to The Cabin and nothing could derail her.

My parents departed for Middleboro, leaving Charlotte, Eric, and me to hit the beach. About an hour after they left, Aunt Moira pulled up a chair to join the porch party.

"I heard they found your dad's phone," Moira said. We all laughed.

"How did you know?" I said sarcastically, since my mom basically announced it to the entire street.

"Word travels fast." We sat in silence for a few seconds, highly unusual for that boisterous clan. The strain of everyone's thoughts hung in the air, but nobody was ready to break the heavy silence. I knew we were all thinking the same thing—that my dad was drinking again. Nobody dared to be the first one to make the suggestion. Probably nobody felt it was their place.

"Well this has been fun," Moira announced after a few minutes passed, "but I'm going back next door to make some appetizers." She headed to the other house and I sat there on the porch for a good hour, staring in the direction of the Cape Cod Canal while Eric and

Charlotte read their respective literature and tried to block out the distracting sounds of summer.

Later that afternoon, Eric was napping upstairs and Charlotte had gone for a walk on the beach, leaving me on the porch to deal with my parents alone.

"Hi, Nik!" My mother came gliding around the corner. "We found the phone!" My dad slunk along behind her and entered the house, this time using his cane.

"Cool. What's up with Dad?"

"I've told you, he has a stomach bug and isn't feeling well. He actually threw up on the drive home. I just feel so bad for him."

"Mom, are you sure he's okay?" My threshold for tolerance of denial was getting thinner and I was about to reach a breaking point.

"Nikki," she said with a subtext indicating not to push her on this, "we're just so glad we have his phone. He just got this one and you know how expensive iPhones are these days.

We're just so blessed that this woman found the phone!"

"Where did she find it?"

"In the parking lot of her restaurant. Dad had stopped at Burger King on his way down here and left his phone on the front seat when he went to use the restroom. He must've forgotten to roll up his windows and some kid took the phone and the dumped it in this nearby parking lot. We're just so lucky. Having to buy a new one would've been awful."

Later that afternoon, before cocktail hour, Eric and I were chatting on the porch when Dad pulled out of the driveway on his way to an AA meeting. He backed into a parked car, shifted into drive, made a left, and kept going. Not wanting to involve my mother, I ran down and apologized profusely to the owner of the car, who had innocently parked for a few minutes to take in the view of the bay. I gave him my number since I didn't have my father's insurance information. At first he was angry and spewed out, "What idiot would do this and just drive off?" I hated that man for calling my dad an idiot. He didn't know the half of it. We were able to resolve things quietly for the time being since not much damage was done to his car. I decided that if I got a phone call from him, I'd deal with it then.

MILE 24

I'm barely moving forward, but I'm moving. And forward is better than backward, or even sideways. I'm never doing this again. My parents are insane. I run to prove to myself that I can. I run to prove to others that I can. I run to protect myself so that if I fail at things that really matter, I can at least say that I ran a fucking marathon. Based on the lack of spectators and runners I'm clearly going to be one of the last to finish, but it doesn't mean I won't finish and it doesn't mean I won't win. Focus on Dad. This is for him. When my father sees me cross that finish line, I'll have won. I'm on the verge of tears due to physical exhaustion and I don't quite have a clear vision of how I'll make it to the end.

"What's your name?" a voice says behind me, interrupting Donna Summers. I turn my head and see a handsome dude next to me. "I'm Todd," he says. He must've seen me struggling.

"Is this your first marathon?" he asks. What gave it away?

"My first and last, yes." I can barely talk.

"Don't be so sure. You'll get addicted. I said the same thing after my first and now I'm on my sixth." Together, Todd and I pass the twenty-fourth mile marker and move onto twenty-five. Two more miles. I run two miles on a bad gym day. I can do this. Todd is pretty fucking slow, actually. I mean, this is my first marathon and I have big tits. Both valid excuses. This is Todd's sixth marathon and he's in great shape. Why is he so slow? He keeps talking to me and I'm so annoyed by the distraction that I'm onto mile twenty-five before I realize I'm already through twenty-four.

—Providence Marathon, 2011.

On a cold day in late December 2010, having upgraded from the Chinatown bus to a double-decker Megabus, I made the trip from New York to Boston. My mother picked me up and then risked worsening her driving record, speeding to get me to the nearest Pizzeria Uno in Revere before I died of hunger. It was Christmas, and usually I treasured getting to go home to spend a few days with my mom. I loved getting out of the city and being able to drive my old car that barely ran with the Act I cassette tape of *The Scarlett Pimpernel* stuck in it, and I looked forward to capitalizing on my mom's take-out ordering skills. Due to my dad's relapse, which was right on cue, I'd considered staying in New York for the holidays that year. I'd had actor friends who couldn't afford flights home, and Jewish friends who were so Jewish that they didn't go home for Christmas, and friends who were waiting tables and didn't get enough time off to actually leave the city. I could've stayed there and I thought about it, but my mother didn't deserve to be alone on Christmas. We arrived safely at our pizza haven, and my mother parked in her usual fashion, slanted across two parking spaces. Something she and my father had in common.

Once safely inside that glorious establishment, we had our pick of tables and I lead us to a booth, since everyone prefers booths. We slid in, sat across from one another, and I threw my purse on the far end of my seat.

"What do you want to drink?" asked a waiter whose nametag read Charles, seemingly annoyed that he had to do his job, probably typical of a waiter at a chain restaurant working a lunch shift in Revere.

"I actually think we're ready to order everything, Charles." Mom answered. We'd just sat down and I hadn't even had a chance to open my menu, but since my mother always ordered the same thing at every "Italian" restaurant we frequented, it didn't come as a shock to me that she knew what she wanted. I decided to go with a deep-dish pizza since carbs always made me feel better during times of stress.

"Happy Christmas Eve!" my mother told me.

"Yeah. You too." Charles returned to deliver our two tap waters, showing even less enthusiasm than before.

"Thanks, Charles," Mom said. "How old are you?"

"Mom!" I interjected. "Leave Charles alone. He's very busy." The restaurant was empty.

"Oh stop, Nikki. We're probably making Charles's day."

"I looked up at Charles, who was unsuccessfully scanning the room for perhaps another co-worker, while shifting his weight from side to side, looking like he was ready to hand in his resignation.

"Tough day, Charles?" I asked trying to alleviate some of the uneasiness my mom had created. No one knew better than I did that there was nothing worse than having to participate in a conversation when you just wanted to be left alone, but if Charles was going to act like such a downer, perhaps he should consider leaving the hospitality industry.

"I'll be back with your food in a bit." Charles made a quick exit stage left and my mother and I were left to face each other.

"How's Dad?" More or less depressed than Charles?"

My mother nearly fell over laughing. She'd have clung to any excuse to laugh that day, but she also thought everything that came out of my mouth was hilarious. She was always my best audience, even when my punch lines were weak, which was why I needed her at every performance of mine.

"I'm going to be honest, Nikki," she said. "He's not good. I've talked to a lot of my Al-Anon friends and my new therapist about my options because I just can't live like this anymore. I can't control him or change him, but I can choose to not be with him." In all the years of my father's alcoholism, I'd never heard her sound that serious about leaving him. In fact, the option had never come up at all.

"Are you going to get a divorce?" I asked, feeling like a little kid.

"I don't know. I don't know that it would financially make sense for us to get a divorce but it's an option. I've thought about separation."

"Where would Dad live? How would he support himself?"

"I'm not sure. There's a sober house for men in Newburyport that would take him. We also talked about staying married and renting him an apartment in Ipswich so we can each have our own space." The thought of my dad at a sober house for men was devastating. I wasn't entirely sure I knew what a sober house was, but I pictured it being an orphanage for older men with addiction problems. I imagined him in a room with four white walls, a small bed, occasionally making a trip to the common area where deadbeats were gathered around watching the Patriots game. My dad didn't belong there. He was a smart man, though he hadn't always acted smartly, and a kind man, though he hadn't always acted kindly. I didn't want him to go to a sober jail even though sometimes I hated parts of the person he'd become. But at the same time, I also hated parts of the person I'd become.

"And who is going to pay for that?" I asked her.

"I would. I've thought about selling the house and getting something smaller. I could use the money to rent Dad and myself separate apartments. The big problem I'm struggling with right now is that your father is currently refusing to go back to rehab so my options seem a bit limited."

"What do you mean? Where is he now?"

"Right now he's in a bed at Lahey Clinic in Burlington. Our insurance covers a ten-day in-patient rehab program that he could go to once he gets out of Lahey, but he doesn't want to go."

"What do you mean he doesn't *want* to go? He's always gone before."

"He's a grown man. I can't force him to go. I just count my blessings that right now, today, at this very moment, I'm okay. I'm relieved he's going to be in a hospital for a few days so I don't have to worry about him falling. I don't remember the last time I slept through the night. You don't know what it's like lying awake listening for a crash, just waiting for him to fall on the way to the bathroom." Her words pained me. My father fell a lot at that point, even sober. Since I'd been relying on medication to help me sleep for the last few years, I couldn't imagine the insomnia that would ensue just waiting for your husband to fall. I thought of the sleepless nights I endured before my sleeping medication when I'd lie awake worrying. Would I die alone? Would I get fired? Would I ever be happy? That seemed minimal compared to what my mother must've gone through, lying there counting down the hours until morning came to the rescue. *Will my husband die tonight? Will I wake up to find my husband immobile on the floor with blood gushing from where he banged his head? Will I make it through the night? One night at a time. One day at a time.* That's what I imagined must've run through my mother's head when she was trying to sleep. Charles brought us silverware, which I hoped indicated that our food was on the way.

"Hey, Charles," my mother and I both said, unplanned in our unison. Clearly wanting nothing to do with us, he quickly retreated to the kitchen. Eventually our food came and we spent the rest of the meal talking about my dating life or lack thereof. If there was anything that might've been more depressing than my father's alcohol addiction, it was my dating life, and I was happy to provide my mother with some comic relief.

"This is more fodder for your show!" she said after I rattled off two recent dating stories, one about a man who'd used his kitchen sink as a shoe closet, and another about a guy who'd claimed to be on Iran's Olympic air hockey team. I'd done a second performance of *Matchmaker* ... that past fall and one of the producers I'd initially invited actually came! I'd taken a page from my recruiting job and blindly reached out to producers based on names I'd seen in playbills from various Broadway shows, exactly how I tried to get business from law firms when recruiting. I realized the formula I was learning at my day job was completely transferrable and applicable to my passion. The producer who came told me that my concept for *Match-*

maker... had legs and that I should consider writing it into an ensemble musical with an original score, which might do very well in the Off-Broadway market. After a series of meetings, Martin, my college friend who'd helped me write and directed the cabaret, and I teamed up with Brendan, a musical theatre composer around our age. The three of us had been writing an original script and score for *Matchmaker Matchmaker I'm Willing to Settle!"* the musical. We decided to keep the title but had transformed the piece from a one-woman cabaret with non-original music to a four-person musical with a full script and original songs. Our first reading of that new version would take place in New York City in January. The one-woman show version that Martin and I had created was soon nominated for a MAC (Manhattan Association of Cabaret) Award. We'd find out the results in a few months. My mom continued to tell me how proud she was and at the end of the meal shared her plan for us to both visit Dad at Lahey on Christmas Day. I had mixed feelings. I was furious and part of me wanted to drown him in vodka myself until he went down with his disease, but more than anything I truly felt sad for him. I'd watched that man fight to kick that disease for nearly twenty years and he just couldn't seem to do it. Yet somehow he was still alive, which did count for something.

It was Christmas morning and thick flakes of snow drifted from the sky, coating my dark hair. Instead of waking up to the traditional Christmas morning rituals, at nine o'clock my mother and I were rushing across the parking lot to the front entrance of the Lahey clinic, moving as fast as we could in order to stay dry. Traffic was light because of the holiday so our travels were considerably easy despite the weather. My stomach was growling; we didn't stop for food because my mother was nervous about the drive, she wanted to get it over with. Though I'd always looked forward to a winter white Christmas, this was not the magical one I'd envisioned.

Sliding across the ice-covered parking lot, I tried to figure out for myself what it was exactly that I wanted to say to my father. This relapse felt different than the others and my gut was telling me that it might be the one that did him in. Being his only child, the onus was on *me* to come up with some life-altering piece of wisdom that would save him, at least that's how it felt. I'd been in that position many times before, but with the gravity of that particular situation, being Christmas and all, my mind went blank. The doors to the clinic opened automatically and we charged in, stomping the snow off of our boots.

Like a mirage in a desert, I saw it over to the left. It was more beautiful than I'd ever expected it to be: the hospital cafeteria. Mom and I decided to make a quick pit stop before going to see Dad. I snagged myself a bagel and she got coffee. While standing in line, my mom placed her coffee on the counter. When she went to get change out of her purse, she accidentally knocked over the cup with her elbow and the coffee spilled everywhere.

"Watch it, lady!" some man exclaimed walking past us on his way to the cereal shelf.

"Sir," I said, "please don't be mean to my mom. It's Christmas." It was funny how I was so rude to my mother all of the time, but when someone else gave her a hard time, I got extremely defensive. My mom started to cry while apologizing to the woman at the cash register. Once my mom collected herself, she led me out of the cafeteria; in the end, she decided against another coffee, she was jittery enough. We made our way down the hall to Dad's room, taking our time, as if both of us were attempting to delay the inevitable, or at least I was. She'd been to Wing H Room 17 yesterday, before she picked me up at South Station.

There was a little hallway inside my father's room between the door and his bed and I stood there, letting my mom go in first. Through a big window at the opposite end of his room, I could see the snow still taking over the sky, blanketing it in white. My mom was talking to my dad but I couldn't register what they were saying. I stood there, immobilized, unable to go into the room and unable to run in the other direction.

After a few long seconds, I managed to put one foot in front of the other and timidly crept to the end of the hallway where I turned to see my father lying in a hospital bed hooked up to an IV. Barely able to look at him, I forced myself to see him, which felt partly like a cruel punishment, but I also didn't want to later regret not having seen him. What if he died? His body looked brittle under the hospital blanket; you could barely tell it was there. There was an oxygen machine at his side. He stared blankly at the wall in front of him, turned to take one look at me, raised his eyebrows so his eyes were wide, and lifted his right hand and formed the Twiddlebugs over the oxygen tank keeping him alive. It was appalling to me. He was trying to make light of the situation, trying to make me laugh with our game from decades ago, but that was the last straw. My mother was silent and I could no longer look directly at my dad so instead I focused on the brown stain on the wall just above his head. From what I could see, he looked child-like and lost, like a ten-year-old who had just stolen a toy from the neighbor and was waiting for his punishment.

"Hi, Nik!" he said cheerfully.

"Hi, Dad." I refused to match his chipper tone which I found utterly infuriating. Nauseating even.

"What's up? How was the trip home?"

"Fine," I said, only carrying on the small talk for sheer loss of what to say to him. Searching for the words that would rescue him, I tried to buy myself some time.

"How's work?"

He pushed me over the edge and I uncontrollably angrily retorted. "Dad, how are you having this conversation with me right now? Are we not going to acknowledge that you're sitting in a hospital bed hooked up to an IV?" I'd reached my breaking point. I couldn't do it anymore. I wouldn't visit him in a hospital again. For a split-second I thought that being firm with him might feel liberating, but it didn't at all. It felt forced and obligatory, kind of what I imagine it feels like to be a parent and having to reprimand a child who you love.

Instead of answering me, he picked up the newspaper sitting beside him and started reading it. My mother exited the room and left the two of us alone. My father was the most stubborn man I'd ever met. Not only did his apathy pain me, it disgusted me, it frustrated the hell out of me. I dug deep within wondering why? Why did his actions make me so furious? I couldn't fathom how someone could run thirty-two marathons full of hills and turns, and not be capable of restricting their alcohol intake. Just don't drink. It seemed so simple to me.

During that piercingly uncomfortable silence, where I tried to search for words that would save him, I realized how similar he and I were, and it made me angry. I was enraged that the man who taught me how to fight had stopped fighting for himself. In between the steady beeping of the oxygen machine, I had a second of clarity. Though he resisted the darkness with deflection and sub-par jokes, it was in his essence, that ooze of depression, and in his half-droopy, half-shell-shocked eyes that I saw myself. Though I wasn't an alcoholic, I knew that depression well, and wrapped up in that depression was the gene that I inherited, of being able to push up hills and mountains and battle through thirty-two mara-thons. Grit.

Grit was the reason he was still alive and it was the same thing that gave me the ability to relentlessly audition and continue to push my dreams forward and to go to work and sell. I got my perseverance from him. Though sometimes the impetus for motiva-tion was depression, it was actually one of the greatest gifts a parent could pass onto their child. My heart flooded with empathy and an-ger and gratitude all at the same time, and instead of continuing to confront him sharply, my approach organically changed.

"How are the other patients? Made any friends?" My voice sounded and felt drastically different. I never thought a person could feel hate, compassion, disgust, and regret all at the very same time. He laughed and started coughing, suddenly wincing in pain. He'd fallen last week and broken a few ribs. Par for the course.

"Don't make me laugh, Nik," he said between heaves. "My ribs still hurt."

"It wasn't funny at all, really." He laughed more. Like a light switch flickering off, any hint of compassion I'd felt was gone. Causing him physical pain made me feel vindicated for the hurt he'd caused me.

"Do you want to live?" I asked him. It just came out and I immediately regretted saying it. I didn't really want to know the answer but at the same time I felt like the responsibility to make him want to get better was mine.

"Yes! Of course I do!" he answered, seemingly shocked, and without hesitation.

"What makes you happy in life?"

"The birds singing!"

"I'm so glad to see you're taking my visit seriously," I said sarcastically. "I don't think you want to get better. I think you're so miserably depressed and unless you figure out what makes you happy you're going to keep subconsciously wanting your life to be over." I knew, because we were the same. Angry and disappointed with myself that I'd just thrown out the greatest life cliché of all time, I stopped talking and stared back at the spot on the wall just above his head. Talking to a parent like that felt unnatural and difficult. I wanted to be strong, but I also just wanted to be the child again, the child that I barely got to be when my father was concerned.

"Have you thought about doing some volunteer work?" I asked. "Giving to others is usually a great cure. Maybe you could volunteer helping to train kids for marathons. You know, something not related to AA or alcoholism. It just seems to me that you've dedicated so much of your life to being sober maybe it would behoove you to be around something else so that your whole identity isn't tied to AA." I sounded like a *Sesame Street* episode. I stared at him, but that time directly at him. He didn't look at me. Instead he took his right hand, held up two fingers and waved them over the oxygen machine once again, that time like a child making bunny ears over someone's head in a photo.

"I just spoke to your doctor," my mom stormed in. "They offered to bring in both a psychiatrist and a therapist and you said no?" She yelled in disbelief.

"I don't want to discuss this now."

"Well when exactly do you want to talk about it?"

"It's Christmas. Can't you just leave me alone?" he said in a tough tone, apathetically. My mother fell silent. I felt the urge to sprint out of that hospital room but didn't. I pierced the window with my glare and rolled my eyes because I couldn't think of anything else to do. I was stuck in that never-ending triangle and desperately wanted out. There seemed to be no way to stop it.

"I'm going to give you guys a minute." I left the room and embarked on a mission to find myself a hot doctor. Not only were there attractive doctors, but they were attractive doctors who were working on Christmas, meaning there was a good chance they would be Jews. After leaving my dad's room, I saw the first reception area and walked towards it. There was a man in scrubs reading today's paper whose nametag read Jordan. He looked up at me and asked,

"Can I help you?" I contemplated responding with, "Yes, yes you can. Will you date me? But instead I simply asked, "Where's the restroom?" He pointed me in the direction of the bathroom and I went in there and pretended to use it.

Eventually I made my way back to room seventeen. Lurking in the hallway right outside my dad's room I heard my parents arguing.

"There's nothing a shrink can tell me that I don't already know. I know way more about AA and alcoholism than any of these psychiatrists," my dad shouted in a grave and weak voice.

"But maybe they can do something. They're experts and something clearly isn't working here," my mom urged.

"Why don't you just go home?" he said, "You're ruining my Christmas." My mother walked out of the room, with tears streaming down the face but not making a sound. I didn't blame her, but instead of following her, I walked back in to look at my father. I wanted to end on good terms in case that was the last time I saw him. He just seemed so out of touch with the man who raised me, the man who dressed up as a woman and took me trick-or-treating one Halloween when I was six, the man who'd let me win Uno, the man that taught me to run my first race.

I looked at him lying there, in the hospital bed, staring straight at the wall. A tear started to form in his right eye but didn't fall. It was the first and only tear I'd ever seen from him. "Merry Christmas, Dad," I said.

"Merry Christmas, Nik," he said without looking at me. I lingered there for a minute, waiting for him to make eye contact, but he didn't and I left. I met my mother in the parking lot and we got in the car without speaking.

MILE 25

Slow down. Don't die. You're already dead. But you're not. At this point I've been pushing myself for so long, I feel like I'd have to consciously and actively make myself stop if I wanted to, not the other way around. Unstoppable is my obsession. The longest training run I ever did was twenty-two miles long. I was told by multiple sources that adrenaline carries you through the last few miles of the race. The crowd will be cheering you on and you'll be on such a high because you're almost finished. I've found this statement to be completely false.

The crowd is nonexistent and there don't even seem to be any runners nearby, aside from Todd. I feel zero adrenaline. At mile two, sure, the adrenaline carried me through, but certainly not now. My expectations were completely mismanaged. Todd proceeds to make small talk which isn't at the top of my list of things to do when I feel like I'm on the verge of cardiac arrest. On the other hand, I half want to keep engaging with him in order to take my mind off death, but I half want to tell him to shut the fuck up. You can't win Todd, you just can't.

—Providence Marathon, 2011.

The morning of my longest training run was in mid-April. I'd started around seven-thirty in the morning, prepared to go for four hours. I'd planned to do nothing later that evening aside from possibly eat an entire pizza, some raw cookie dough, and maybe watch some World War II dramas which I was really into at the time (it was a phase). It was around eight o'clock, I'd been going for about thirty minutes, and I could still see my breath in front of me when I exhaled. I was running uphill and it was cold. That twenty-two mile training run was critical because, based on what I'd read in the blogs, it was essential that my body became used to logging miles so that I had the physical and mental stamina when marathon day came, which was in just two weeks.

After extensive research, I'd chosen the Providence Marathon because it was rumored to be the flattest course in New England. I'd debated long and hard as to whether or not to actually register. But, at the end of the day, Providence was driving distance from Massachusetts, and the perfect Hail Mary pass to throw to my father. Since I couldn't seem to find an effective way to communicate

Dry Run

with him, maybe seeing his only child run 26.2 miles, continuing his legacy and passion, would make him understand the things I wasn't able to express to him in words. Maybe he'd get a second wind in life and be motivated to get better and stay sober.

Central Park was full of other runners that morning, in both directions. My fleece hat kept my head warm and the temperature outside was certain to heat up over the next few hours. My pace was slow as I rounded the south side of the park, but it was okay that I was slow, since the goal was just to maintain the endurance to complete all twenty-two miles. It was nuts and I felt a little crazy.

Part of me wished I'd asked my dad for marathon advice but we hadn't spoken since Christmas, about four months earlier when I'd left him with the Twiddlebugs at Lahey Clinic. That same day, unable to compose herself, my mother hit three parked cars in the span of forty-eight hours. Ironically enough, her biggest piece of wisdom in terms of marathon training was that speed didn't matter, it was just essential that I got in the mileage. Take it slow. I was sure it disappointed my dad when I went to my mother for training tips instead of him, and while part of me felt guilty, the other part of me felt satisfied, like the feeling you get when you use a sharp knife to cut a soft piece of cheese. My father was difficult to love. It was such a strange sensation to genuinely care so deeply about someone and in some ways, want to be like them, but to also want to hurt them at the same time.

Central Park was an amazing place to train. It was full of hills, which ultimately could only be a good thing. The more hills I had under my belt, the easier the alleged flat marathon course would feel on game day. At least, that was the plan. My mom told me that the absolute longest distance I should run when training was twenty-two miles, even though twenty was probably fine. The extended runs were hard on your body and should be done sparingly because come race day, the adrenaline from the cheering crowd would carry me through the remaining miles, apparently.

I started to run up the west side of the park and passed Tavern on the Green on my left, which I'd heard marked the iconic finish line of the New York City Marathon. It made me think of having a glass of wine on their terrace, and I did think a cold glass of Pinot Grigio in my apartment would be an iconic end to my training run.

My body felt warm at the core, but the crisp, cold air pricked my sweaty hands. The trees were still somewhat barren. In between songs I could hear the sound of my feet hitting the pavement, as they covered ground bit by bit on the way up the west side of the park, the Great Lawn on my right. For the most part, it was fairly quiet; the barrage of strollers and tourists who thought a bike ride through the park would be fun didn't usually appear until after nine. After several runs in Central Park I'd perfected the passive aggressive head shake and disapproving eye roll, which I gave bikers who biked in the running lane.

Physically, I felt okay during that training run. Mentally, it a weird juxtaposition of sensations. On one hand, every tenth of a mile I ran made me feel slightly more powerful, but at the same time, each stretch of incline became more difficult. The more tired I got, the more beaten down I felt, even if it was just a little bit. I'd always been of the school of thought that if it wasn't difficult, if you didn't have to suffer at least a little bit for it, it must not be correct or worthwhile. It was for that reason that I thought I created more unnecessary work for myself in every facet of my life, because I wasn't worthy of a positive result unless I'd fought tooth and nail for it, whether it was to book a show or close a deal at work or even just to run.

I missed my father. I hated myself whenever I screened his voicemails, during which he'd rattle off something about the weather or the score of last night's Celtics game. It did occur to me that perhaps sports scores were his attempts to relate or connect with me on some level. He finally did succumb to the claws of an outpatient rehab facility after the new year, and I didn't have the courage to call him and tell him I was proud. Instead of calling him back, I trusted that my mom had kept him up to date on my life. And while my mom consistently talked to him about her favorite subject (me), I did what he taught me to do. Run. Whether it was toward something or away from something, I still wasn't sure.

There was a water fountain I knew of, just ahead, next to the brown mystery building that looked kind of like a log cabin. I looked up to tried to find it. All I had to do was arrive at that fountain. Once I was there, I could find the next landmark. "You have to get up this hill because if you don't you're worthless." That's what one of the voices in my head said to me that morning. There was another one, slightly louder: "You're so strong. You're going to get up this hill because you're unstoppable and determined and a fighter. Perseverance is in your blood." A gust of chilly air slapped my face while snot dripped out of my nose. My legs kept going and I picked up speed ever so slightly. Then the first voice was back, "You're so slow. You're too weak to make it to the top of this hill. If you haven't made it as a Broadway star, what makes you think you'll make it to the top of this hill?" I tried to run faster, just to make both voices stop. My music was already turned up all the way, blasting in my ears, and I wished the show tunes would drown out the voices in my head.

Minutes later, I dragged myself up that hill and arrived at the water fountain where I stopped for a quick stretch. The water in Central Park wasn't yet turned on for the season, but I almost felt like if I poured water down my throat it would've frozen anyway. I only had approximately twenty miles left until I could check this activity off of my to-do list for the day. At least I'd feel proactive. I was moving apartments the day after the marathon. It was aggressive but I was excited. Analise was getting engaged and would be moving in with her fiancé, but it just so happened that two of my other girlfriends from NYU had a third roommate who was also getting engaged so I would take her spot in the apartment.

My legs felt stiff but I knew I needed to keep going so I forged ahead to mile three. There was another fountain that was usually accompanied by a food cart at the base of the reservoir, so that would be my next landmark. I doubted the food cart would be stationed there that early in the day, but that was probably for the best. I shook my shoulders, letting my arms droop rag-doll style, in an attempt to loosen my body as I ran down a hill. The sun started to peek through the trees. Maybe it wouldn't rain that day after all.

I'd started a new job two months earlier and I was scared but happier. Another eDiscovery staffing firm recruited me directly and I was able to use my hard-won book of business from my previous job as leverage for more money, as well as a bargaining chip to keep my flexible schedule and freedom to come and go for auditions. Though having a sales quota was still stressful, I thought that the new company would be a better fit for me. And although I hadn't been auditioning as much because I'd been preparing for the upcoming production of *Matchmaker Matchmaker I'm Willing to Settle!* I was able to miss work in order to do so as long as I was still hitting my numbers.

Through a connection at my former recruiting job, *Matchmaker…* was offered a workshop production at a reputable theatre in Boston, where several shows that had started there later transferred to Broadway. It felt like we'd achieved the impossible. Thinking of that filled my entire body with adrenaline and I ran faster. Unstoppable.

There was a woman ahead of me wearing green shorts. I noticed them because the only other person I could think of who wore shorts in cold weather was my father. They also stood out because the woman had clearly crapped in them. From the back, she looked to be fairly young, and I knew she was moving more slowly than I because I was gaining distance on her. Ever since I'd made the decision to run the Providence Marathon, I'd started collecting marathon war stories and the one common denominator among marathon alumni is that you would sometimes see people shit their pants. Maybe it was due to the physical state of the body, or maybe it was simply that someone was so concerned with their race time that they didn't bother to stop to shit and figured they could save time by doing it in their pants; there didn't seem to be a consistent explanation. But when I saw that woman, instead of being completely grossed out, all I could think was, good for her! I hope that if I shat my pants during a marathon, I too could keep going.

The voices in my head had grown quiet and I was about to reach the reservoir on my right where I knew I'd find the non-working fountain and phantom food cart. I decided to turn right into the reservoir, even though it was colder around the water, because I wanted to give myself some flat road. Leaving the woman with the spoiled green shorts in the dust, I started to make my way around the reservoir. I tried to think positive thoughts. I had this. I had yet to crap my pants. I would make him hear me.

It was funny to me how things changed. I remembered that first Turkey Trot so vividly, specifically thinking how I never wanted to run another race, ever. I'd run just a handful since, which was odd because the aversion I had towards that first race was so strong. I remembered being annoyed at Mitch for trying to criticize my stretching regime, which, in his defense, was completely fake. I remembered slogging through mud and seeing a man fall. I remembered crossing the finish line when my dad wasn't there. I remembered being torn between relief that he wasn't there to tell me I hadn't run fast enough, and disappointment that maybe he didn't have faith that I'd be as fast as I was (which to be clear, was not fast). I never found out where he went that day. I never asked. I didn't think it was important, really. What was significant was that he wasn't there, and

Dry Run

truthfully, in the grand scheme of things, it was fine. Though that moment still haunted me.

There were a few scenes from my past where my father was concerned that stuck with me, one being the day he picked me up a South Station and swerved ever so slightly off of the Route 1 exit on the way home. What if he'd had a few beers before he got in that car? I'd honestly rather not have known. But it also could have genuinely just been his bad driving. And besides, maybe it was just the darkness and the sharp turn.

By mile eight in that training run, all I could think about was my dinner. Maybe if I was really feeling wild I'd even bake some of the cookie dough I'd planned on eating. Those long runs screwed with my brain and at some point, there came a flip in perspective. For the first ten miles or so I thought about logging miles, getting them under my belt, thinking of each mile as an accomplishment. But after mile ten, my mentality flipped from recording miles I'd completed to, "Look at the miles I still have a head of me, the ones I have yet to climb."

MILE 26

I can see the final mile marker. Twenty-six fucking miles. Todd sprints off ahead of me and I miss him. I feel a sense of loss. I typically hate talking to people when I run but I don't know that I'd have gotten through the last few miles if I didn't have Todd to distract me. I wonder if I'll see him at the finish line, or if he'll always just be two-mile-Todd. I wonder if my father ever tried to talk to someone while they were on the verge of death at mile twenty-five of a marathon. My guess is probably not. He was never much of a talker, at least not to me. I hate that I just thought of him in the past tense. There was a time when I didn't think he'd ever recover. My acting coach once told me that the only certain thing in life is that there will be loss. Maybe that's why I stopped answering phone calls. Maybe the way I dealt with the potential loss of him was to create an actual loss of him. But he's still alive. I can see the marathon volunteers starting to collect orange cones behind me. I really am cutting it close. "Last Dance" starts for the eleventh or twelfth time. Either way, I'm now alone to finish what I started. My scalp is still on fire, there is blood between my inner thighs, I'm freezing, my breath is short, my quads are aching, my right calf is twinging, I'm nauseous. But I'm here.

—Providence Marathon, 2011.

It's May 1, 2011, and I'm standing near the starting line of the Providence Marathon dressed in a white tank top, three sports bras, and the shortest pair of shorts I was able to locate in the entire New England region. I see him standing there in the crowd, beside the road, practically motionless, next to my mom. His feet are firmly planted with the help of a walker of sorts that he's leaning on, and his eyes are subtly scanning the crowd, I assume looking for me. The sun reflects off of his puffy silver jacket, which looks like it's made out of tinfoil. I smile, because my father has always had a thing for flashy clothing. For a while I didn't understand it, but I've come to the conclusion that it has less to do with brand-name fashion and more to do with a fear of getting old, maybe even a fear of losing independence, and a desire to dress the way he thinks young people do.

My mother can't seem to stand still. She's walking in circles next to him, lifting her sunglasses and squinting to get a better look through the camera lens of her outdated flip phone. I know she's

Dry Run

desperately searching for her soon-to-be marathon champ so she can proudly snap a picture that she'll undoubtedly set as the background on her phone and use to brag to all of her friends. A photograph that she'll tag on Facebook without my permission and which we'll later argue over her taking down.

My dad, unlike my mom, doesn't need to take a picture. Just having this moment is enough for him. After nineteen years in and out of rehab, he probably doesn't have the energy or even the desire to take a photo. When your life has flashed before you that many times, a moment of joy, no matter how short, a moment untainted by AA meetings or by relearning how to walk with a walker, must feel, I imagine, memorable enough without a photograph to capture it. He's officially been sober for five months and I still haven't spoken to him since Christmas. This past week he's reached out to me five times and left me three different voicemails that I've ignored. I've deliberately chosen not to listen to him ever since his last relapse. I'm not entirely sure why, but I think it may have something to do with his lack of credibility and years of empty promises. The image of him making bunny ears over that oxygen machine while my mother cried silently is stuck in my mind and I can't get it out. That moment was lasting enough without an actual photo. Sometimes I wonder if he hates himself as much as I hate myself. Maybe that's where I get it from.

There my parents stand, next to each other. It's complicated. I grin. I almost wish I could take a photo so I can ensure this moment is saved long after they're gone. It's funny how the images we want to remember are the ones we so easily forget, and the ones we wish to erase haunt us forever.

In an attempt to focus on the task at hand, I hit the play button on my iPod and MC Hammer's, "Can't Touch This" (obvi the uncensored version) comes on. There's a light breeze in the air and I jump up and down in sync with the bass of the music in order to get warm. It's the type of spring morning where you suffer through goose-bumps because you'd rather be cold than overheated when running later. I didn't have any warmer tops I could bear to part with further along the course, and no one wants to be crossing a finish line with a sweatshirt wrapped around their waist like a middle school field trip chaperone from the nineties, so I'd decided to dress lightly and tough it out. I think about going over and saying hello to my parents but don't. It feels unnatural and I don't want to distract myself before the race. It's one of those rare moments in my life when

I want to go unnoticed. Besides, it's a massive coincidence that they happen to be camped out right in the area where I'm preparing.

I look back at my parents, unable to take my eyes off of them, and it strikes me that that is such a classic moment for them: My dad waiting patiently and silently next to my neurotic mother who is spreading her excited, frazzled, contagious energy that only my father is immune to. He showed up. When he'd heard his only daughter was attempting to carry on his legacy, I'd hoped he'd come. Though there was actually a very real possibility with his rapid decline in health that he might not have been able to come. But he did. Both of my parents have come to everything I've ever done in my entire life, with the exception of the soccer games and family vacations my dad missed when he relapsed. They were there for every history fair, every choral concert, every talent show. I knew my mother would be here today without question. I could be competing in a basket-weaving competition in Uzbekistan and she'd be on the next plane there, one of the perks of being an only child.

I've got a bit of a headache, likely due to a lack of sleep the night before. A slightly stronger breeze sends a shiver down my spine, interrupting my thoughts. But I suppose I deserve to feel cold in my sparse ensemble that I've admittedly worn more for social media photos than for practical reasons. Then again, maybe the cold feeling is just nerves. The three sports bras are an attempt to avoid chaffing and are all black. Thankfully, my hair stays in place despite the light wind, since I'm sporting pigtails, a hair style that hasn't been worn by yours truly since 1995. I have extra lip gloss tucked into my running pouch next to my flip phone; I plan to reapply during mile twenty-six, assuming I get there. I'm no fool and am certainly not planning on running one of these ever again making Providence a once-in-a-lifetime social media photo opportunity. As far as more practical supplies go, I have a packet of gel shots for energy and a five-dollar bill in case of an emergency.

As I join the other runners gathering in the corrals leading up to the actual starting line, I think to myself, how did I get here? How did a former straight-A student living in New York City, head hunter by day, aspiring actress by night, end up here in Providence, Rhode Island, listening to the uncensored version of "Can't Touch This" on her iPod, with twenty-six point two miles ahead of her? It seems like a lifetime ago that my parents and I were all eating over-cooked meatloaf together.

Many people around me have earbuds in their ears, others appear to be silently focusing and in the zone. My brain is split between enthusiastic thoughts like, "You can do this!" and "You're going to have the biggest meal of your life tonight" and not so positive thoughts like, "I might die" and "Why the hell am I doing this?" I justify it all with, "Nikki, you will be so skinny after this marathon." Really, I just want to think about the race, not my parents' reaction; just for a few minutes, I want to be free. But we're all prisoners of our thoughts to some extent and can't necessarily choose when visiting hours take place.

There's a man right in front of me wearing a bright yellow shirt that says "AIDS AWARENESS," in all capital black letters across the front, who looks to be a little overweight and at least fifty. If he can run this marathon, I can run this marathon. Is that rude of me to think? He stands on his left leg, grabs his right ankle with his right hand, and stretches. Following his lead, I do a little lunge and plaster a confident look on my face, trying to appear like I'm doing a regular warm-up routine. I don't pretend to be an elite runner or to have any real concept of strategy in terms of what I am doing. All I know is that I need to get from point A to point B, which unfortunately in this case are twenty-six point two miles apart so it's going to take a really long time, and that's that. During the months leading up to the marathon I'd done more carb-loading than I had actual running. "Sorry, can't meet you for a drink, I actually have to carb-load tonight." It made me sound athletic, trendy, and in the know.

Immediately to my right is a girl who looks to be about my age and is sporting a long blond ponytail with just the right amount of volume and curl. I wish I could get my ponytails to look like hers, but mine are always so messy. She's wearing black leggings and for a moment I feel self-conscious about how short my shorts are. The excitement and nervous energy of all the runners continues to ripple through the starting corrals. I hear quite a bit of superficial laughter, the type you force when you know the next several hours are going to be painful don't want to acknowledge it. The vibe is similar to that of a funeral, when people try to overcompensate by making surface level jokes, just to have something to laugh about, or like when you make Twiddlebugs over an oxygen machine. Other runners around me adopt a more serious approach, taking deep breaths, shaking out their legs and getting in some last-minute stretching. An announcer comes on over the loudspeaker and proclaims that the race will begin shortly.

I wonder why everyone around me is running today. After all, you don't just wake up one day and decide to run twenty-six point two miles for kicks. I'm running because I can, because I can run and he can't. I'm running because I can't stop. I'm running because moving feels safer than standing still.

My mom warned me that if I started off too fast I might not finish. The goal is just to finish. This is a foreign concept for me because I never "just finish" anything. I need to finish and be the best. The simple act of completion has never felt good enough. My dad's words from years ago echo in my brain: "Crossing the finish line of a marathon makes me feel unstoppable." God, why couldn't he have just stopped drinking? I glance down to make sure my shoes are double-knotted.

It's now just minutes before the race starts. The turnout isn't huge. Actually, there are only a few thousand runners, less than the number of participants in some of the shorter races I'd run in Central Park. My dad finally spots me and I pretend not to see him. Maybe it's because I don't actually forgive him. Maybe I do, maybe I don't; I don't know anymore. Someone once told me that the definition of forgiveness is accepting someone and genuinely not wishing things were different. Hopefully over the course of the next few hours, I'll figure that part out.

With five seconds to go, I look over to my left and see a man and woman who appear to be running the race together. The man kisses the woman quickly on the lips before she bends down to tie her left shoe. How nice. My parents ran six marathons together before he started drinking. I think about the story of how when they ran the Cape Cod marathon in Falmouth, my dad finished so long before my mom that he drove home, showered, changed into a new outfit, drove back to the marathon, re-parked the car, and made it to the finish line in time to see my mother cross.

With four seconds left, it occurs to me that I want him to see me cross this finish line but I don't want him to see me seeing him see me. I don't think I'll be equipped to handle the intensity of any interaction at all between us, even just looking at each other, when I'm so exhausted. So I've decided that, assuming I do reach the finish line, I'll most likely pretend to search for my parents in the crowd even though I'll know exactly where they are.

Dry Run

With two seconds to go, I hear my dad's words in my head again: "If you ever run a marathon, you'll feel unstoppable." Despite his total lack of credibility, on some level, I must've believed him.

The gun goes off. I start running. Running away from him yet towards him at the same time. Twenty-six point two miles. People around me start moving too. Oh, my God. I can't believe I am doing this. I'm not a quitter so there's no turning back. I'm past the point of no return. "Poor Life Decision" runs repeatedly through my head. If this is what it takes to save him, then here I go. This is how I'll make him listen to what he cannot hear.

MILE 26.2

I'm nearing the finish line and my body is being ripped apart in places I didn't realize existed before today, like the skin on the underside of my arms, just below my armpits, where I'm now bleeding. Neither of my parents warned me that by mile fifteen of a marathon my scalp would be throbbing and sunburnt. Or that at mile twenty, I'd feel short of breath running up a hill to the point where I'd consider yelling for a medic, consciously telling my body to breathe in through my nose and out through my mouth. Or that by mile twenty-six the skin between my legs would be completely torn apart, leaving two red gashes on my inner thighs.

Seasoned marathoners I'd talked to had told me that the sense of accomplishment and pride they felt when crossing a finish line was unparalleled. But here I am at age twenty-seven, about to finish my first marathon, and all I feel is disoriented. I have about two hundred yards to go and I can hear what's left of the dwindling crowd positioned right at the line cheering which is confusing because I don't think that moment is worthy of applause and I don't feel accomplished or proud. But in just a few minutes, God willing, I'll cross that line.

Fear overwhelms me to the point where had my body not been physically overcome with exhaustion, the thought of crossing that finish line would be crippling. My dad is on the other side and in about one hundred-fifty yards I have to face him. I always thought apologizing to my father would be harder than accepting one from him. Now I'm starting to think it's the other way around. I slow down further to brace myself for the end, to delay the inevitable, which is also the thing I've been working towards. I'm not quite ready to out-run him, but I know eventually I have to pass him. I have to cross that line.

My dad ran the Boston Marathon in two hours and forty-eight minutes and loved running to the point where it became an addiction. He taught me that the line between passion and obsession is often dangerously thin.

I thought approaching the end would feel different. I guess I expected to be clear-headed and resolved, and that I'd know exactly what to say to him. But what I learned is that despite the blood

Dry Run

dripping from my underarms, my sunburnt scalp, and the torn skin between my legs, running 26.2 miles was easier than having an honest conversation with my father. I thought running would make me understand my father, but at 26.1 miles I still don't. I'm actually not completely sure I understand myself. I'd sworn I'd never run a marathon, but here I am running my first and, what I'm certain after this torturous and brutal physical experience, will be my last.

Of course the last stretch is uphill. How could it not be? The sun is shining way too brightly and everything is in slow motion. To my left a man is collecting the last of the orange cones that marked the boundaries of the course. It takes me what feels like hours to run past him. By the time I do, those barriers are gone. I must be one of the last runners to finish. Part of me thinks I've intentionally slowed down because I'm not quite ready to face what's waiting for me. Now, as I near the finish line, I have no choice but to face him. I've run twenty-six miles, there's literally no turning back now.

I try to look calm and energetic, but I'm certainly not energetic and I'm the opposite of calm because I don't know what I'm going to say to my father. I try to give myself one last big push and pick up the pace about twenty feet from the finish line. If there's one thing I've learned from my father and my years of Turkey Trotting, it's that you always want to look like you're running fast when you cross that line. It almost doesn't matter what you've done for the other twenty-six miles, because the last twenty yards are really all anyone else sees.

As I get closer, I see my parents are two of the ten or so people still waiting there, standing right beside the huge digital clock. The flashing red numbers read 5:45. I think about the months I've put into training for these thirty seconds. I wonder how my father ran thirty-two of these. And how my mother ran six. I'm fatigued, but not necessarily changed. I am awakened, but not resolved. I see him there, right in front of me as the numbers on the clock change to 5:46.

My right foot crosses the finish line and at first I look directly at my father's face because there is literally nowhere else to look. There he is. Here I am. There's my mother is freaking out over my accomplishment as usual. My dad is silent but wearing the biggest grin I've ever seen. It's the happiest I've ever seen him look. If I could save that smile and show it to the world, I would. He's standing there. Smiling at me. It's almost like the past doesn't matter. All of the miles behind us, the same miles that brought us here. I try to stop myself from smiling as I run past him but can't, so I avert my eyes, stare straight ahead, and fixate on the ambiguous space behind the line.

– Providence Marathon, 2011.

PART II:
STILL RUNNING

CHAPTER 1

A few days after the Providence Marathon, I decided to wean myself off of antidepressants for multiple reasons, but mainly I think because I was ready to face myself, including the parts of myself that scared me. Seven months later, after a few physical withdrawal episodes and a handful of minor mental breakdowns, I was walking down Third Avenue, medication-free.

It was an afternoon in December after the Providence Marathon Day, otherwise known as the day I was convinced would change my life but didn't, at least, not in the way I'd anticipated it would. Walking downtown from the office on my last day of work before the holidays, reflecting upon my year, my mind was flooded with thoughts and experiences from the past seven months as I tried to organize them in time for New Year's resolutions. I passed by the Chinese place I'd always ordered takeout from and thought about going in just to get a cookie to see if the fortune would shed any light on what my upcoming holiday visit home might bring. Avoiding the patches of ice by my feet and last minute Christmas tree vendors on either side of me, I headed to the gym, planning to get in one last run before traveling home to Boston.

A few Christmases prior, someone had gifted me perfume and I'd saved the nice box it came in. It was a perfect cube made out of flimsy cardboard that was purple and white and sat on top of my piano, just to the left of the music stand. In that box, I kept every fortune from every fortune cookie I'd eaten since 2009; I'd be lying if I claimed I'd never ordered Chinese just so I could read the fortune, hoping it would provide some direction in my life. I placed a lot of stock in fortunes even if they were nothing but the reassurance I needed to get through that night. Also, after fighting to control every outcome in my life for so long, I'd grown to find comfort in giving that up and sometimes just blindly trusting fortunes. Much like in running, the only thing I really could ever control was forward movement, if I was lucky, but trying to manage what happened to me along the course felt impossible and exhausting. Sometimes it was easier and less stressful to just abide by what the fortune told me. Plus, I learned select Chinese words. I'd saved all the fortunes, storing them out of harm's way in my little box.

I guess I wasn't really sure what I'd pictured happening after that finish line. In an ideal world, maybe my dad would've thrown down the walker on the way to the restaurant and miraculously been able to walk again like that scene from *Forrest Gump*. And he would have said something like, "Nikki, because of you, I will now be sober forever, and we will live happily ever after." My braids would still be perfectly in place, my lip gloss glistening in the sun. What ended up happening was that my dad hobbled a few paces behind my mom and me, almost tipping himself over trying to maneuver around a parked car and up onto the sidewalk with that walker.

When I crossed the finish line of the Providence Marathon, my dad was proud, but nothing really changed between us. As far as I knew he'd been sober for about a year come that December, which was positive, but we still didn't talk much. I'd had dinner with my parents immediately following the race and while it wasn't what I'd envisioned, it was fine. They both told me how impressed they were and I thanked them for coming. The three of us then sat around a table mostly in silence. After putting in an order of chicken fingers, fries, and a Diet Coke, I excused myself to the bathroom, where I tried to wash my face in the sink, ripped my tight braids from my sunburnt head, then vomited. My dad phoned me the next day and I screened his call. He wasn't the problem.

Seven months later, on that December afternoon, haunted by thoughts of the marathon past, I was hoping the gym would be fairly empty since New York City did clear out around the holidays. My feet were a little frozen. I should've worn boots, but instead I wore patent leather flats in an attempt to look nice for my celebratory work lunch. Also, I'd grown to detest the shoe switch, because my winter boots took up so much space in my bag when I wasn't wearing them, and my bag already contained my running shoes. My hands were shoved deep inside my pockets in an attempt to keep warm. Accompanied by the sounds of New York City taxi cabs and the occasional Salvation Army holiday bell, my mind continued to wander.

The week that followed the marathon, during preparations for the production of *Matchmaker...*, that would open in Boston that summer, Martin, who'd been watching me perform since college, told me that I was half the actress on antidepressants that I was off of them. I absolutely hated hearing that and I knew I was going to have to find a way to survive without medication. That was really the trigger for me to want to face myself. All of me. If something was preventing me from being the best that I could be, especially where my art was concerned, it would have to change. Another marathon.

"Do what scares you." That was my acting coach's advice the second I started class, just days after running the marathon. It wasn't a phrase you'd find in a fortune cookie, but it resonated with me. The class was a Meisner studio that had come very highly recommended and met twice a week for four hours a night. The time commitment was intimidating for a twenty-seven-year-old who was trying to do it all, but I'd been told by multiple sources that if I really wanted to learn how to act, I needed to be in that studio. The mantra of the studio was "get out of your head" which was also, ironically enough, what I needed to do to get off of medication. Get the best acting training and get off meds. The miles of my life had led me there and I could kill two birds with one stone. I never missed a class.

Meisner training was very specific. It was a style in which the objective was to get your attention off of yourself and completely onto another person so that your body would respond before your brain could judge or manipulate your instinctual behavior. The golden rule of the Meisner Technique was that words and the mind could lie, but the body and true behavior could not. There were countless videos on the Internet that I'd come across as I did my due diligence, demonstrating Meisner Technique where students would often repeat the same phrase over and over again. The point of the exercise was that while the words remained the same, the body and behavior changed. It oddly reminded me of my father, and how he could lie, but his body still betrayed him each time.

"Write me a two-page monologue about something in your life that is true and difficult to say. Memorize it word for word, and be prepared to deliver it to the class a week from Tuesday." That was what I was told my first day of class, and that was the assignment that changed my life. A student raised her hand and commented that she had two different ideas and wasn't sure which one to pursue. Our teacher, a muscly, good looking, middle-aged Italian man with dark hair and a tight black t-shirt said that the story you wanted to avoid was probably the one you were actually dying to tell and that we'd know was the right choice. I knew mine. I thought of that day often because it marked a few milestones for me. Most importantly, it was the day I started telling the truth.

I went home after that class, ordered Chinese, got a fortune that said "A short saying oft contains much wisdom," put it in the box, learned how to say "plant" in Chinese (*chang*), and wrote my monologue in twenty minutes. A week and a half later, I stood on a well-lit stage, looking out into the darkness and felt my knees start to shake as a pit the size of a grape simultaneously formed in my stomach. But it was different from the knot I felt when my dad relapsed. Different than that sick feeling I got when my mom called and spoke in the doomed, nervous tone I'd learned so well, because I always knew what she was about to say and didn't want to hear it. That uneasiness in my stomach on stage was a fear of the unknown. A fear of my unknown. My less medicated unknown.

The teacher chose a student at random, and asked them to go stand against the office door, which was directly in front of me, about ten feet from the edge of the stage. I was instructed to make eye contact with that person and to speak my monologue right to them. I'd never felt so vulnerable or exposed in my entire life, but the goal was to do what scared me. So I took a few seconds, looked directly into those unfamiliar eyes, and began.

I love my Dad. I don't always tell him or mean it when I do tell him but I really do love him. Dads are weird. I find myself getting irritated because he'll always call me when I'm in line at the grocery store juggling my wallet and iPod or when I'm at work, not actually doing work, but in theory he knows I'm working. In reality, I'm just avoiding his phone calls. I get angry when he leaves me voicemails rambling on about the Red Sox scores that I already know. Couldn't he just leave me a message rather than wasting thirty seconds of my life that it takes to dial my voicemail then hit three seven to skip to the end and delete? I'm an awful person.

That monologue went on to talk about how I ran twenty-six point two miles to save my relationship with my father in a drastic attempt to rescue him from alcoholism. Delivering that two-page piece woke me out of a downward spiral of self-loathing that, until then, had been tempered by medication. I didn't even realize I'd written the line, "I'm an awful person," until I was on stage saying it out loud to a theatre full of twenty strangers. Completely immune to self-hate, I realized I'd been running through life treating the negative voices in my head like neighbors who belonged there. I'd even gone as far as to bring some of them housewarming gifts when they moved in. Sentences carried such a different weight when said out loud and that day, on that small stage on the fifth floor of a building on the corner of Forty-Third Street and Eighth Avenue, performing the rest of that monologue, I felt dangerously bare but unexpectedly empowered. In front of that audience, I realized that while running the Providence Marathon didn't save my father, it *did* make me feel like I could accomplish anything in the world, like I was unstoppable. And though it seemed impossible, I knew then that the relationship I needed to repair wasn't the one with my father. It was the one with myself.

I turned right onto Fifteenth Street making my way closer to the gym, and even though it was around four o'clock, it seemed particularly dark. As I approached the gym, my brain shifted focus from meta moments of my life to more practical things, like getting out my key card to enter the gym and starting to unbutton my coat so I could change quicker when it was go time in the locker room. Just as I was about to walk inside, my mother called. I would've called her earlier in order to kill time on my walk, but I assumed she'd be giving piano lessons since it was still late afternoon. Also, it was really too cold to hold the phone or have my hands anywhere except my pockets.

"What's up?" I answered.

"Nikki, I have some news to tell you and I don't want you to be upset." I knew that tone. And that call was extra devastating. A part of me somewhere truly believed that after he saw me run the Providence Marathon, I'd cure his alcoholism and he'd stop drinking for good. He only made it seven months.

"Okay. What's going on?"

"It's Dad."

"Okay." She went on to tell me that earlier that week he had a bad relapse and that he was really wanting to call me himself that time, but a few days had gone by and she didn't want to keep me in the dark. She explained that she'd warned him that if he didn't tell me himself, she would.

"Dad fell in a parking lot. He went to the Sylvan Street Grill after an AA meeting this past Monday. His meeting was at six so when he wasn't home or answering his phone by ten I called the police. They found him passed out in the parking lot. He fell on his way to the car and was rushed to the ER and is going to be fine."

"Jesus fucking Christ. Mom, what the fuck?" I startled myself. Usually I withheld myself and stuck to with one-word monotone answers. "What if he got into that car? He was on his way to get into that car. He could've tried to drive home and killed someone!"

"It's a blessing he didn't get in that car," she said, raising her voice. It was painfully obvious how hard she was fighting to stay calm. "An angel had to have been looking out for him."

"What a blessing. You're right, Mom. We're so blessed! My God, are we lucky. I mean really, what the fuck?" I felt rage like I'd never felt before, furious that every single mile of that race, every individual hour upon hour of training, every piece of skin that was ripped from my body leaving scabs that took weeks to heal, my sunburnt head, were all for nothing. The February days I'd trained in the rain, sometimes almost slipping on ice, only to return home with my limbs frozen, were for nothing. I was wrecked, like a bulldozer had just slammed me all the way back through time, erasing all of the headway I thought we'd made.

I stood in the foyer of the gym, a quasi-warm space in between the sweat coming from inside and the bitter cold coming from outside. Sick to my stomach, I didn't care if anyone else overheard me on the phone. The one thing I'd forgotten being off of antidepressants was that the highs were euphorically high and the lows were dirty, raw, and sometimes miserably low. I'd trained my brain to remember the perspective I'd learned while on medication and tried to remind myself that while emotionally that moment felt like rock bottom, my dad falling and breaking more ribs wasn't the end of the world. I fiercely tried to combat my rage with that logical thought, kind of how the week prior, when I'd had a panic attack at work when a candidate placement I'd made fell through, I was able to mentally remind myself that the result would not be me getting fired. I'd reminded myself that even though I physically felt like I was dying and could barely breathe, my throat wasn't swelling on the outside and I needed to trust that I was fine and that the panic was just inside my head. Sometimes it felt like I had two selves. Calm Nikki, and Panicked Nikki. Panicked Nikki's mind spun out of control, but she'd learned to blindly trust calm Nikki, birthed from antidepressants, the logical voice with perspective, who, for what it was worth, had yet to be wrong. And I'd never have learned that perspective without antidepressants. It was time to move past them, but they had saved me.

"Mom, how could you not call me sooner? I'm so pissed off at you both." My mom started to cry. "You know what, Mom, I have to go." I needed to control my fury before exposing myself to others.

"Nikki, I'm so sorry. I love you. I didn't want you to be upset."

I hung up the phone without saying anything and went inside to the front desk to scan my key card. My mother didn't deserve the indiscriminate anger I'd speared at her. The exhaustion of fighting that battle alone paired with my reluctance to share the burden, had taken a toll on me. At that point in my life, sure my friends were supportive, and yes I'd told boyfriends and dates and confided in people, but it still felt lonely as fuck. I understood that my mom, like many mothers, felt it was her job to protect and fix, but I was sick of being treated like a box marked fragile.

Once inside the women's locker room, I ignored two calls from my mom. The third time I answered.

"What?" I growled.

"Nikki, are you mad at me?"

"No, Mom, I just don't want to talk to you right now, I'm busy. Don't you get that?"

"Nikki, I'm not the enemy here. Will you at least talk to me?"

"Mom, stop trying to steal my serenity." I hung up the phone feeling very proud of that line. Thrashing out of my work ensemble, I tore through my bag for my leggings and sports bra. When I'd crossed the finish line, my dad told me he was proud of me. And what was funny is when I threw up in the restaurant after the race I didn't view it as punishment for what I'd put my body through; it felt like a sick badge of honor.

Due to the nasty weather and time of year the gym was, as I'd hoped, fairly empty. I threw down my bag now full to the brim with my work clothes, and got on the treadmill, starting my pace at 6.4 since I clearly had a ton of energy to burn. Adrenaline fueled me to the extreme point where I was able to run, despite the fact that I'd eaten a four-course holiday meal less than four hours ago. It was hot in the gym since the heat was turned up with it being so frigid outside, so I started to sweat. I just kept thinking to myself that my dad was not my problem. My mother was not my responsibility. I couldn't control either of them, but what I could control was myself and forward movement on that run.

I tried to focus on other things, which I was sometimes able to do when the act of running transcended my brain. My date from two nights ago wanted to go out again next week, which surprised me. I'd suspected the date had gone well, but I guess I'd just learned to expect a "no" and if I got a "yes" that was an added bonus. Either that or maybe since the one consistent man in my life had disappointed me so many times, I just waited for any date or potential boyfriend to do the same. It was funny how I could be so genuinely confident that I was a great first date, but equally as confident that my date wouldn't be able to recognize that or wouldn't show up for me a second or third time. Speed: 6.5. Distance: .5.

My life had become a series of waiting for rejection. Waiting for a deal to fall through, waiting to find out I didn't book the show, waiting for my date to cancel. I'd deliberately and unconsciously built a world for myself where every aspect of my life was centered around rejection. But I ran hard to counteract that waiting because the greatest gift I could give myself at the time was the ability to move forward, with a clear head and speed. It felt powerful. There was no waiting when I ran. Speed: 6.6. Distance: 1 mile.

The few times my dad and I did speak after Providence, there was a complete lack of substance to our conversations, most of which lasted under sixty seconds. I really thought he was getting better, but I guess I couldn't run a marathon for him. I was sure I'd never run another one. It was hands down the most challenging and exhausting thing I'd ever done. I guessed I couldn't save him anymore than my mom could. I couldn't even begin to imagine what it was like to be in her position. What it was it like to have spent so many years with a partner, the first several of which were carefree and truly happy. Speed: 6.7. Distance: 1.5. More distance behind me. More distance between myself and where I started. The space in between.

A few years ago, for my twenty-fifth birthday, I'd really wanted to buy myself an adult-looking watch. I'd always felt like a nice watch, as opposed to a stop watch, was a sign of maturity. I knew I wanted the watch to emulate sophistication, but needed help deciding on color and style. I'd saved up money to buy it for myself and thought a fashion and shopping related activity would be fun for me and my dad to do together. My mother was adamant that I should buy the watch in NYC and on my own time and not involve my father, because she thought not being able to pay for the watch would break his heart. I remember being so upset that she thought I was doing something inconsiderate. Now looking back, I saw she was just trying to protect him. I ended up going against her wishes and taking Dad with me to buy the watch I wanted. I still wore it and thought of that day every time. Speed: 6.8. Distance: 2.0.

Speed: 7.2. Distance: 4.0 After finishing four miles, I immediately felt better. My breathing had returned to its normal rhythm and my thoughts had slowed down dramatically. I threw on my jacket and was walking east, back to my apartment, when my phone rang. It was my father. My first instinct was to avoid the call but instead I answered.

"Hi, Dad," I said quietly into the phone.

"Hi, Nikki." The shame in his voice was so evident, his tone was soft and his words were hollow. "Mom said she talked to you."

"Yes, she did, and I would've appreciated a call from you." That was the first time I'd ever confronted my father in that way. No paper airplanes, no more listening to him tell me he's stick to his stomach over what he'd done. I was demanding answers.

"I know. I'm just sick to my stomach." I didn't say anything. After a few seconds, he continued. "I'm just so sorry. Dad fucked up again and I feel terrible."

"Yeah, Dad. It really sucks, I'm not going to lie to you. And I don't want an apology. No offense, but your apologies don't really carry much weight with me. I want to know what happened. I'd like to hear it from you."

"I relapsed."

"But how? I'd like you to explain this to me." I was impressed by how calm and level-headed I was remaining.

"I went to the Sylvan Street Grill after AA and ordered two tall beers."

"Two tall beers? Dad, that's lame." He laughed.

"I fell on the way to my car." I couldn't stop thinking about what could've happened had he driven, and wondered if he'd driven drunk before. And most alcoholics got drunk immediately, after a couple of sips. It's how their bodies eventually processed booze. At least, that was the case with my dad.

"Dad, what went through your head when you were going to get in that car? I need to understand." He tried to deflect by telling me that he broke some ribs when he fell, which wasn't the first time he'd suffered that specific injury. I didn't respond and instead initiated an uncomfortable silence and waited for him to find the words.

"I don't know. Nothing I guess. Relapse is a deeply-rooted psychological science. Sometimes it's hard to understand what makes a person do it. I don't even understand myself."

"I feel bad for you, Dad, I really do but I just feel like you need to make some serious life changes."

"That's good advice. I'm just so sorry." He started to cough.

"Okay, Dad. I should go."

"I love you, Nikki."

I hung up. I was so tired of fighting, but something about that post-relapse conversation felt different, maybe it was because I was actually participating instead of remaining silent and afraid of what I'd say, or rather what I wouldn't say. In an odd way, I felt like I was standing up for myself, but also holding my father accountable. There was a lot of freedom in having a conversation you dreaded. I was working toward a different kind of finish line. Or maybe I was just trying to get from one landmark to the next.

CHAPTER 2

It was a Thursday in mid-July, the best kind of Thursday, because it was my twenty-ninth birthday. On my continued quest to do what scared me, I'd decided to take a trapeze lesson. My body wouldn't stop trembling and I kept reminding myself not to look down. It hadn't occurred to me until that moment, standing twenty-three feet or so in the air at the edge of a platform on the roof of the Trapeze School New York, that I did in fact have a fear of heights. It was mild, but still a very genuine, fear of heights. The wind kissed my face, taking one or two strands of my hair with it, blowing in the direction of the Hudson River.

My hair was in a half ponytail, which I loved because the half pony-tail part kept the hair out of my face while the rest of it flew free in the wind, making me feel like a little girl again. I'd spent the past two minutes climbing up a rickety ladder to try to get back to a time in my life before I knew anxiety, or fear, or self-hate. Back to a time when I could blissfully do backflips on a trampoline.

I could feel my knees shaking and I wondered if the rest of the students in the trapeze class down below would be able to see that. Overwhelmed by the sensation of being up so high, I couldn't tell if the shivering was just on the inside and I actually appeared super confident and composed to anyone looking at me. The instructor standing on the platform next to me unclipped my harness from the safety cable attached to the ladder that had protected me during my ascent, and fastened it to the wire that would connect to my harness and keep me from falling were I to slip or let go of the trapeze bar at the wrong time. I took a deep breath, closed my eyes, and tried to focus on the shirtless instructor with the chiseled abs standing behind me. I wasn't going to let fear cripple me. I wouldn't be like my mother, driven by anxiety, and I wouldn't be like my father, trapped in an unstoppable pattern.

The shirtless trapeze instructor helped guide me to the edge of the platform and offered me some chalk for my hands before handing me the bar. I graciously accepted the chalk, not because I was worried about my grip, but because it seemed like a great way to prolong my life before jumping off of the platform. Not that I actually thought I was going to die, but standing up there, so high, everything else felt, well, heightened. Much to my dismay, the chalking process didn't last as long as I wanted it to and the instructor handed me the bar. I thought of the bars I'd set for myself in life, bars I needed to learn to let go of. I gripped the bar tightly, first with just my right hand while clutching a wire attached to the platform just behind me with my left.

I was instructed to slowly remove my left hand from the wire and place it next to my right on the bar. The experience was so unnatural because my hips needed to be thrust forward and my knees slightly bent so the cables supporting the metal bar in front of me weren't pulled taut. I stood on that platform twenty, maybe even thirty, feet in the air, leaning forward, with my hands in front of me, gripping a metal bar that wasn't taught. The only tension I felt was from the hottie standing behind me, holding the back of my harness. If he let go I would one hundred percent fall to my death. Not really, but that's what the sensation felt like. Still trying to look anywhere but down, I turned to my right and fixated on the Hudson River while taking a few deep breaths.

The Hudson River. The previous summer there was a day when I'd decided to go swimming in the Hudson River —disgusting, I know. Forced to stay in the city Fourth of July weekend because of a wedding, resentful that I wasn't able to be at CWTF and really missing the beach, I'd planned to spend the day with myself in NYC, doing things out of my comfort zone. I had this idea that if I did physical activities that were out of the norm, it would be good muscle memory for my soul in a metaphorical sense: To never be afraid to make choices that may not seem so safe, like quitting my job to pursue my art full-time, which I had yet to do. Or, like putting a musical about my dating life out in the universe, which I had done. That musical went on to have five professional productions, two of which were Off-Broadway in New York City. It was amazing and frightening at the same time. The script was authentic and true, that was for sure, and that was the scary part. If people didn't like it, or thought it was too risqué, it was my life they were commenting on. But there was also something about that concept that was awesome. It was my life people were commenting on. And though I hadn't yet fulfilled my childhood dream of being on Broadway, in many ways *Matchmaker...* seemed like the epitome of all I'd ever wanted. When I looked back on my life, I'd worked very hard to evaluate my success not based on what I thought it should look like, but on what my eight-year-old self would think of me today. Because really, wasn't that the opinion that mattered? And the minute I started giving up what I thought my life should look like was when my life started taking shape. Eight-year-old Nikki would've been so psyched that twenty-nine-year-old Nikki was currently standing on top of a building about to go trapezing for the first time.

The day over Fourth of July weekend that I'd decided to go swimming in the Hudson River started with a solo run along the East River. Afterwards I Citi-biked for the first time over to Pier 40 where I'd heard there was free kayaking. I'd never ridden a bike in the city before and the thought of getting hit by a car had always frightened me, so I decided to invest in a helmet and give it a shot. I discovered that I loved biking and made quite a few friends by offering up high-fives to fellow bikers and drivers at red stop lights.

Kayaking on the Hudson was awesome. I remembered sitting in an orange kayak wearing a yellow life vest fastened just a hair too tight. The sun hit my legs, warming them while the river water occasionally splashed them, keeping me cool. I sat there floating and looked at my city from the water. New York, New York, the place that took me in when I was eighteen. Eleven years later, I was still there. Though I'd always be a loyal Boston sports fan, New York truly had my heart. And while it wasn't CWTF on July Fourth weekend, it was nice to be on a body of water. When I got out of the kayak, I asked the life guard, who I found out was working on a volunteer basis (not the most comforting fact to discove) if people ever swam in the river.

"Do you want to swim in the Hudson?" he asked me very pointedly. I gave him a look that clearly screamed, "Yes I do, but I'm afraid I might die from a disease" and he threw an oar off the dock and told me to jump in and retrieve it. Before I could think, I jumped. It was the most glorious cannonball and everything about that moment was perfect. The way the sun was high, the coolness of the water on my submerged body, even the racerback, oversized navy blue shirt I was wearing that multiple people had told me they'd hated (but it was my favorite so I wore it anyway) clinging to my skin when I resurfaced. That memory came flooding back as I admired the river from above.

I was broken out of my New York City/Hudson River love fest trance when the second instructor on the ground yelled, "Ready?" He'd explained that after ready, I'd hear, "One, two, three, hep," and that was the actual cue that I was supposed to wait for. I was to jump right after the "hep." Despite my best efforts, I glanced down for a second just to make sure the net was still there. It was.

"One," the man on the ground started. My hands involuntarily clung tighter to the bar, to the point where my knuckles felt like they were going to pop off. "Two." Oh God it was almost time. What would I do? Would I hesitate or would my body just be able to go? "Three." Here we go. "Hep!"

I experienced a second of panic just before that "hep," but I immediately reminded myself that I couldn't hesitate. I needed to act before I could think, just like in Meisner training, just like when I cannonballed into the Hudson River. I needed to get out of my head. My knees bent and my legs pushed off of that platform. For a few seconds, I was gliding through the air into the unknown and it was pure liberation. In that slice of time in space I was free. I was so out of my body and head that I wasn't capable of stressing or agonizing or wondering or controlling. I was simply existing, moving through the air, holding onto a bar as it changed heights, swinging back and forth. I kicked my legs back and forth, let go of the bar and threw my knees over my head, resulting in a backflip. After landing on my ass on the net, I bounced a few times then took a minute to sprawl flat on my back and look up at the sky.

I wished my dad could do that. Technically he didn't need his legs to fly, but there was no way he could've climbed that ladder. His walking had gotten so bad over the course of the past year that he now used a walker full-time. While my mother and I both assumed he'd been drinking again, after multiple trips to a neurologist, it turned out he'd in fact been sober, but had had three strokes in the past year that went undiagnosed. When I learned that news, I called him and asked him how he was, and let him know that my mom had told me what had happened. He said he was scared, but that he was in physical therapy and able to walk very slowly on the treadmill. I liked hearing an update from him. And while I didn't know that we'd ever really be able to connect on a deeply emotional level, we were at least able to connect at all.

I rolled over and started to make my way off of the net and back to solid ground. Luckily, there was still an hour left in the class, so I'd definitely get to relive my fears a few more times. If I could train my body to let go of the bar and physically give up control, hopefully at least a fraction of that muscle memory would transfer to my mentality. I'd found it to be so crucial to continue to practice that fearless way of living. Since going off antidepressants, there were absolutely still weeks at a time I felt hopeless, there were dark and endless nights I couldn't sleep and laid awake feeling trapped but I had an understanding that those feelings were temporary. I was able to fight to trust that they would pass and accept them for what they were in that moment. I was able to embrace the discomfort instead of fear it.

A few minutes later, knots once again crept into my stomach when I clipped the safety wire from the ladder onto my harness and began the ascent up the rickety ladder, a second time, continuing the cycle.

CHAPTER 3

"I'd cut back on the mileage. Be healthy. Sun's out. Be strong and healthy going into race day. Stop & Shop. Mom good. Good luck at marathon. Good stuff. No more miles. No Pats injuries except Collins. Did you run today?" That was what my dad's text said. I responded.

"Not running today. Ran fifty-one miles this week. Thanks for the advice! Sucks about Collins." After the strokes, some of my dad's cognitive functions had started deteriorating and his quasi-in-coherent texts messages gradually stopped phasing me. I'd thought about going for a run that morning, even doing just a quick five miles, but I was so spent when I woke up from all of the training I'd been doing. Not that thirty-two was old, but it was not twenty-seven. It had been five years since my first marathon and there was also a tense knot in my right calf and I wanted to be kind to my body considering I only had two more weeks until the 2016 New York City Marathon. Instead of getting up to conquer the day on that particular Saturday morning, I laid in bed snuggled under my duvet.

I remembered the exact moment I'd decided to run it. It was about a year and a half prior in March of 2015; I was standing naked in the middle of my bedroom in my apartment in Stuyvesant Town about to get into the bathtub. I'd just run the New York City Half Marathon, which I'd done with a friend who didn't want to do it alone. I was kind of his Todd. The day was gloomy and I was freezing; the 13.1 miles-worth of sweat stuck to my body turned cold during my subway ride home. A guy I'd dated a few years earlier, ac-tually the one referenced in Mile 22 who was looking for a swinging partner (confession, I did go out with him again), saw my post on social media about running the race. Like most flings of Internet dates past that resurfaced, he took that Facebook announcement as an opportunity to reconnect and messaged me asking if I was trying to qualify for the New York City marathon.

I wasn't sure why that blast from the past was asking if I was trying to qualify for the marathon. Maybe he was just rekindling conversation and it was as simple as that. But he went on to message me that if I ran nine New York Road Runner races and volunteered at one in a given calendar year, I'd gain automatic entry to the New

229   *Dry Run*

York City Marathon. I didn't have to think twice about it and before I even got into the bathtub to warm up my body, I took the gift card that my parents had given me for Christmas last year and immediately registered for eight more races in 2015. Despite swearing that I'd never run another marathon, something about this was pulling me. Maybe it's because the first one, in many ways, four years later, still felt unfinished. And the more time passes, the easier it is to forget the pain, which is both a blessing and a curse.

The very first time I ever went to New York City was with my mother when I was eight years old. Mom never let me eat fast food as a kid, so naturally I always had a burning desire to live on the edge if ever presented with the opportunity, perhaps at a friend's house, to taste a McDonald's fry. We were walking through Times Square, down Broadway, the winter of 1991 and she asked what I wanted to eat for dinner before going to see *She Loves Me*, my first Broadway show ever. I looked up and saw those golden arches at Forty Sixth Street and said, "Let's eat there!" It was also at that time that I knew I'd live there one day. The day of the New York City Half Marathon, I ran through Times Square (all of the Midtown streets were shut down), and when I saw those exact same magnificent golden arches lighting up the block, something came over me that was bigger than me. It was almost like I'd traveled back in time, gave my eight-year-old-self a hug and told her that she would in fact live in New York City one day. I ran by the Wintergarden Theatre where I'd seen *Mamma Mia* several years earlier and, past the Stardust Diner where I'd overdosed on vanilla milkshakes and sung karaoke as a kid. I recalled turning onto Forty-Second Street and at Ninth Avenue, spotting the Laurie Beechman, where I'd had the first production of *Matchmaker*. The crowd of spectators lining Forty-Second Street were going wild, and for the first time, getting applause while running made sense, probably because I was running down the street of my childhood dreams. My body felt strong and the adrenaline made me feel like I could run for days. I ran by the corner on Ninth Avenue where two years earlier I'd watched my dad nearly fall, grabbing onto the scaffolding like his life depended on it, on our way to dinner. Across the street from that corner I saw the diner where I once had lunch with my acting coach who made me perform the monologue that changed my life. The more landmarks I passed, the more memories ran into my heart, filling it faster than the rain hit the streets. The feeling of power I was able to harness during mile seven of that race was unlike anything I'd ever felt before. For the first time in my life, I felt invincible.

During the past year and a half between the New York City Half Marathon, and that day when I laid in bed mentally preparing for the New York City Marathon, I'd run nearly twelve races, four of which were half marathons. I was getting faster and faster and couldn't stop. One could probably argue that I'd developed an addiction of my own. I'd found that running was the one constant in my life that I could control. It was the one thing where I wasn't set up for rejection and where it was completely in my power to continue moving forward. And my favorite thing about it was that I wasn't reliant upon anyone but myself. I wasn't dependent upon a candidate accepting a job, or beating out another girl for a role; the only person I was ever competing against was a prior version of myself. I finally understood what a PR was! It was a different kind of pressure than what I experienced in an audition room or at work, but I'd come to find that it was a much more important kind of pressure. Because the only one who could possibly benefit from the results was I. It was a way to maintain a relationship with myself. At that time, I'd increased my daily running to five miles a day and was actually getting faster. It was amazing to me that even when my life was in shambles, on a week when nothing was going my way creatively, and every deal I had on the table fell through, and my dad had a bad fall which put an unbelievable amount of stress on my mother, that my runs held all of the chaos together like a tiny piece of thread. It was my one constant in a world of ambiguity and the unknown. My dad's passion had become my lifeline.

"You're selfish. You don't work hard enough. You're a bad friend." I was thirty-two and had been off antidepressants for six years by the time the New York City Marathon rolled around, and I still experienced negative voices often. But lately I'd found that when I had a run under my belt, I had a much easier time combating them. Over the past few years I'd picked up a tactic where I'd stop trying to block out the negative voices, and acknowledge them instead. Sometimes I'd even yell back at them: "You can't tell me I'm a lazy piece of shit, I ran five miles this morning!" In many ways, running had become an inexpensive gift I could give myself every day. It was no longer a punishment, but a way to do myself a solid. Though it was by no means an elixir, I did find that I typically experienced less negative self-talk on days that I ran.

Dry Run

A few weeks ago, my parents came to NYC to celebrate my mom's seventieth birthday, though my dad almost didn't make the trip. His ability to walk unassisted was gone, making NYC a very difficult city for him to function in. Despite his great intentions, over the past few years, every NYC trip had had some misfortune revolving around my parents. Two years ago, my dad lost his dentures and the hotel maid eventually found them in between the mattress and the bedframe. Earlier that year, my parents came in for the weekend to help me move into my first, very, own one-bedroom apartment. After one trip up two flights of stairs, empty-handed, my dad napped for four hours. The next day, my mom nearly had a panic attack trying to parallel park her car outside my new apartment and wound up leaving me alone on the sidewalk with all of my belongings, where a homeless woman tried to steal my television.

During that particular seventieth birthday weekend extravaganza, I remembered helping my dad get out the door of our hotel and watching my mom support him while he crossed the street. I hung back a little bit, needing a short break from the intensity of the situation and saw my dad putting so much weight on his arms, that it seemed like his legs were ghosts, floating just above the pavement. I remember looking to my right to make sure there were no cars coming, and realized that I was a block away from where I'd run the New York City Half Marathon on the day when everything in my life unexpectedly changed. I looked back at my dad and my heart broke, right there on West Forty-Fourth Street.

It was a shattering and disorienting experience watching a parent deteriorate. It was also bizarre, seeing the man who raised me when I could barely walk, evolve into a co-dependent child himself. I'd officially passed him. It was a unique and unexpected kind of heartbreak. I just felt so sad for him. And how demoralizing it must've been to have my mother have to comb his hair before going out at night, and for him to be ushered to and from a restaurant across the street like a kid. And what was that like for my mother? Despite everything, she'd stuck by him. What that must've been like to go from being someone's life partner to their caretaker. She made her decisions and she owned them. They both did, really. And as devastating as it was for me to watch, I was happy that I was finally able to feel empathy for both of them, probably because I was at last able to feel empathy for myself, at least some of the time.

Part of me was disappointed my parents wouldn't be able to make the trip to watch my race; it was just too difficult for them with my dad's walking. Another part of me thought that it was fitting that I cross that finish line alone. I'd spent so much of my life trying to prove myself to others that I couldn't even identify who those "others" were. But it didn't matter because what good was impressing anyone else, if I wasn't truly happy with myself? I'd taken some time off from auditioning the past few years because it had become more about having to show others that I was talented enough to be on Broadway and less about fulfilling my childhood dreams of being a performer. My eight-year-old self would've hated seeing me come home crying every day, exhausted from being up so early, singing a rock song that was painfully too high for me, because I wanted to convince someone whose opinion didn't actually matter that I could be in *Rock of Ages*.

My eight-year-old self would have, however, been so excited to see me running through Central Park listening to the *Hamilton* soundtrack. My eight-year-old self would've died over the fact that when I took a break from auditioning for Broadway, I started writing and performing in my own one-woman shows all over New York City and after having some success, eventually got to perform in a cabaret concert next to my childhood idol, Donna McKechnie, at Birdland. My childhood idol called my cell phone, and asked me to perform with her. When I saw her name on my caller ID, I remember thinking how, in many ways, that was all my eight-year-old self would have ever wanted. She would've been freaking out. She would've been so happy. To be clear, I thought being happy and feeling satisfied were two very different things. If I were satisfied, I'd have no need to run. It's the wanting to be slightly more fulfilled that made someone run one more mile over and over again.

I was elated to be able to ask my dad for running advice that time around. As far as I knew, he'd been sober since that legendary two tall beer Christmas almost five years earlier, aside from the one Thanksgiving he'd accidentally tasted salad dressing that had balsamic vinegar in it. The Antabuse he'd been taking kicked in right away, causing him to become violently ill at the slightest hint of alcohol consumption, and it took him a few days to recover. He'd been volunteering at an assisted living center in Beverly where he spent his days keeping senior citizens company and I think it made him feel young. For the past three Christmases, my mom and I gave a concert at that assisted living center; she played piano, I sang, and my dad sat in the audience. My mother had since started five different Alateen programs at high schools across Massachusetts and continued to run her own piano studio.

In the spring of 2016, my dad decided that in addition to his work at the assisted living center, he wanted to donate his time to hospice and was the only male in his class of thirty female volunteers to complete the full training. He was specifically studying to sit with people during their last few weeks or days of their lives. At the end of the course he was denied a certificate because he failed the background check due to a DUI on his record from eight years prior (which I never knew about) It was then that I understood how my dad was able to run thirty-two marathons. What a tremendous person it took to have the will power to keep going, even when the universe wouldn't let you repent for your mistakes. That was unstoppable. And that was the gift both of my parents had given me. Tenacity and grit weren't always pretty, in fact sometimes they were very ugly, and very messy, but always awesome.

The way I saw it, life was a series of marathons, which was why it made sense that my dad ran so many. Once a race was complete, it was only a matter of time before another one began. And there would be tenuous up hills, steep down hills, and stretches of nice flat road. No two courses or runs were ever the same.

I'd stopped keeping track of how long my dad had been sober because alcoholism was a battle he'd be fighting for the rest of his life, just like self-love was my eternal war. I often still contemplated whether or not I had forgiven my father, and I truly didn't know the answer to that question. Sometimes I was furious with him, other times I felt astounding compassion for him. Other times I admired him. But above all, I accepted him. I had zero expectations of him. And ultimately I was grateful for the gifts he'd passed onto me, the good, the bad, and the ugly. The determination to run miles, the drive to produce *Matchmaker...*, the insanity to swim in the Hudson River, the courage to let go of the trapeze bar, and the endurance to keep going.

I looked at the clock on my bedside table which read 10:47. It was time to get out of bed even if I was too tired to run. For all of their faults, one trait neither of my parents passed onto me was laziness. My phone vibrated and I had another text from my dad. "Have good run. Dad luvs you." I decided not to respond.

CHAPTER 3.1

November 4th, 2016 was my day. I mustered up everything I had to speed up just a little for the part of the race that people saw, and crossed the finish line of the New York City Marathon, my second full marathon. And though my hands were numb and trembling, I was lightheaded, and felt strongly that I might puke, my knee-jerk reaction was to call my father. He was clearly waiting by his phone, as he answered instantly.

"Congratulations, Nik!"

"Dad, I just crossed the finish line!" I was so short of breath I could barely get the words out.

"I know! I was tracking you! I'm so fucking proud of you." While it felt amazing to hear him say those words (and also nice that he figured out how to work the tracking technology), I was surprised by the fact that I genuinely didn't need his approval that time. I didn't need anyone's validation, really. I was just so thrilled that my dad was happy and that we'd shared that minute, which was a minute worth the last five hours and five minutes that preceded it. And that minute was fleeting. I tried to hang onto it for as long as possible, but there was nothing else to say to my dad so I hung up and the moment was gone. I couldn't take a picture, nor did I need one. It was in the past. Poof. A disappearing act. I looked down to see a text from my mom that said "Call me!!!!!!!" No surprise. My mother had always been my biggest fan, and no one got anywhere in life without a fan. I smiled and rolled my eyes at the same time, still struggling to catch my breath. For a second, everything in the world seemed balanced. I finished five minutes slower than my goal time but that was alright, because life was a series of resetting goals and readjusting expectations. You always wanted to pace yourself and never start out too fast, or get carried away and speed downhill just because it felt easy; that easy feeling could be deceptive. My parents weren't perfect, and neither was I, but despite it all they'd given me one of the greatest gifts I could ever have imagined—a legacy of grit, perseverance, and the ability to have a sense of humor about everything. They were both arguably heroes, at least in my eyes.

Once upon a Turkey Trot I swore I'd never run a marathon. I ran the Providence Marathon to prove *something* to a world whose opinion ultimately didn't matter, and to rescue my dad from self-destruction. I achieved neither. But I ran the New York City Marathon because I wanted to feel —for myself —unstoppable. And I did. And I was. My original belief was that running a marathon would save my father, but it actually saved me. The Providence Marathon was a dress rehearsal, my dry run. My dry run for the New York City Marathon, and for all of the races, the auditions, the miles, the rehearsals, for the learning to let go on the "hep." For learning to let go when the man who took me trick-or-treating wasn't able to be at the finish line anymore, when he no longer just let me win, because he was no longer capable. Though flat roads were nice, and understandably his favorite, the richness was always in the hills, the pain, the euphoria, the cold, the blood, the rehabs, the tears and the laughs that happened at the same time, the compassion, the hate, the kindness, the truth. No, I didn't wish things had been different. We were unstoppable, after all.

Acknowledgements

A very special thanks to the following individuals who played an integral role in the development and publishing of this manuscript:

To **Mary Allen** for your long-time editorial guidance and for helping me to develop the foundation of *Dry Run*. **Ben Hodges**, my attorney and trusted advisor —you are the best. **Melanie Rud**, my copy-editor/editor, your work and advice have always been top notch. A huge thank you to **Shirkrishna Singh** for your belief in me and willingness to take a chance on publishing *Dry Run*. **Ani Sarkisian, Deborah Stone**, and **Rita Waggoner**—your valued input and tremendous editorial feedback has dramatically shaped what is, *Dry Run*. **Mimi Weinberg-Clark**, thank you for editing the original cover photo, and helping to make my vision a reality. **Sarah Cooper** — you've been an inspiration. Thank you for creating the final cover of *Dry Run*. Thank you to **Sarah Eldridge** for the production and design of both the electronic and print versions of the book.

A heartfelt thank you to **Matthew Corozine** for giving me the original two-page writing assignment that evolved into *Dry Run*. **David Gazzo**, thanks for shooting the About the Author shot— your photography is exquisite. **James Huntley**, thank you for editing the About the Author photo your expertise never disappoints. **Kevin Martinez**, thank you for your marketing guidance, branding expertise and most importantly your support and friendship. And thank you to **Tessa Faye Mosier**, my coach and my friend, for giving me that final push to make *Dry Run* a reality. **Josh Rivedal**, thank you for being a trusted advisor, friend, and mentor throughout every iteration of *Dry Run*. **Mike Waggoner**, thank you for advocating for this book and for introducing me to Auctus Publishers. Without you, this would not be possible.

From the bottom of my heart, thank you to the following individuals who have taken time over the years to read and comment on various drafts throughout the different stages of *Dry Run*. Without your crucial feedback and undying support, *Dry Run* would not exist: **Michael Abbott, Amy Burgess, Alison Carroll, Will Cohen, Brooke Chaffee, Barbara Delinsky, Ryan Driscoll, Carlynn Finn, Matthew Friedman, Nisha Gupta, Brandon James Gwinn, Matthew Josepher, Kalina Leopold, Grace Lykins, Becky McBride,**

Kelvin Moon Loh, Simone Morris, Adrian Pena, Emily Popp, Michael Quartararo, Jen Reiss, Anne Rothenberg, Thayer Surrette, Joel Waggoner, and Andrea Weinberg.

And of course, thank you to my entire family for all of your support and for the richness and memories you've gifted to me. You have shaped me, shown up for me, empowered me, and most importantly, laughed with me. I'm forever grateful.